Children and television

Television is often blamed for the increased breakdown of family life and for encouraging violent and anti-social behaviour amongst adolescents. How much of this criticism is justified?

Barrie Gunter, a chartered psychologist, and Jill McAleer, a qualified teacher, are both media research specialists. They examine research evidence on the way children use television, their responses to it, and the effects it has on them. They describe children's interactions with television in a readable, non-technical style, dispelling many of the myths about television's hold over young people. Taking a balanced view of the medium's impact on children, they show how television can be a valuable tool in the home and at school, and has an important role to play in children's intellectual and social development. Gunter and McAleer conclude that children are more selective and critical viewers than we often give them credit for. Children control television far more than it controls them.

An invaluable source of information for students and researchers in communications and social sciences, *Children and Television* will also be of special interest to teachers and educational policymakers and, of course, to parents.

Barrie Gunter is Head of Research at the Independent Broadcasting Authority and an Honorary Research Fellow at University College, London. **Jill McAleer** is a researcher at the Polytechnic of East London. They are both media research specialists and have been active researchers on children and television.

Children and television

The one eyed monster?

Barrie Gunter and Jill L. McAleer

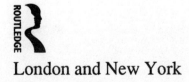

London and New York

First published 1990
by Routledge
11 New Fetter Lane, London EC4P 4EE

Simultaneously published in the USA and Canada
by Routledge
a division of Routledge, Chapman and Hall, Inc.
29 West 35th Street, New York, NY10001

Typeset by LaserScript Limited, Mitcham, Surrey.
Printed and bound in Great Britain by Mackays of Chatham PLC, Kent

British Library Cataloguing in Publication Data

Gunter, Barrie
Children and television: the one eyed monster?
1. Children. Influence of television programmes
I. Title II. McAleer, Jill L., *1944–* .
305.2'3

Library of Congress Cataloging in Publication Data

Gunter, Barrie.
Children and television: the one eyed monster?/Barrie Gunter, Jill L. McAleer.
p. cm.
Includes bibliographical references.
1. Television and children—Great Britain. I. McAleer, Jill L., 1944–
II. Title.
HQ784. T4.G86 1990
791.45'013—dc20

89-70262
CIP

ISBN 0-415-04728-5
ISBN 0-415-04729-3 (pbk)

Contents

Tables

Preface

The 'child' viewer: the myth and the reality

How does today's society perceive children and television and the interaction between the two? Are youngsters really spending a high proportion of their waking hours staring fixedly at a television screen, making little attempt to communicate with the rest of the household? Do they passively absorb all they see and hear irrespective of content or format? And has the continuous bombardment of media 'messages' been a prime factor in increased breakdown in family life or encouraged spates of violent and anti-social behaviour amongst adolescents? If some of the sweeping generalisations quoted regularly in the daily press are to be believed, this and more is the 'true' effect of television – or is it?

Back in the nineteenth century and earlier in this one, concerns were expressed about the harmful effects that the growing avalanche of 'pulp literature' such as 'penny dreadfuls', cheap novelettes and comics would have, both on the young and the less well-educated. Nowadays, although some concern is still expressed about the content and quality of children's literature, notably comics and the ubiquitous Enid Blyton, it is a mere 'drop in the ocean' when compared with the amount of criticism levelled at television. But how much of this criticism is based on 'myth' and therefore unjustified and how much is reality?

The concerns: what are they?

In Britain today, 98 per cent of all homes possess at least one television set, the majority of them (particularly those with children) more than one, yet in the early 1950s only a handful of people had the desire or the means to purchase a set. However, from the late 1950s onwards, there was a phenomenal explosion in the number of television households, with a parallel increase in the amount and type of programming. More and more, educationalists, politicians as well as other authority figures started to voice their fears about the social and educational impact that this new medium might have, fears that continue to be expressed today. For example, it is not uncommon to read stories in the press about individuals committing a violent crime, the idea for which arose from something seen on television. We are told that television can provide examples of bad behaviour which young viewers especially may copy, or that seeing well-known television characters using violence to solve their problems provides some justification for young viewers to emulate their heroes. 'If the members of *The A-Team* can do it, why can't I?'

It is said that television can teach lessons about the world, but that this is a world in which certain types of people predominate, a world in which they behave towards each other in certain ways and play certain types of roles. Television, in other words, is a very stereotyped world. Women, for example, tend to be portrayed in domestic roles more than professional ones and, as opposed to men, are more often the victims of crime. They are also portrayed as more emotional and less independent than men on television. These portrayals, it is claimed by some writers, can cultivate, especially among children who know no better, stereotyped beliefs about the sexes which serve to limit their career aspirations and their attitudes towards men and family life.

Educationalists have been worried that television viewing would displace reading and harm children's school performance. Other critics of television have argued that it is a disruptive influence in the family context both through its presence in the household and through the lessons and values it may teach.

Television is criticised as giving a low priority to family life in that it rarely depicts happy, intact families on screen. It is seen as having a deleterious influence on family interaction – family members no longer talk to each other as they used to – leading to a breakdown in the essential bonds that are so crucial to a stable family environment and to the development of socially responsible children. These then are the concerns, but how justified are they?

In this book, we shall examine evidence for the role television can play in children's intellectual and social development. Despite the emphasis given to possible social ills of television, we believe a more balanced view of the medium's impact on children is warranted. Television can be of general benefit to children. It can bring them into contact with aspects of life they would not otherwise become aware of. It can provide a valuable tool in the home and at school not simply to keep children occupied but also, if used appropriately, as a constructive way to use their time.

There are many myths about television and children. These include misconceptions about how youngsters use it, how actively they respond to it, and how much and in what ways they are changed by it. There is a bias towards thinking ill of television when the medium deserves a fair hearing. Television is not a 'one eyed monster' lurking impishly in the corner of the living room, kitchen or bedroom waiting to exert an evil influence over young members of the household. It is a channel through which a range of entertainment, drama and learning can be obtained and experienced and increasingly these days is under the control of the viewer.

Chapter one

What is the nature of children's viewing?

Viewing patterns

Television may be almost a universal feature on the domestic scene, but it is not used in the same way by everyone who has access to a set. To begin our look at children and television, we shall examine some basic questions about television viewing:

1   When do children begin to watch?
2   How much viewing goes on?
3   What kinds of programmes are watched?
4   In what ways does viewing change with age?
5   How does viewing interact with other activities?

Measuring television viewing

There are various ways of finding out from people how much and what kinds of television they watch. The techniques used include traditional data collection via *questionnaires*, *diaries* and, more recently, *electronic meters*, none of which is able to produce figures of guaranteed accuracy, plus *observation methods*.

Questionnaires, popular with researchers because they are cheap and convenient to produce, invariably require viewers to estimate retrospectively the amount of television they have watched for a given period of time. *Diaries*, which usually consist of a weekly booklet divided into timed segments or programme listings, have to be completed by a pre-selected panel of viewers as they watch. However, the measuring tools most heavily relied upon by the broadcasting industry to estimate audience ratings (i.e. the number of people who have watched a particular programme) are either the *electronic set meters* or the more sophisticated *people meters*. *Electronic set meters*, commonly used in conjunction with diaries, record when and how long a television set is switched on, and which channel it is tuned to at a particular time. *People meters* are also set meters, but with an electronic rather than a paper and pencil diary, whereby individuals push buttons on a handset to indicate their presence or absence when the set is switched on.

However, all of these methods are totally dependent upon the reliability of viewers themselves. For example, how many people who complete questionnaires really remember the exact number of hours they watched the previous day or week? How many more fail to push the button on their people meter, each time they enter or leave the room *and* once their viewing presence has been registered, how much of their attention is then directed at the screen?

Observation

On rare occasions researchers have observed television viewing directly. These studies that have been undertaken – either via participant observation where an observer joins a household, or via direct film or video recording of behaviour in front of the screen – offer insight into the use of television by families which are, by and large, unattainable by more traditional methods.

Photographic records of a family's viewing behaviour have been made by placing either a time-lapse still camera or video camera in the home. Observers may record activities by using a structural log or by less structural note taking. These methods can produce a wealth of detailed information about how people watch television; they also raise questions about the accuracy of viewing figures obtained by more traditional methods.[1]

An investigation of the way people watched television in the United States started out with the principal aim of testing the accuracy of viewers' personal questionnaire or diary estimates of how much they watched. Video cameras were installed in the main television viewing room at the homes of twenty families who volunteered to take part. One camera was mounted over the TV set and filmed the family while watching; the other camera was aimed directly at the set so as to film the programmes actually being watched. These pictures were then relayed to a video recorder in an equipment truck outside the home.[2]

Participants also filled out a variety of questionnaires designed to estimate viewing behaviour. These consisted of a five-day diary, with each day broken down into fifteen-minute segments. Families had to mark off the intervals during which they watched television. Two questionnaires were also administered. One asked the families to indicate which programmes they had watched on the previous day and how much time they spent with each programme, and a second given at the end of the observation period asked for an overall estimate of amount of time spent watching over the five days.

The level of agreement between what people entered into their viewing diaries and what they were observed to watch ranged from 92 per cent agreement in the best case to 54 per cent in the worst case, with an average agreement of 71 per cent. They found that under-reporting of viewing time (5.5 per cent) was rare, whereas over-reporting was relatively frequent (24.8 per cent).

Questionnaire estimates of viewing produced less agreement with observational evidence than diary measures. When required to produce an estimate for the five-day period, the average level of agreement with camera evidence was only 44 per cent. One complicating feature of this study was the fact that the researchers unfortunately did not determine whether families were basing their reported viewing simply on the amount of time they were present in the viewing room while the TV was switched on or the extent to which they were actually watching the screen. Observational evidence has revealed that people do not always look towards the screen when the set is switched on.

More recently, similar in-home, video-recorded observational studies of viewers' attention to the television screen have been reported by Anderson and his colleagues. They installed time-lapse video cameras in the homes of ninety-nine families and recorded family viewing behaviour and what they were watching for ten full days in each case. The equipment automatically began recording when the set was switched on. In this study, emphasis was placed on children's attention to the screen.[3]

The relative accuracy of diary methods of viewing depended on the precise observational criterion used to corroborate viewers' own estimates. Anderson found, for instance, that families overestimated viewing when the criterion was eyes actually directed towards the TV screen. When diaries were compared with presence in the viewing room, viewers' estimates proved to be much more accurate. The diaries may therefore have been accurate records of what most people consider to be 'watching TV', normally being present in a room with a set in use.

It was found that parents' diary estimates of the children's viewing were accurate when compared with camera evidence of their youngsters' presence in the room when the set was on. Parents were generally better at keeping accurate records for very young children than for their older offspring, who more often viewed independently of parents.

As with all other methods of audience measurement, however, the direct observation technique is not without its problems. Many people are reluctant to be observed in the privacy of their own homes; low acceptance rates are therefore quite common. We must also ask questions about those people who do agree. For example, are they representative of viewers in general? How much of their behaviour is normal, given that participants know they are being observed? Sample sizes are also limited by the expense of producing and controlling equipment and by the time taken to obtain the data. Usually few pieces of equipment exist and if placements are for a week or longer, it may take many months or even years to build up worthwhile samples. Bearing all these problems in mind, what do we know about the time children spend watching television and how it fits in with other activities?

When do children begin to watch?

The television is an integral piece of the household furniture and practically every home has at least one set. Thus, children are born into a world in which television is present from the start. But at what point during early childhood does viewing actually begin?

There are different sources of evidence on this. Parents' reports about their children's viewing have indicated that consistent viewing begins between 2 and 3 years of age. Wilbur Schramm and his colleagues reported 2.8 years as the average age of regular television viewing based on the testimony of parents.[4] More recent published observations revealed a gradually growing attentiveness from about two years. Under more contrived conditions researchers have observed a sharp increase in the frequency of looks at a TV screen at the age of 2½-years. This increase was correlated with a similar sharp increase in the amount of viewing the same children were reported by parents to do at home.[5]

Even though children are obviously beginning to look at television even as infants, the set by no means commands their constant attention. When 3- to 5-year-olds were monitored while watching *Sesame Street* the children looked at and away from the TV set about 215 times an hour. Nearly 75 per cent of the looks were under six seconds in length. Lower frequencies of looks have been observed elsewhere, but even those corroborate the rapidly shifting nature of infants' attention to the screen while watching television.[6]

How much viewing and when?

It has often been claimed that television can harm children. But anxieties about its undesirable side-effects tend to be founded on ill-informed assumptions about the nature of children's television watching. We are told, for instance, that children watch too much television and stay up late to watch programmes that are unsuitable for them.

Another common belief is that children increasingly are exposed to heavy diets of violence-laden programming which can teach them examples of anti-social conduct or condition in them a callous attitude towards violence and its victims in real life. What are the facts of the matter? Are children spending large proportions of their waking hours slumped in front of the box? Are children staying up past what should be their bedtimes, watching programmes they are not ready for? And are children feeding off a television diet of violence, which may only bring out the worst in them? Such worries are understandable, but are they substantiated when we take a careful and considered look at children's viewing figures?

The official viewing figures in the United Kingdom are published by the Broadcasters Audience Research Board (BARB). They are drawn from a national panel of some 3,000 households recruited and run by Europe's biggest market research company, Audits of Great Britain. Data are collected electronically through a meter system. Each TV set in panel households has an electronic meter attached to it which keeps a record of when the set is switched on and the TV channel it is tuned to. In addition, householders are supplied with a remote control handset, referred to as a 'people meter', with which they indicate their presence in front of the screen when the set is on. All this information is stored in the set meter which is automatically telephoned over night so that the day's viewing data can be pulled off and entered into a central computer. Projections from these data then provide estimates of viewing for the population as a whole or for particular sections of it.

Table 1.1 shows BARB estimates of average amount of viewing per day for a range of age groups each year from 1982 to 1987. Focusing on the 4 to 15 years age range, two trends can be highlighted. First, viewing levels rise through ages 4 to 11, and then show signs of dropping off during early teens; viewing sinks to its lowest point during late teens and early 20s. At this age, of course, young people tend to go out a lot more. As they discover the delights of pubs, clubs, discos and so on, television, inevitably, becomes a far less important feature of their lives. Second, between 1982 and 1987 the average amount of daily viewing done by children increased from around two and a half hours per day to three hours. To put this finding in context, however, a similar increase in average daily viewing also occurred over the same period for every other age group. This increase in viewing time probably reflects a response to the expansion of hours of television output, beginning in 1982 with the introduction of Channel 4, followed by breakfast television in 1983, daytime television from late 1986, and late-night services from mid-1987. It should also be noted that the BARB measurement system changed its definition of viewership in 1984. A person was classified as a viewer if he/she watched for at least eight minutes out of any quarter-hour time segment. This definition was changed to three consecutive minutes in any fifteen and produced a slight overall increase in apparent viewing levels.

Before leaving Table 1.1, it is worth noting that despite claims that children are nowadays spending far too much time watching television, they are by no means the heaviest viewers. Every adult age group (except the youngest one) exhibits a greater average number of hours a day watching television than children do.

Table 1.1 Number of hours of TV watching each day

					Age groups				
	4–7	8–11	12–15	16–24	25–34	35–44	45–54	55–64	65+
1987	2.8	3.3	3.2	2.4	3.8	3.5	4.1	5.1	5.7
1986	3.0	3.5	2.9	2.5	4.0	3.6	4.2	5.0	5.5
1985	2.9	3.5	3.1	2.5	3.9	3.5	4.1	4.9	5.4
1984	2.6	3.0	2.6	2.2	3.5	3.2	3.8	4.6	4.9
1983	2.3	2.6	2.1	2.2	3.4	3.1	3.5	4.0	4.2
1982	2.4	2.9	2.5	2.4	3.4	3.2	3.6	4.0	4.4

Source: IBA/BARB/AGB
Note: Channel 4 started 1982
     Breakfast programmes started 1983
     Daytime (BBC, then ITV) from late 1986 onwards
     Late-night services from mid-1987
     BARB measurement system changed December 1984

And when do children watch?

This is an important question and is becoming more so as television hours expand. The main worry is about children staying up late at night to watch television. One reason for this worry is that after nine o'clock in the evening, which broadcasters regard as a watershed, programmes may be shown which are suitable for adult viewing, but not necessarily for children.

Viewing figures produced for the television industry for 1987 and 1988 show that substantial numbers of children these days watch television until quite late (see Table 1.2). For the youngest children on whom data are available (4- to 6-year-olds), the viewing figures show that around one in twenty are watching television between 10.00 pm and 11.00 pm while around one in five 10- to 15-year-olds are still up at this time on the average weekday.

The proportion of 7- to 9-year-olds and 10- to 12-year-olds watching between 11.00 pm and midnight falls dramatically to just 2 or 3 per cent, while one in ten 13- to 15-year-olds are still watching at this late hour. On Saturday night the numbers increase.

Table 1.2 Child audiences watching at different times on an average weekday

	Age							
	4–6		7–9		10–12		13–15	
	1987	1988	1987	1988	1987	1988	1987	1988
7.00 am	2	2	2	3	1	4	2	1
8.00 am	10	14	10	15	10	14	9	8
9.00 am	9	7	9	7	7	7	4	4
10.00 am	7	6	6	7	6	6	4	4
11.00 am	6	7	4	5	4	4	3	3
Noon	14	5	6	3	5	5	5	4
1.00 pm	8	8	5	5	6	7	5	6
2.00 pm	11	9	6	6	7	6	5	9
3.00 pm	6	8	5	7	7	6	6	9
4.00 pm	39	35	31	35	25	23	14	17
5.00 pm	48	42	42	47	46	41	33	34
6.00 pm	36	30	34	34	37	36	31	32
7.00 pm	35	30	34	34	37	36	29	32
8.00 pm	32	23	37	37	47	39	32	33
9.00 pm	16	12	23	23	38	29	31	26
10.00 pm	8	5	11	11	23	18	25	22
11.00 pm	2	4	4	5	9	8	12	12
Midnight	0	2	0	3	3	3	4	7

Source: IBA/BARB/AGB
Note: Average percentages viewing over four weeks in February

Across the day during the week viewing levels suddenly jump at 4 o'clock in the afternoon when children are returning home from school. Peak-viewing time for children up to the age of 15 years occurs between 4.00 pm and 8.00 pm. Viewing levels then begin to drop slowly at first and then more rapidly after

10.00 pm. Among 10- to 15-year-olds, however, one in five is still watching after 10.00 pm.

On Saturdays, the viewing profile changes (see Table 1.3). There are two peak times. The first occurs in the morning at around 9.00 to 10.00 am, particularly among children aged up to 10 years. Around three to four in ten of these youngsters watch television at this time. Older children watch in much smaller numbers. Viewing levels fall away after lunch-time on Saturday, but pick up again between 5.00 and 6.00 pm. They reach a peak at around 8.00 pm on Saturday evening when more than four out of ten children will watch television. Among 7- to 12-year-olds up to half the children in this age group in the country will be watching television at 8 o'clock on Saturday night. Children's audiences begin to fall away after 9.00 pm, though much more slowly for 10- to 15-year-olds than for younger children.

Table 1.3 Child audiences watching at different times on an average Saturday

| | Age groups | | | | | | | |
| | 4–6 | | 7–9 | | 10–12 | | 13–15 | |
	1987	1988	1987	1988	1987	1988	1987	1988
7.00 am	2	3	3	4	0	2	0	3
8.00 am	21	16	26	23	12	11	4	8
9.00 am	38	34	42	43	27	26	10	12
10.00 am	40	31	40	39	32	27	17	16
11.00 am	32	27	28	27	26	21	16	20
Noon	22	21	22	27	23	23	16	19
1.00 pm	16	17	15	17	18	21	14	15
2.00 pm	17	11	16	15	18	15	13	11
3.00 pm	14	12	12	13	16	13	12	11
4.00 pm	13	14	12	15	16	16	12	13
5.00 pm	24	24	21	22	24	23	21	22
6.00 pm	47	40	45	42	38	44	35	35
7.00 pm	43	41	47	49	49	47	36	38
8.00 pm	40	40	37	53	51	50	30	39
9.00 pm	25	26	34	45	48	48	33	38
10.00 pm	14	14	22	26	36	36	32	30
11.00 pm	8	7	11	14	19	15	24	20
Midnight	4	5	5	9	11	7	17	14

Source: IBA/BARB/AGB
Note: Average percentages viewing over four weeks in February

Which programmes do children watch?

While concerns have been voiced that children may watch not simply too much television *per se* but also too much of certain types of programmes, a close analysis of children's viewing diet shows that it can be as varied as the television schedules. The major television channels in the UK offer a varied mix of programmes and children tend to sample liberally from the full range of material that is normally made available.

First of all, which are the most popular programmes with children in Britain? One way of finding this out is to look at which programmes attract the biggest child audiences. Tables 1.4 and 1.5 show the Top Ten programmes among 4- to 9-year-olds and 10- to 15-year-olds for the week ending 10 April 1988 and the Top Ten programmes and Top Ten children's programmes among 4- to 15-year-olds for the week ending 1 May 1988.

Both tables clearly show the striking popularity of soap operas, with the Australian serial *Neighbours* clearly emerging as the most watched programme of all. It is also evident that relatively few children's programmes finish among the Top Ten. This cannot be entirely accounted for by scheduling, since *Neighbours* was screened at the off-peak time of 5.35 pm. Among children's programmes, serialised drama once again features prominently plus children's news and magazine programmes. Thus, a long-standing belief among media researchers that news is of little interest to children is not borne out by these tables. Provided it is packaged in the right way children switch on to the news as much as adults do.

Table 1.4 Top Ten programmes ranked by TVR

		Channel	*Day*	*000s*	*TVR*
	Children aged 4–9				
1.	Neighbours	BBC1	M–F	1,560	37
2.	Knight Rider	ITV	F	1,418	34
3.	EastEnders	BBC1	Tu/Su	1,405	33
4.	EastEnders	BBC1	Th/Su	1,369	33
5.	Jossy's Giants	BBC1	Tu	1,212	29
6.	Running Scared	BBC1	W	981	23
7.	Real Ghostbusters	ITV	M	951	23
8.	Snow White's 50th Birthday Special	ITV	F	947	22
9.	Million Dollar Duck	ITV	F	898	21
10.	Blue Peter	BBC1	M/Th	896	21
	Children aged 10–15				
1.	Neighbours	BBC1	M–F	1,981	45
2.	EastEnders	BBC1	Th/Su	1,703	38
3.	EastEnders	BBC1	Tu/Su	1,680	38
4.	Knight Rider – The Movie	ITV	F	1,317	29
5.	Jossy's Giants	BBC1	Tu	1,240	28
6.	Wildlife on One	BBC1	Tu	1,193	27
7.	Running Scared	BBC1	W	1,188	27
8.	Top of the Pops	BBC1	Th	1,187	27
9.	You Must be the Husband	BBC1	Th	1,070	24
10.	Clash of the Titans	BBC1	Sa	959	21

Source: IBA/AGB Programme Profiles

Table 1.5 Top television programmes

Top Ten TV programmes among children for week ending 1 May:

1.	Neighbours	BBC1	(Tues)	35.3
2.	Neighbours	BBC1	(Wed)	33.7
3.	Neighbours	BBC1	(Thurs)	32.3
4.	Neighbours	BBC1	(Fri)	30.8
5.	Neighbours	BBC1	(Mon)	27.8
6.	Running Scared	BBC1		27.8
7.	Degrassi Junior High	BBC1		27.2
8.	Blue Peter	BBC1	(Thurs)	23.9
9.	Top of the Pops	BBC1		23.8
10.	Newsround	BBC1	(Wed)	22.8

Top Ten children's programmes for week ending 1 May:

1.	Running Scared	BBC1		27.6
2.	Degrassi Junior High	BBC1		27.2
3.	Blue Peter	BBC1	(Thurs)	23.9
4.	Newsround	BBC1	(Wed)	22.6
5.	Yogi Bear	BBC1		22.2
6.	Gentle Ben	BBC1		21.7
7.	Take Two	BBC1		21.7
8.	Around the World with W Fog	BBC1		21.7
9.	Newsround	BBC1	(Thurs)	21.4
10.	Blue Peter	BBC1	(Mon)	19.0

Source: IBA/BARB/AGB
Note: Figures refer to the percentage of children in the UK, aged 4–15, watching

Do children watch too much violence on television? Youngsters may well name certain action-adventure series among their favourites. This does not, however, provide an accurate reflection of what their viewing diet contains. For example, one study in which children kept personal viewing diaries revealed that, on average, children watch two action-adventure programmes and two televised feature films a week. These, however, are interspersed among many other types of programmes. In fact, the programmes most popular with children are comedy and light entertainment made for the family.[7]

But boys and girls differ in their programme favourites. Boys watch more action-adventure and sport, girls watch more soap operas, while boys tend to watch more children's programmes than girls. With increased age, viewing of programmes made especially for children drops significantly, while viewing of general programming, particularly of feature films and light entertainment, increases substantially.[8]

Does television displace other activities?

The introduction of television on a widespread scale in Britain in the late 1950s prompted concern among educationalists that viewing would displace reading and harm children's school performance. Although research at the time did not indicate an across-the-board reduction in all kinds of children's reading, once their family had acquired a set, some displacement was evident.[9]

Thirty years on, the question of displacement of some activities, media-related ones in particular, by others has risen once again. The first half of the 1980s saw an unprecedented growth in availability and use of new electronic media. Increasingly today, homes possess not just one, but two, three or even more television sets. Furthermore, the set has acquired a range of accessories and attachments – video-recorders, personal computers, remote controls – which have significantly modified the way it is used.

Typically, children are more comfortable than their parents with each new medium or gadget as it comes along. They do not have so many hardened media habits to unlearn; they are more receptive to new ideas because they have fewer old ones to abandon and they often take to new gadgets as 'toys', if not for more serious purposes.[10]

Essentially, children are less threatened by new media than are grown-ups. But time is a limited commodity. Greater use of new electronic media or gadgetry must mean that less time is spent doing other things and this possibly includes using more established media, such as books, magazines, newspapers and radio. Displacement of some activities – particularly something like reading, if it occurs – is as worrisome today as it ever was. To what extent, though, do television viewing and also these days the use of television-related equipment result in less time being devoted to other intellectual and social pursuits?

Television viewing uses up time. One observation is that if people spend more time watching television, they must be spending less time doing something else. This is a very simple statement, or at least it appears so on the surface. But in fact it has some very important implications concerning the impact of television. For instance, the displacement effects of television may be a crucial issue when they occur among young viewers during the developmental years of early cognitive and affective growth. The richness of children's learning environment can be measured in part by the quality and variety of available sources of lessons. Consequently, there is reason for concern about conditions under which a youngster's repertoire of activities may diminish due to displacement from a competing activity. But which activities among children become squeezed when television viewing increases?

Two principal approaches have been used to ascertain whether or not television viewing displaces other activities. One method has been to monitor the effect on amounts of time devoted to other activities when television is intro- duced to a community for the first time. As television has become practically universal, however, it has become increasingly difficult for researchers to find virgin territory with totally naive television audiences on whom such tests can be run. The available evidence obtains from the efforts of far-sighted researchers during the earliest days of television in Britain and the United States, similar investigations conducted in countries to whom television came rather later and from studies of anomalous cases of communities in otherwise widely penetrated television nations who, because of their geographical location, were unable for many years to receive a television signal.[11]

A second method is to find out relative amounts of time devoted to television, other media and non-media leisure activities among current television generations. The critical question is whether heavy users of television spend less time on other activities than do light users of the box.[12] A more interesting question which we shall also examine is whether viewing certain types of television (rather than overall amount of viewing *per se*) is related, either positively or negatively, to time spent with different leisure pursuits.[13]

Early research reported mixed and largely inconclusive evidence that television viewing displaced participation in social, recreational, hobby or work activities among children and families. Studies of early television generations in the United States indicated that children and teenagers soon learned how to accommodate large amounts of television watching without sacrificing other activities. Generations of children reared with television found ways to integrate extensive use of this new medium without finding it necessary to neglect other pursuits.

'The more, the more'

As television becomes increasingly pervasive throughout the world, it becomes more and more difficult to find people who have no experience of the medium. During the 1970s, however, several natural experiments emerged in which television-naive communities were introduced to television for the first time. Fortunately, researchers were on the spot to record and measure the impact television had. Broadly these found that television did not simply replace time devoted to all other leisure activities, but bit into it selectively. Those activities or pursuits most likely to suffer were ones where television could provide the same sort of gratification, but more easily. In one natural experiment in Australia, researchers studied 98 families in a town without television (no-TV), 102 in a town with one year's experience with one government-run channel (low-TV) and 82 in a town with at least two years' experience of two channels. Parents were interviewed about the amount of time they and their children spent in each of seventeen categories of leisure activities.

Children in the no-TV town spent more time in other leisure activities than did children from the TV towns. The increased presence of television was related to less time spent playing sports, watching sports and other outdoor activities. There was also less cinema attendance, radio listening and record playing among television communities.[14]

A major study conducted in Canada (directed by Tannis Macbeth Williams) examined the impact of television on a community which previously had had no television reception. Once again, three towns were compared. These three towns were labelled Notel, Unitel and Multitel. At the start of the study, these towns had no TV, one channel only and four TV channels respectively. By the end of the research, Notel had one TV channel, Unitel had two channels and Multitel still had four channels. The three towns were compared at the outset and then again two years later in order to find out what impact television had had on other activities.[15]

Television apparently had little, if any, influence on the number of community activities available to people in each town, but it had a noticeable negative effect on participation in those activities. People, especially children and teenagers, were much more active when there was no television, and became progressively less so as the amount of television available increased. The introduction of television in Notel produced a marked reduction in many community activities and participation in sports. Television decreased attendance at dances, suppers and parties. In other words, in the case of activities which cannot easily be time-shared with television, participation tended to decrease when television was introduced or when the amount of it that was available grew.

One interpretation of the finding which revealed a relatively frequent usage of television along with regular participation in other leisure activities consisted of a notion termed 'the more, the more'. This posits that those motivations which drive an individual to view large amounts of television will similarly compel that person to pursue other leisure activities. In this view, television watching and alternative leisure activities are not seen as competitive but serve rather to reinforce one another – in other words, an interest in one activity stimulates an interest in others.

On the evidence accumulated so far, there are no firm indications that television viewing invariably has a negative impact on how much time is spent doing other things, although, and almost inevitably, not all researchers are in agreement about this. There is mounting evidence that television may replace some alternative activities, though not others, among children and teenagers. Different activities bring different pleasures. Young people today have an unprecedented array of media, media-related gadgetry and in-house entertainment facilities at their disposal. The decision to choose one item or activity over another may depend on which one is judged to give the most satisfaction, given the young person's needs at the time.

Researchers in the United States have considered what they call the 'opportunity costs' of television viewing for young people. Among one group of American adolescents it was found that, among other things, heavy television viewers forfeited taking part in some formal social activities with peers, were less likely to play musical instruments and gave up on some sleep.

Interviews were carried out with children and teenagers aged 12–14 years who were asked about the television programmes they normally watched, the times they watched, their use of other media such as radio, records or tapes, newspapers and video games, their membership of groups or clubs, and other miscellaneous hobbies, pastimes, sleeping patterns and musical instruments.[16]

Modest support was found for the claims of 'the more, the more' explanations of time use. As television viewing time increased so did time spent listening to records and tapes, and to a smaller degree listening to radio and engaging in hobbies. There were some at-home activities which competed with television viewing. The playing of home video games (which may be in competition not only for viewing time but also for viewing equipment), sleeping and playing musical instruments stood as trade-off activities with television viewing. As involvement with television increased, these activities were seen to decline. Belonging to clubs and the holding of group memberships which take the young person away from the house are in direct competition with watching television. If the child or teenager is out of the home, he/she is unlikely to be in a position to view television. If the amount of television viewing is allowed to increase, therefore, these other activities are likely to be among the first to decline.

One recent survey among children in Britain explored which media they have available to them and what use they make of these media. From this research it has become clear that children have access to and make use of a wide range of media – and that the use of older established ones does not invariably diminish in the face of competition from the new.[17]

Television viewing diaries and questionnaires were completed by a nation-wide sample of 468 young people aged between 4 and 12 years. In their diaries, the children logged the programmes they watched on television during the survey week. On the questionnaire they were asked about ownership and use of a range of media and media accessories.

All children surveyed had a television set in their homes, as a condition of being in the panel; national data indicate that 98 per cent of all households have at least one television set. These, then, are the availabilities of seventeen other forms, grouped in terms of their pervasiveness:

—96 per cent said they had a computer at their school
—94 per cent had a shelf of books at home
—93 per cent had a cassette player for listening to music tapes
—83 per cent had a paintbox or set of colours to make pictures
—83 per cent had a record player
—70 per cent had a musical instrument to play
—68 per cent had a cassette player or radio with earphones
—65 per cent had their very own radio
—62 per cent had a pile of comics

—52 per cent had a video-recorder at home
—52 per cent had a computer at home
—49 per cent visited a friend who has a video-recorder
—43 per cent had their very own television set
—41 per cent had a television set with a remote control

—35 per cent had a toy which operates by remote control
—25 per cent had a push-button telephone in the home
—18 per cent had a teletext receiver at home

This listing does not exhaust all possible media available to children. For example, questions were not asked about the availability of newspapers and magazines. Nevertheless, it does indicate a media pervasiveness that is on the whole quite extensive; a majority of the children claimed to have most of the items asked about.

How often do children use different media if they have them? If we take a look first of all at what may be called 'TV-media' comprising video-recorders (VCRs), teletext and remote control channel changers, then there is clear evidence that VCR usage is fairly extensive. Nearly half the children from VCR households (49 per cent) said they used it regularly. Slightly more claimed a similar level of usage of teletext if they had a set (52 per cent) and a substantial majority of children from homes with remote control claimed to use it often (82 per cent). Frequent use of personal computers was less widespread but not uncommon either, especially for playing games. One in five children with personal computers at home, however, claimed to use them for non-games purposes.

More than four out of ten said they regularly played records (42 per cent) or listened to music on the radio (44 per cent). Far fewer claimed to play any pop music videos, though, and nearly 80 per cent of youngsters from VCR households said they never did.

Despite the obvious use of quite an array of electronic media in the home, there was no indication that print media were being ignored. More than half the children said they read a newspaper at least occasionally. About one in four (26 per cent) claimed to read one fairly often. The same applied to books (32 per cent) and comics (24 per cent).

Even more enlightening were findings which revealed how the use of different media – old and new – fit together. Was there any evidence, for instance, that the most modern media were ousting the traditional ones? The answer is no, with rare exceptions. Not only do the new fit with the new, but some of the old do too.

For example, children who claimed often to watch films and television programmes on their VCR were indeed more likely to have played pop videos, used teletext and a radio/cassette player with earphones, but were also more likely to have been to the cinema recently. Children who said they regularly played computer games were less likely to read comics, but were slightly more likely to read newspapers and magazines. Playing pop videos was also positively associated with reading newspapers and magazines, but makes no difference to how often books or comics are read.

More detailed results indicate that there are children who are media rich – having access to and making use of many media – and there are those (far fewer in number) who are media poor. The latter tend to make do with fewer sources of amusement. Among the media-rich children, however, the new media are not totally replacing the old. Displacement can occur and does so possibly when a new medium provides the same gratifications as an old one, but in a more attractive package. For instance, although total TV viewing was not significantly related to the use of any reading materials (books, comics, magazines or newspapers) children who watched more TV drama read fewer comics (frequently regarded as being 'bad' for children anyway).

In this multi-media era, today's children may be learning to identify the unique benefits and gratifications that can be derived from different media and divide their time between the many that are available, according to their personal needs and wants.

But what are these personal needs and wants when it comes to television? This chapter has examined the extent to which children watch television and types of programmes; it is now necessary to investigate the reasons behind children's viewing behaviour.

Chapter two

Why do children watch TV?

People rarely sit mindlessly watching just anything on their 'box in the corner'; invariably some kind of choice has been made as to which programme they are going to watch. Children, as can be seen from the TV ratings, are no different. They too have their likes and dislikes. For example, Channel 4's sometimes controversial programme *Network 7*, screened at the unpopular time of 11 o'clock on Sunday morning, has consistently attracted large members of young viewers even though its overall audience is relatively small.

As we have seen already, television programmes can be divided up into various categories or types, some of which are watched more often and by larger numbers of viewers than others. Furthermore, patterns of television viewing and programme preferences are linked to the demographic and family characteristics of audience members. Thus, some young people exhibit a taste for one type of programme, and other young people show preferences for a different sort of programme.[1] Although these relationships are interesting for what they show about the pattern of television watching behaviour and the character of programme tastes across mass audiences, they do not reveal much about the reasons why people selectively choose to watch one type of programme in preference to another or why they become 'hooked' on a particular series. Are there psychological reasons why some programmes are preferred by certain people? Do particular programmes satisfy special needs for individual viewers?

There is emerging psychological evidence that both transient and enduring motivations and temporary moods can and do influence the way people use the mass media. Children are no different. In the context of television viewing, their individual personalities and current moods can affect how and why they watch television as well as the specific programmes they select to view.

Reasons for watching television

Researchers have for many years talked about the 'uses and gratifications' served by the media. This means that the media are thought to satisfy various needs of their consumers – to be entertained, to be informed, to have company, to relax and so on. Such needs may direct people to seek out particular mass media or, in the case of television, to choose to watch particular kinds of programmes. Television viewers are therefore motivated to watch television in order to satisfy their various wants, needs and desires at the time. This does not mean that viewing behaviour is always pushed by strong psychological drives. But, for most of the time that people watch television, and this applies to some extent even to the young, they do so for a reason. This reason may be as simple as 'to pass the time'.

There is a belief among some scholars of media consumption that if the gratifications sought by people are met by watching specific television programmes, listening to particular radio shows, and reading certain newspapers or magazines, they will return to those programmes and reading material again when motivated to do so.[2] Thus, viewers may be drawn back to a television series for episode after episode, not simply because they want to see the outcome of the next bit of the story, but also because by watching the series they are gaining some form of satisfaction which is important to them. Viewers may return to the news for information, magazine shows for advice on personal or social problems, soap opera for companionship, drama for excitement and escapism, comedy to be cheered up, or any of these to have something to talk about with others the next day. One early observation, made during the 1940s, was that women who were lonely or socially isolated, or who experienced more anxiety and frustration in their lives would listen more to radio soap operas. These serials compensated for social or emotional vacuums in their own lives. Women also used radio serials as a source of 'advice' about how to deal with everyday problems.[3]

In the early 1960s, Wilbur Schramm and his colleagues outlined three main uses of television by the child. The first referred to the positive pleasure of being entertained. Television offers a fantasy world in which the child can escape real-life boredom and problems. Schramm observed that children would sit with absorbed faces when watching favourite programmes. Second was information, for example about how to dress, behave and so on. Third, he identified 'social utility' as a major function. Watching in mixed company, he argued, gave young men and women an excuse to sit close together and often provided topics for conversation.[4]

Several surveys carried out in Britain and the United States have aimed to identify the major reasons children report for watching television. Around six to eight reasons have usually emerged, although there is considerable overlap between them. One survey by Bradley Greenberg was carried out among children in London who were aged 9, 12 and 15 years. The children were asked to write an essay on the subject 'Why I like to watch television'. An in-depth analysis of the essays yielded eight groups of reasons why children claimed to watch television. These were 'to pass time', 'to forget as a means of diversion', 'to learn about things', 'to learn about myself', 'for arousal', 'for relaxation', 'for companionship' and 'as a habit'.[5]

A similar survey carried out among young people in the United States identified six reasons why children and adolescents watch television: learning, habit or to pass time, companionship, escape, arousal and relaxation. Viewing to pass time, for relaxation and arousal were the most salient motives. Thus, children and adolescents report a variety of reasons for watching television.[6] Even those identified above, however, each cover a cluster of needs, motives and gratifications sought by the younger viewer. We turn now to examine what each one means.

Viewing as habit or as time filler

One of the most prominent reasons for watching television mentioned by most people is simply as a means of passing or filling time. In his work with British children in the early 1970s, Bradley Greenberg found that this was the most important kind of reason given, though its significance weakened with age. Thus, viewing out of habit or because there is nothing better to do is something children are less likely to say they do at age 15 than at age 9 or 12.[7]

The particular reasons children give for watching television are related to the types of programmes they watch and what they think about those programmes. Children who say they watch television out of habit or to pass time tend to be less likely to watch news and current affairs and more likely to watch comedy and light entertainment. There is some evidence also that children who claim to watch out of habit are more eager to talk about television.

Viewing to learn

People may turn to television as a source of learning. Learning motivations do not simply direct viewers towards strictly informational programmes, though. Certain kinds of learning benefit can also be obtained from drama and entertainment.

Television's dramatic characterisations and plots, for example, may convey lessons about how or how not to deal with other people, solve personal or family problems and disputes, make friends and influence people, and get on in life – professionally and personally. In other words, not only does learning from television consist of improving one's knowledge of what is going on in the world, that is, political, economic, industrial and foreign affairs, but also television is a major source of social learning. This learning may be an incidental by-product of watching ostensibly for entertainment-oriented reasons, though for many people it may be the most significant kind of learning from television.

Most studies of learning motivations and television watching have looked at television in general rather than at specific genres of programming. But while young people may be able to report their most important reasons for watching television, it is likely that such reports are based upon their reasons for watching specific programmes.

Young viewers then may turn to television as a source of various kinds of learning. Through television, children may learn about themselves, about life, about how to behave in different situations, about how to deal with personal and family problems and so on. In learning about life, television programmes may be selected because they contain information about people, places and the way society operates. They may offer insights into the way people in distant places feel and behave. The child may learn about different social and racial groups, different occupations, life-styles and events that are happening in the outside world.

Television programmes can sometimes provide helpful suggestions about how to do things that you have not done before. They can provide young viewers with some indications about the appropriate ways to act in certain situations. They may offer hints about current fashions and fads. They may offer advice on how to improve your technique at playing games, a blueprint for losing weight, information about holidays, cooking tips, getting ahead in a job and so on.

Television can also be a source of advice for young people. Television programmes may be selected because they can provide useful guidance for decision-making or problem-solving regarding some particular matter a child has to deal with in life. Television may offer some insights which can help young people to make their mind up what to do. Some programmes can offer advice on how to deal with parents and problems within the family. Others may give advice on how to deal with health problems, making and keeping friends, having a romantic relationship, being successful with the opposite sex and so on.

Research has shown that where information about how to cope with certain important emotional and social needs is unavailable in their own environment, children will look for alternative means of satisfying these needs. Under these circumstances television may become particularly significant to youngsters for their schooling in life. Socially disadvantaged youngsters can develop a dependence on television for learning about life, getting to see what people are like, learning how to solve problems. At the same time, youngsters may also depend more on television for excitement and for thrills than better-off counterparts.[8]

The survey of London children referred to earlier identified and measured two sets of learning reasons: 'learning about things' and 'learning about myself'. Children were asked if they watched to learn about things happening in the world, to learn about things they have done before, to get new ideas, to learn things they do not learn in school, to learn things about themselves, to see how they are supposed to act, to learn about what could happen to them and to see how other people deal with the same problems they have. Practically all these reasons were perceived as pertinent to the viewing experience.[9]

Viewing for companionship

Watching television can provide a source of companionship both by bringing the family together to share in the enjoyment of programmes and by supplying a collection of fantasy friends with whom the child can vicariously become involved. It is the latter involvement to which most children probably refer when they say that television provides company. Indeed, within the family setting much use of the television set these days is solitary. Although watching programmes off-air is more often done in the company of others than alone, the opposite is true when the set is used for playing back videos. Furthermore, with the growth of two- and three-set households, there is even more scope for solitary viewing.[10]

Television as baby-sitter

Recognition of the function of television as a source of companionship occurs not simply as a perception of children themselves but also within the family context. One role of television these days is as surrogate baby-sitter. Although it cannot perform all the usual and expected duties of normal baby-sitters – it does not break up fights, it cannot tell the child when to go to bed, it may not keep the child from wrecking the house – it may be effective at keeping the kids quiet for a while or at least keeping mischief-making down to a more manageable level.

Television's potential as baby-sitter was first remarked upon over thirty years ago. Eleanor Maccoby, a prominent TV researcher in the 1950s, found that mothers in one of her surveys mentioned using television as a 'pacifier'. A majority mentioned that television made it easier to care for children in the home. Evidence to substantiate the belief that television can keep children occupied has emerged from the observation that children become more passive while watching, self-absorbed and less likely to misbehave or require constant parental supervision.[11]

How do mothers use television to occupy their child's attention? How widespread is television's use as a baby-sitter? Do parents talk to their children about television and in what way? Do mothers rate television highly as a baby-sitter?

In one recent American survey, mothers generally believed that television is used quite widely as a baby-sitter, but they saw it as something which goes on in other families rather than their own.[12] These mothers did not condone habitual television viewing and felt that it is not something they would like their own children to spend all their time doing. Playing with friends was usually seen as preferable to watching television and most of the mothers tended to feel that their kids would rather watch television than play on their own.

When asked what they usually told their children to do when they needed to cook, do some housework or relax, television was mentioned as often as friends, though they claimed to ask their children to help with the chores more often. Many, however, simply told their child to do whatever he/she wanted to do, or to get out of mummy's way.

The majority of these American mothers felt that most other mothers of children aged between 2 and 12 used television as a baby-sitter. On average, they estimated that other mothers might use television to keep their kids quiet for up to several hours a day. They were much less likely to admit to this amount and kind of use of television in their own homes, however. In other words, mothers are less inclined to admit to using television as a baby-sitter than they estimate its use among other mothers. We do not know how typical this behaviour is. Nor do we know how well mothers are aware of how other mothers use television with the children. It seems likely, however, that in so far as mothers are prepared to admit to such things at all, television is deliberately used by many to occupy their offspring at times when they cannot be bothered to look after their kids themselves or when they are preoccupied by other matters.

TV people as companions

A different aspect of television's role as companion stems from the various relationships which often develop between viewers and the characters and personalities who enter their homes with regularity through the television set. Young viewers may form close associations with certain characters, identifying with these people as desired models whom they aspire to be like.[13] For children who have few friends, TV people may provide substitutes with whom they can engage in what researchers have termed 'para-social' relationships. In other words, although they cannot really be friends with their TV favourites, they can pretend that they are.

Para-social interaction is especially likely to occur with those television celebrities who appear frequently and whose performance simulates face-to-face conversation with the viewer at home. One belief is that in addition to identifying with TV characters, viewers retain their own personas and respond to people on television in the same way as if they might upon meeting them in the street. A great deal of viewer involvement in television programmes derives from the familiarity viewers develop with television characters. This experience leads viewers to feel that they know the characters and can, as a consequence, predict their likely next actions. This illusion of 'knowing' may be especially likely to develop around those TV personalities who give the impression of talking directly to the viewer; for example, the personality who regularly hosts chat or entertainment shows.

Viewing as a source of conversation

Both children and adolescents cite television as a major source of conversation material. Programmes provide a fertile ground of common experience for the next morning's conversations in the classroom. Unless you have watched the most popular programmes of the day, you are likely to be left out. Those children who cannot talk about the latest happenings in the plot of a popular soap are not able to join in the conversation. Thus, a programme may be selectively watched by children to ensure that they will not be left out if it is raised as a topic of discussion the next day or at some later time.[14]

Viewing for escape

Television can offer a fantasy world for the vicarious pleasure of viewers into which they can escape from everyday problems or the humdrum of ordinary living. The escapism function of television operates for children as well as adults and is one of the central mechanisms of television's entertainment functions. Television provides a source of distraction from everyday realities. Through its fantasy material more than anything else, viewers can become vicariously involved with the characters and events and act out in their minds ways of dealing with their problems. Television's fantasy is also the stuff of dreams which, though unlikely ever to come true, provide some temporary hype and respite from the less desirable everyday realities with which many individuals have to contend.

Various motives have been identified as underlying the need to escape through vicarious involvement in the fantasy world television can bring into the home. One idea is that children subjected to harsh parental discipline may use television to escape from an unpleasant home environment. Alternatively, the need to escape may stem from an unhappy experience in school. Early evidence indicated that children of lower intelligence and poorer educational performance sought out programmes through which they could forget about their problems.[15]

Another important factor which seems likely to underlie the use of television as a means of escape is how well children get on with other children. Early observations indicated that children who become addicted to television are found not only to have lower intelligence and come from poorer walks of life, but also to be shy and retiring, have few friends and be ill-at-ease with others. Thus, not only might television provide such lonely young people with some form of companionship, but also it may help to take their minds off their loneliness.[16]

And what about children who choose to escape via televised violence? Preferences for media violence have been shown to relate to transient mood states of individuals. People who have been put into an angry mood or aggressive frame of mind have been found to exhibit stronger preferences for violent over non-violent media content when compared with non-angered people.[17] Some researchers have found that when people have been induced to fantasise about behaving aggressively this can create a further preference for violent films over non-violent films especially among male viewers.[18]

Much of the research literature concerning television violence has focused on the impact of violent TV material on viewers' attitudes and behaviours. Much less attention has been paid to whether or not violent programmes are viewed selectively, in particular by individuals whose personalities are already characterised by strong aggressive dispositions.[19] And, if so, whether and to what extent this may account for the relationships so frequently observed in correlational surveys between the viewing of violent programming and personal aggressiveness. A number of surveys carried out in the United States during the early 1970s reported relationships between delinquent aggressiveness and preferences for violence-containing programmes. These results have most commonly been taken as evidence that watching television violence encourages the development of anti-social tendencies among young people. But another way of looking at the findings is that they may reveal a different sort of connection whereby those youngsters who are already aggressive tend to prefer to watch programmes which contain violence.[20]

Evidence supporting the thesis that aggressive predisposition may underlie the enjoyment of violent television content has emerged from several studies. In one of these a panel of young people was surveyed twice across a period of one year. Measures of their attitudes towards the use of aggression and their television viewing habits over time were taken. Although general patterns of viewing changed little over the year, some evidence did emerge that individuals who exhibited aggressive attitudes at the beginning of the study expressed particularly strong preferences for violent programming after one year, even when other important variables such as sex, age and initial viewing patterns had been statistically controlled. The reverse relationship between viewing television violence initially and the development of aggressive attitudes over time was much smaller.[21]

Viewing as arousal

Psychologists have long recognised that human beings have basic needs for stimulation. It is well documented that people have a natural curiosity and that their seeking after new and varied experiences reflects these drives. According to some media scholars, television viewing preferences are underpinned and shaped by these stimulation-seeking tendencies.[22] The aim, however, is not to seek endless stimulation, but a sufficient amount to achieve an optimal state of arousal. There is a point at which the individual attains an ideal level of arousal, while to be either above or below that level is less comfortable. In their pioneering study of the role of television in children's lives, Wilbur Schramm and his colleagues reported that television is viewed predominantly for the simple pleasure of being entertained. Entertainment can derive through various gratifications being satisfied. One major ingredient in respect of the entertainment value of many programmes is whether or not they excite or amuse their viewers in some significant way.[23]

Television offers various forms of entertainment – serious drama, science fiction, romantic serials, situation comedy, music and variety shows, game shows among them. The emotions aroused will often differ from one type of programme to the next. Viewers' tastes in these programmes will vary as well. General liking for one kind of drama or entertainment may be linked to enduring dispositions which characterise a viewer's personality. At the same time, the extent to which a viewer will want to watch one particular type of programme – even one that is normally liked – may depend on how he or she feels at the time. As moods change so too does appetite for certain programmes. Thus, television viewing may provide a means for 'mood management'. Programmes are chosen in a selective fashion according to the individual's need to achieve a satisfactory level of arousal.[24]

Overcoming boredom

One aspect of the arousal function of television is that it may be used as a means of overcoming boredom. It provides a source of stimulation – both mental and emotional – and can brighten up a dull day or night. Programmes can vary in their arousal properties. Thus, the choice of what to watch can depend on how much stimulation we are in need of. Bored viewers have been found to select exciting programmes which increase their level of arousal. Individuals who are already in a state of excitement (or stress) have been found by contrast to select to watch calming or relaxing programmes.

Improving on bad moods

Another way in which television functions to influence a viewer's arousal is when it is used to make a person who is in a bad mood feel better. Programme selection in this context will rest not simply on whether or not it is arousing, but in what way. Comedy, drama and game shows, for instance, may all be entertaining in their own way, but the events they contain may not invariably be the most appropriate kinds of material to cheer up someone who is feeling down. Drama and game shows can offer suspense and tension, and sad moments along with a few happy ones. Comedy, in contrast, is aimed at inducing laughter, merriment and euphoria. It may offer a better guarantee of cheering viewers up. Research has shown that to some extent this is all true. Choice of comedy, however, can also vary depending upon the mood state and type of comedy on offer. Certain forms of humour are hostile and aggressive. This sort of comedy may have a particularly strong appeal to viewers who are in an angry mood (more so than does non-hostile comedy), although the latter pattern is more likely to be found amongst males than females.[25]

Reassurance and comfort from TV

The information contained in programmes can offer crumbs of comfort in addition to being entertaining. Thus, programmes may be selected and used by viewers not because of expectations regarding the excitement and pleasure they might bring but because they contain soothing, comforting information. Thus, just when it seems like the world is becoming an increasingly hostile, unpleasant place to live, programmes which depict acts of kindness and generosity may serve to restore faith in human nature. There is evidence that people faced with hostile environments may turn to television and movies not simply to escape but in search of reassurance. Research with pre-school and infant children has shown that even at a very early age, television programmes may be used in this way. Children who had recently experienced an unpleasant situation, in which an adult had criticised them, opted to spend more time watching a programme in which children were treated nicely than did children who had previously had their appearance praised. Thus, television can provide a means of coping with a harsh, cynical and unfriendly social environment.[26]

Children's reasons for watching television then, are multiple and varied; they seek to gain information, to be entertained, to pass time and so on. However, research into the reasons behind children's viewing preferences frequently assumes high levels of attention to the screen. But is this necessarily the case? What factors influence *how* children watch TV? It is to this issue that we turn our attention next.

Chapter three

How do children watch TV?

The previous two chapters have already pointed out that on average children watch television from two and a half to three and a half hours per day according to age and that the reasons why they watch are multiple and varied. However, the *way* they watch is another important factor to take into account when investigating the nature of children's relationship with the media. Children do not just sit, glued to the screen. The way they watch varies considerably from one day to the next and even from one moment to the next. How do children watch? How much attention do they pay to the screen? Is television viewing a shared activity carried out alongside other activities?

People themselves frequently report that television does not command their exclusive attention. Often, viewing is carried on intermittently, as the individual leaves and re-enters the room where the set is on, or divides attention between looking at the screen and doing other things while in front of the TV. Consequently, time spent viewing is only a superficial indicator of how people use television.[1] Familiarity with having a set in a family household, for instance, is often associated with an increased ability to accomplish other activities in conjunction with TV watching. Thus, children may report doing homework or household chores while watching television. Some surveys have found that a majority of people, children included, report doing something else while watching, for over half of the programmes they watched the previous day. Few programmes are reportedly watched from beginning to end.[2]

Direct observation of how children watch television has further revealed that television holds the child's constant attention a lot less often than we might think. Pioneering research using a time-lapse camera revealed that people may leave their sets on even when they are not actually watching. For a large portion of the total time sets are switched on, they are playing to an empty room. And even when people are present they may be engaged in a variety of alternative activities at the same time as viewing the television.[3] As we shall see, children have been observed to be frequently doing other things such as eating, drinking, dressing, sleeping, playing and fighting. Often they are not actually looking at the screen at all and leave the room for extensive periods while the set is on. As the number of small children in a household increases, however, so too does total set in-use time but there is also a corresponding increase in the length of time the room is empty while the television set is switched on. How children watch television is also related to their understanding of programmes and to their reactions to different features of programme areas; these are covered in more detail in the next chapter.

The child's attention to the set

As we observed in Chapter 1, children start to pay attention to television from very early on in their lives. A major bone of contention among researchers, however, has been whether children's attention to the screen is mainly an 'active' or a 'passive' phenomenon. In recent years there has been increasing support for the active notion despite frequent adverse publicity which accuses television of turning children into mentally and physically lethargic 'couch potatoes'.

Adherents to the passive view believe that much of television washes over children and disengages their minds and requires only shallow effort in following what is happening in programmes. This impression of the way in which children watch television implies that programmes are more likely to be absorbed passively as a series of disconnected scenes rather than as events which link together to form a coherent whole.[4] Increasingly over recent years, evidence has emerged which indicates that this impression does not reflect the real nature of children's viewing.

Researchers who have observed children watching programmes both in controlled laboratory settings and at home have noticed that children rarely sit quietly and stare at the television the whole of the time viewing takes place. One study of infants watching an episode of *Sesame Street*, for example, found that children frequently looked at and away from the screen, averaging about 150 looks at and away per hour. The child would usually change his or her attention after no more than fifteen seconds of either looking towards or away from the television.[5]

How is the child's attention to the screen controlled?

There are two opposing points of view on this subject. One viewpoint is that children's attention is controlled by the formal features of television, that is by changing physical stimulation accompanying visual scene changes, background music, sound effects, and so forth. Another view is that children themselves learn to control their attention in relation to things which happen on screen which have meaning for them.[6] But what is the evidence on these ideas about children's viewing? Are youngsters reactive to the events happening in programmes? Or is their attention driven actively by their understanding and interpretation of what is going on?

Viewing as reactive

Children's attention to television involves looking and listening. Researchers have studied both. Studies of children's visual attention to the screen have tied its onset and offset to specific events or happenings in programmes. This research has provided clear evidence that some attributes of television which children watch are associated with much more looking at the screen than others. When there is a sudden change in the pace of the action, or the occurrence of funny voices, loud noises or appearances by children, young viewers are likely to turn their eyes towards the screen. Such research suggests that these attributes have some control over children's viewing.[7]

If a child's attention is governed by the physical features of a programme, infants and toddlers would be the most tied to such control since they are recognised as being more 'stimulus bound'. One noted researcher, Jerome Singer, has suggested that the orienting reaction is the basis for television viewing.[8] This is a natural response we all make towards something new or different which happens in our immediate environment. It stems from a primitive need to know what is going on. Since this response is already established in toddlers by about the age of 3 months we might expect to find it happening amongst very young infants while they are watching television. One study has reported that 6-month-old infants when kept near the television at home in a playpen without toys do pay some visual attention to the screen (49 per cent attention measured over sixteen minutes; 'chance' attention would be about 4 per cent). Under less restrictive viewing circumstances, however, toddlers' attention to television appears to be less frequent.[9]

The length of visual looking at the TV set has been found to increase fourfold from 12 to 48 months of age. This increase is partly connected with increases in the length of looks at the screen, but seems primarily to be due to a dramatic increase at about 30 months in the frequency of looking at the television. At about the age of 2 to 2 ½ years toddlers exhibit a significant shift in amount of looking at the television.[10]

Up to this age, children appear to show only sporadic attention to the set when it is switched on. Older children begin to develop what seems to be a concept of 'watching television'. This is indicated by the way they position themselves physically towards the set. Thus although they may still be playing with their toys, the centre of activity is the television, and looks towards it become more frequent. Subsequently, visual attention to television increases throughout the pre-school years until the child starts school, after which it tends to level off.[11]

One view is that children's mode of response to television changes systematically as they grow older and pass through progressive stages of intellectual development. As infants up to the age of 5 years, they are considered to be 'perceptually bound'; this means that very young children are most likely to have their attention drawn to the screen by overt visual or sound effects. As they grow older, those sorts of features, while not irrelevant, become only aspects of a programme's content likely to attract a child's attention. Young children tend to focus on concrete aspects of the programme, most notably changes of pace in physical action and the character types who are involved. Older children are more sensitive to abstract features of programmes such as relationships between events and characters whose meaningfulness derives from youngsters' understanding and following of the storyline as it unfolds.[12]

Proponents of the theory that children react to television, rather than actively seek to pay attention to those things which have meaning for them, also believe that it is sudden, often gimmicky changes in visual action or sound effects in programmes which is what really controls children's viewing behaviour. Thus, television which is rapidly paced with lots of physical changes, visible or heard, will gain and retain a child's attention. However, this style of presentation is not conducive to learning and understanding. If the content is presented too quickly, very little of it will stick. Assuming that this explanation of how television grabs the attention of youngsters is correct, as attention gets greater, understanding should get poorer.[13]

But is this really what happens? The active theory of viewing makes a substantially different assertion. It proposes that the child attends to things he or she can understand. Thus attention is driven by comprehension. On the latest evidence, the active theorists would seem to have it.

Viewing as active

An alternative impression of the nature of children's television watching has emerged from other evidence. Some scholars have proposed that the degree of attention that children give to the screen is actively and strategically guided by their attempts to understand and follow programmes. They also propose that children begin to learn to do this before 3 years of age and that this process may occur almost automatically, purely as a function of their early experience with television.[14]

As with adults, children don't need to pay constant attention to the screen to follow what is going on; they are able to detect changes in serials or significant events in programmes even when looking away. Just listening to the sound-track can provide clues as to when something important is happening and when they should look back at the screen. Even children as young as 3 years have this ability to monitor the sound-track on television whilst looking elsewhere and have been observed to shift their attention back to the screen when appropriate.

Other studies point to young children's motivation to understand television as a prime driver of their attention. In other words, there is increasing evidence to suggest that children actively direct their attention to television content that has meaning for them. In one study 5-year-olds' level of attention to an episode of *Sesame Street* was observed by placing one group in an empty room and another group in a room that contained potentially distracting toys. Under these conditions, children were found to differ greatly in the amount of time they watched the screen, but there was no difference in the extent to which youngsters followed and understood the programme. However, within the 'toys' group, looking at the screen and understanding were correlated, providing some evidence that attention may be directed by comprehension.

Nevertheless, as had been expected, the presence or absence of toys did make a difference to how much the children looked at the screen. The children who were placed with toys watched on average for 44 per cent of the time, while among the other children, watching averaged 87 per cent. Significantly, the two groups did not differ in how much they could remember overall from the programme. However, there was a connection between the particular aspects of the programme the children could remember and whether they had been paying attention at the moment those parts of the programme were being shown. In other words, if the child's attention was distracted by toys at the precise moment when an important piece of information was being presented, that item was unlikely to be recalled later.[15]

The finding that there were no differences between the two groups is the important one, though. It suggests that even among children whose attention may have been divided between watching the programme and playing with toys, attention to the programme was strategically organised and distributed between the two activities so that viewing occurred for the most informative bits of the programme. This strategy was so effective that giving the TV more attention did not improve their ability to remember it.

Further evidence that the ability to follow the programme underpins looking at it derives from the fact that when the programme is re-edited and jumbled up, it ceases to hold the attention of very young viewers (aged 3–6 years) for very long. Youngsters report thinking most about parts of programmes they can understand and choose not to think about those which have little or no meaning for them.[16]

It is now known that, as they mature, children acquire the intellectual skills necessary to organise specific elements of TV programmes into coherent and meaningful wholes. Through their primary school years, children are more capable of following dramatic plots. They become able to distinguish central from peripheral events in programmes. With such newly acquired comprehension skills, young viewers' attention may be selectively directed towards what they perceive to be the more important story elements in a programme. In other words, children's attention concentrates more decidedly on the main theme or plot, while they become much less concerned about or able subsequently to remember incidental, subplot elements from a programme.[17]

Children then learn to monitor the sound-track of programmes and listen for things which mean something to them. They are already fairly active in this regard by the time they have started school. Anything they hear which is significant and has meaning encourages them to look up at the television, while anything they cannot relate to inhibits attention. Children continue to look at the screen as long as they can follow what is happening. The programme must not simply be meaningful, however, if it is to maintain their attention; there must also be a certain degree of unpredictability about it.[18]

As children grow older their dependence purely on sound effects decreases. For instance, 11-year-olds exhibit greater depth of understanding television programmes than 5-year-olds, whereas the younger age group follow a programme much better and look at it more often when significant sounds occur. This difference is much less pronounced among the older children. Young children are very responsive to sound effects and other exciting events in the programme. Older children's attention is dependent upon deeper aspects of their understanding of the programme. At this level of viewing, an attention-grabbing event in a programme might consist of a significant development in the storyline, which in itself may not involve exciting changes of pace. The event's significance is only apparent to the child who has followed the storyline and is thus able to place what happens in a context which lends it meaning.[19]

Attentional inertia

The longer a young viewer continuously maintains a look at television the more likely it is that he or she will continue to do so. This tendency increases up to a period of about fifteen seconds of looking, after which the probability that the child will continue to look at the screen does not change substantially. Anderson and his colleagues have noted that the inertia pattern characterises *not* looking at the screen as well. In other words, the longer it has been since the viewer last looked at the screen, because of doing something else, the less likely it is that he or she will look back.[20]

To what extent is attentional inertia specific to the types of things being shown in programmes? Do children continue to watch a programme if it is interesting to them or involves them in some way? And to what extent do they fail to return to it if they find it boring? The evidence would suggest that, although attitudes to a programme do depend on what kinds of things it is about, a switch from one item to another is no guarantee that attention will suddenly change. In other words if one part of a programme is interesting and commands the viewer's attention, there will be a tendency to continue looking even after a change to a new item or different kind of content which may be less interesting and involving.

Researchers believe that 'attentional inertia' is an important aspect of the way the child watches television. It reflects the fact that even young viewers are actively monitoring television while viewing in order to identify meaningful content. It can drive the child to continue paying attention even when the material being shown is not easy to understand. So for a while, the young viewer tries to make sense of the complex, the new and the difficult. Although in general the child stops paying attention when the going gets really tough, attentional inertia serves to maintain attention further than it might otherwise go. As such, attentional inertia may be part of the means by which the child comes to process a programme that is poorly understood. This may lead the child to explore difficult territory, to work at understanding the unfamiliar and generally to stretch his or her ability to make sense of television.[21]

Programmes and the nature of watching

Children's viewing styles can vary with the type of programme they are watching. We have already seen that children have obvious programme preferences. Some programmes are watched more often and liked more than others. Levels of attention vary too across different kinds of programmes.

American surveys have found that levels of attention to television as reported by families can vary from programme to programme. Claimed attention levels were generally higher than average for peak-time drama series and family shows. Usually, there was greater deliberation and planning to watch these shows. And there was a greater likelihood that family members would report watching these shows all the way through. Programmes receiving relatively little attention were variety-comedy or variety-music, educational and sports programmes.[22]

Daniel Anderson and Elizabeth Pugzles Lorch have reported a wide variety of viewing styles among children on the evidence of video-tapes of families viewing in the home. They speculate that style of viewing is a function of age, viewing environment, relevance of the programme to the viewer, and viewer intention. They cite as an example a 5-year-old girl who looked intently at a favourite programme on Saturday morning but never looked at a hockey game in the evening. In the first case, it seemed likely that the girl wanted to be entertained by television, while in the second instance she was concerned mainly with playing with her father, who was trying to watch the hockey game.[23]

Levels of attention to the set vary with the type of programme. One study which observed children watching television at home through installed video cameras indicated that films were the programmes most attended to; on average, viewers exhibited visual attention to the TV screen for 76 per cent of the movie's duration. In descending order, children's shows received the next most attention (71 per cent), followed by suspense series (68 per cent), religious programmes (67 per cent), family series (66 per cent), game shows (66 per cent), talk shows (64 per cent), melodramas (59 per cent), sports events (59 per cent), news (55 per cent) and lastly advertisements (55 per cent).[24]

The sample was divided into three age groups: children (1–10 years), adolescents (11–19 years) and adults (20–75 years). Overall, the children looked at the screen 52 per cent of the time they were with television, adolescents 69 per cent and adults 65 per cent. Furthermore, interactions were found between the age of the viewer and type of programme being watched in influencing level of viewers' attention to the screen. Children attended most to children's programmes (86 per cent) and least to melodrama and sports (8 per cent). Adolescents paid most attention to suspense programmes (84 per cent) and least to sports (43 per cent). Adults looked most at films (78 per cent) and least at commercials (52 per cent).

The ability of children to follow a television programme is affected by the pace at which things happen in it. The view that young children respond to television in a predominantly 'perceptual' fashion suggests that fast pace, short scenes and frequent changes make the best combination to obtain and hold on to children's attention. Despite the fact that many physical features of television programmes have been found to affect young viewers' attention, little evidence has so far emerged which shows that rapid pace *per se* has this influence.[25]

The significance of pace on attention can vary with the type of programme. One American study found that children attended to high-paced cartoons more than to low-paced cartoons, but when the content was changed to a magazine format (segments taken from *The Electric Company*), pace had no effect on visual attention. Moreover, children aged 8–9 years had their attention held more strongly by fast-paced cartoons than did pre-school children, an age trend opposite to what the researchers expected.[26]

More detailed analysis of what actually is going on during viewing reveals one reason for the complex and inconsistent ways in which children's attention to the screen is affected by the pace of a programme. Pace can actually be composed of several ingredients: changes to a new scene not previously shown in the programme; changes to a familiar scene; and changes in the cast of characters present. These changes are often marked by visual features, such as fades, dissolves, zooms, or pans, or by auditory features, such as changes in music, sound effects or speech.[27]

Changes of scene sometimes elicit attention from a child who is not looking, but for a young viewer who is already watching the screen, scene and character changes can sometimes prompt a temporary interruption of looking. Older children, presumably better able to pursue the flow of a programme, can use scene-change points as the occasion for both starting and stopping a look more so than do younger children. This suggests that, as they get older, children become more aware of formal feature cues marking breaking points in the programme. It appears that for school-age children, scene and character changes are points at which the young viewer decides whether to begin or stop or continue paying attention to a television programme.

Increasingly with age, young television viewers come to attend more consistently and strategically to programmes, and understand more effectively what they view.[28] Other interesting work with young television watchers has further revealed the varying significance of pace with the type of programme being watched. Fast-paced programmes do not consistently receive greater attention than slower-paced programmes. In general, programmes with a continuous story-line receive greater attention than segmented, magazine format shows. The former tend to be better remembered than the latter as well. Pace appears to have a greater impact on the tempo of looking among older children primarily when they are watching programmes with a continuous story. Increasing the pace of magazine shows makes them more difficult for children to follow and with older children in particular does not cause them to pay the programme more attention.[29]

The implications of this evidence for children's programming are that fast pace does not often enhance attention and may interfere with young viewers' abilities to understand and learn the content of a programme. Children attend more effectively to material presented in story format than in a magazine format.

Conclusion

In conclusion then, it seems that children's attention to the screen is neither constant nor passive. The amount of attention they are prepared to give to individual programmes is directly related to whether the visual and audio message has meaning specific to them, and whether they are given sufficient time to absorb that meaning. In this regard, the format of programmes is all important. Therefore, a major controlling factor over how and why they watch particular programmes is to do with how well they are able to follow and understand the information they are offered. But how does their ability to follow and understand television develop? Are there particular factors that hinder or enhance this development? In the next chapter we attempt to answer both these questions.

Chapter four

How well do children follow and understand TV?

A commonly held belief about television viewing is that it requires little effort. Indeed it is true that for most viewers for most of the time television is watched as a source of relaxation. Yet in order to get any enjoyment or satisfaction out of television at all, there has to be a degree of understanding. In other words if programmes cannot be understood, it is unlikely that they will be enjoyed. The ability of viewers to follow a programme and to understand at least part of what's going on is essential to being able to get anything out of television at all – even relaxation. This is just as relevant to children as it is to adults. Since we are not born with an intrinsic understanding of television, it must therefore represent a skill or set of skills which we learn. This learning begins in early childhood from the time we start to watch television.

As we saw in the last chapter, understanding television dictates and even determines attention to the screen. The nature of children's attention to programmes changes with age as their understanding of programmes develops. Among relatively inexperienced young viewers, attention to the television can be affected quite significantly by physical happenings in programmes. Reaction to a change of events is less discriminating among very young children than later on in their viewing lives. As children learn about different types of programmes and develop the ability to recognise the particular characters of programmes, they become more selective in the way they respond to visual and sound effects and other sources of physical stimulation which programmes contain. This happens as these physical features themselves acquire meaning. Eventually, it is the meaning that children respond to rather than the physical event.

In this chapter we will take a closer look at different aspects of understanding about television. An implication associated with many common-sense beliefs about the importance of television is that it 'injects' viewers with new attitudes and examples of how to behave which they take on board without question or resistance. This belief is at best misleading and at worst wrong. Viewers are not empty vessels – not even young viewers. Nor do they passively accept all that television tells or shows them. There are a number of ways in which children learn to understand television and make sophisticated judgements about programmes. We shall examine some of these under the following headings:

1 children's understanding of the format features of programmes
2 children's abilities to follow television narratives
3 children's discrimination between what is real and what is fantasy on
   television
4 children's judgements about television characters and their actions.

Children's understanding of the format features of programmes

Researchers have found that young children's attention to television varies with
a variety of content and presentation format features. The implication of this
work is that children's visual attention to the screen is largely governed by how
much they understand what is going on. Two kinds of format attributes have been
investigated – visual attributes and sound (or auditory) attributes. The major
difference between these is in the way they are able to affect and control attention. Clearly, visual attributes can have influence only when they are seen, in
other words when the child looks at the screen. Sound attributes, on the other
hand, can draw the young child's attention to the television even when he/she is
not looking directly at it.[1]

In one study, researchers observed children aged 3–5 years continuously while
they watched a mixed compilation of programming over a three-hour period.
Snacks and toys were available while viewing took place. The children were
assessed, principally for the extent to which they looked towards or away from
the screen, and according to how much their attention was influenced by visual
and sound attributes of the programmes. Which features of the programme made
children look back towards the screen when their attention was diverted elsewhere? And which features could maintain the child's attention while he or she
was actually watching the screen?

As might be expected, audio or sound effects proved to be the main means of
regaining a child's attention while visual attributes were best at maintaining the
child's attention. In other words, some kind of change in the spoken dialogue,
background sounds or music could encourage a child to look at the screen, but
this look would be prolonged only if what was happening visually proved to be
of interest. Both the audio and visual attributes were then examined to assess their
potential for either eliciting or inhibiting attention.

In all, seven different types of change in the sound-track produced visual
attention from among inattentive young viewers – change in sound volume,
special sound effects, laughter, women's voices, children's voices, peculiar
voices and instrumental music. Three sound features inhibited attention – men's
voices, individual singing and slow music. Two sound features had mixed effects
– the onset of lively music or rhyming elicited attention but only for a few
seconds. Finally, two sound features made no difference to visual attention –
group singing and applause. If the child was looking at the television, both visual
and sound attributes maintained attention. In all, six visual attributes were found
to maintain attention, six visual attributes terminated attention, eight visual

attributes were non-significant, three sound attributes maintained attention, three sound attributes terminated attention, and five were non-significant.[2]

Children's abilities to follow television narratives

The next question on children's understanding of television concerns how well young viewers are able to follow the narrative or storyline of programmes. Children may pay attention to the screen because of the physical stimulation caused by a programme, for example, because of significant voices they recognise, changes in the tone of the music or other sound effects. But how well do they actually follow what is going on?

Most of the research on children's understanding of television has focused on developmental changes with age. Age trends are not the only important factors, however. It is important to look at the form and content of programmes and how they affect comprehension and growth of understanding. Evaluating the state of knowledge about these matters is not always easy. Comparability of research is often hindered by lack of consistency in the definition and measures of comprehension used by different researchers. Sometimes comprehension has been defined in terms of what children can recall from programmes they have watched. On other occasions understanding has been indicated by the ability of children to place scenes from a programme in correct sequence. It is unlikely that such different methods measure the same thing. A convenient way to divide up the research is by the age of the children studied. Some researchers have been interested principally in school age children, while others have focused on infants who have just begun or have yet to start school.

Research with infants and pre-school children

Before they start school, children can experience particular difficulties in being able to understand the programmes they watch on television. Children of 4 and 5, for example, may be able to recall isolated episodes or scenes from programmes they watch but are unable to put all the pieces of a story together to form a coherent whole. At this age, children's thinking is concerned totally with life in the present and they have difficulty connecting the beginning, middle and end bits of programmes which occur at different points in time.

At the age when they are about to start school, children usually have trouble following the plots of programmes and do not necessarily recount the events in a story in their proper, original sequence. Even programmes made especially for this age group can cause them difficulties.[3]

Communicating deeper meaning

Even if a programme is carefully produced and succeeds in getting across a good grasp of basic story ingredients to young children, they may still fail to understand the deeper meaning that may underlie it. In one Swedish study, producers tried to communicate an understanding of the situation of immigrant children from Finland. They did so by describing the day-to-day lives of a Swedish and a Finnish girl. The underlying message of the film was 'We are quite alike, after all'. The film did not succeed, even though the children were able to follow the story and relate various details. In order to grasp the message, young viewers had to draw conclusions from the material presented, that is, they had to be capable of inferential reasoning, something they were unable to do since their thought processes were not yet sufficiently developed.[4]

Young children's understanding of television has been investigated in a project begun in 1969 at the Swedish Broadcasting Corporation (Sveriges Radio). Rydin and colleagues have been investigating pre-school children's understanding not only as a means of providing insight into the way they comprehend television, but also as a formative research exercise designed to help produce better programmes.

At the time when interest in pre-school programming was growing, in particular following the introduction of *Sesame Street*, Sveriges Radio produced a successful but controversial programme *Two Ants are More than Four Elephants*. The pre-schoolers and their parents seemed to enjoy the programmes but educators and other critics claimed the 'pace was too fast and the content was packaged knowledge out of context which would not stimulate deeper, activating processes within the young viewers'.

This criticism stimulated further research on a programme called *The Tale of the Seed*. This study assessed children's understanding and retention of information and investigated the effect of accompanying material that was irrelevant to the central theme. Rydin found that repetition of information enhanced learning from the radio version of the programme, but irrelevant details neither increased nor decreased children's retention of factual material. In a subsequent study of the televised version, the inclusion of irrelevant details resulted in reduced ability to remember the factual material.

Younger children (5 years) were more distracted by the lack of agreement between audio and visual (e.g. when irrelevant verbal information was not illustrated in the visual display). Rydin suggested that one of the major problems inherent in much of the television programming of the western world is the fragmentation of the sequence of the programme. This applies both to children and to adults. Thus, the viewer is unable to move with the flow of the programme. This fragmentation, she argues, is the result of the domination of much of the western world's television by commercial interests. Programmes are fragmented because advertising can be more easily inserted.

School-age children's comprehension of television

Between the ages of 7 and 12 years, children's thinking is still very different from adult thought processes. At the same time, however, children at this age show some signs of mental maturity. Their command of language, for example, is nearly complete. They also show a growing ability to see other people's point of view. In terms of television, what particularly distinguishes school-age children from younger ones is their ability to draw conclusions from the material presented to them. Their thinking is more flexible and not so closely bound up with the situation in which they find themselves at the moment. When recounting a story, they frequently introduce their own interpretation, which was not part of the original version. Making one's own interpretations and drawing conclusions are part of the mental processing by which we all create structures and contexts for what we perceive in the world around us and help us to remember the things we have experienced.

This development does not happen all at once. Thus, some studies have found that children's understanding of television up to about 8 years of age is poor. In general, up to the age of 8, children retain a relatively small proportion of depicted actions, events and settings in typical programmes; memory for pro-gramme content improves significantly between the ages of 8 and 12 years.[5]

Although young viewers attend to aspects of programmes that are obviously salient and have meaning or relevance for them, particularly in programmes produced for children, they apparently lack the abilities necessary for a proper understanding of more complex programmes made for older viewers. While 8-year-olds can follow major, explicitly presented ingredients of a plot, they are significantly less likely than 10- to 12-year-olds to 'go beyond the information given' and make more subtle connections, e.g. relationships between an early and a later scene in a drama. Indeed, younger school children seem able to perform at little better than chance when tested for their understanding of programmes at this level. Thus, while viewing is active and discerning to some extent even among young children, the strategic skills necessary for mature viewing of complex programmes develop markedly over the primary school and early adolescent years.[6]

Drama programmes consist of a series of discrete scenes which are tied together by an underlying theme or storyline. Most peak-time programmes, even though they attract large numbers of young viewers, are not made specifically for children but for a general audience including adults. Consequently, stories must be somewhat complex and subtle in order to appeal to the adult audience. To understand and follow a plot fully, it is often necessary to make connections between two or more sequences in a programme that are separated by other sequences. Thus, there may be a scene early on in the programme involving a quarrel between two characters, and a later scene towards the end of the programme in which the same two characters are portrayed in altered circum-stances in which one attacks the other. The motive for the attack lies in the earlier scene, but viewers must remember that scene and make the connection. Such linkages are essential for understanding plots. Adults who are experienced viewers are usually able to make connections; young children, however, may often be less able to do so.

Researchers have found, for example, when children are shown a typical hour-long, action-adventure programme and tested afterwards for what they can remember and understand about the story, that those up to the age of 8 are able to remember accurately only about half to two-thirds of what adults have judged as central to the plot. However, by ages 10 through to 14, 80 to 90 per cent of the central plot is remembered and understood.[7]

Comprehension of TV dramas, however, relies not simply on how much viewers can remember from programmes (although, clearly, accurate memory for events is an important component), but also on the ability to make inferences about what will happen next based on what has just gone before. Storylines often tend to be fairly predictable. Adults learn to predict what may happen next because they have learned how stories typically unfold. Young children, however, have to develop this ability as they mature. Certain studies have attempted to investigate the development of this ability.

One way of examining the relationship between this ability and children's comprehension of TV dramas is to interrupt the programme while children are watching, and ask them at different points in the story what they think will happen next. Studies show that it is not until the age of 10 that children begin to make adult-like inferences. Below the age of 8, usually only a quarter of children are able to make these kinds of inferences, and show that they have followed the story.

As a concrete illustration of this, one American experiment showed groups of children a programme which was interrupted at different points. At one stage, the programme was stopped after a scene in which one of the main characters was asked by an old man, down on his luck, for a dollar. The character, guilt-ridden over his murder of a similar derelict old man earlier in the show, impulsively gives the old man 40 dollars. After this scene, children were asked to guess why the younger man reacted as he did. Children aged 10 and over were able to make the connection between the scene they had just watched and the earlier murder, whilst younger children were largely unaware of any such connection.[8]

Familiarity with programme settings and understanding the story

As children mature their understanding of their own environment and the world at large improves. When faced with a new experience, they attempt to integrate it into their existing framework of knowledge in order to make sense of it. Does this mean that, when young children are offered a television narrative with settings and character types of which they have some real-life experience, they are better able to follow the plot? In a study designed to investigate this question Andrew Collins asked if children's recall from programmes would vary with their social background. Children from certain social or ethnic backgrounds were expected to show better understanding of programmes which featured characters and settings similar to those found in their own home environment. The study involved white and black children, from working- and middle-class backgrounds, and represented three age-groups, 7-, 10- and 12- year-olds. One set of children drawn from each sub-group saw a sit-com featuring white, middle-class characters, while another set viewed a sit-com with a similar plot line, but featuring black, working-class characters. In both stories, the father is offered a better job in another city; his accepting it would mean that members of the family would be separated.

After viewing the programmes, the young viewers were tested for their understanding of the plot, reasons or motives underlying particular actions, their perceptions of how characters felt in different scenes, and their memory of other aspects of the programme not central to the main storyline. Regardless of the programme seen, 7-year-olds' memories of all these things were poorer than 10-year-olds, who in turn were worse than the 12-year-olds. Among children who viewed the middle-class family programme, middle-class 7-year-olds remembered more story content overall than did lower-class 7-year-olds. Among children who viewed the working-class family programme, the reverse was true; compared to middle-class 7-year-olds, lower-class 7-year-olds were better at remembering the main storyline, making judgements about classmates' feelings and recounting other aspects of the programme. There were no ethnicity differences.

Throughout, though, age differences were important, regardless of social background. Older children exhibited a better grasp of the main storyline, were better able to identify causes of events, had better recall of the emotional state of an actor in the scene concerned, and were more likely to remember peripheral content if the main story was understood.[9]

Children's discrimination between what is real and what is fantasy on television

Are the events and characters depicted in programmes to be believed or taken for real? How well do children distinguish between reality and fantasy on TV? The reality–fantasy distinction is seen as an important issue because research has shown us that the effects of television on children's subsequent attitudes and behaviour can be significantly modified by their perceptions of how real televised events are. In general, more realistic events have more profound effects. However, most children's viewing is devoted to fictional programmes; there is relatively little attention paid to the news before the age of 10. It is cartoons, fantastic heroes and funny situations which attract most of the young viewer's attention. But even amongst fictional programmes there can be considerable variation in how real different portrayed situations and characters appear to be.

For example, with a programme such as *Tom and Jerry* we all know that the characters are nothing more than animated drawings, and that when they hit each other, nobody really gets hurt. This realisation develops quite early on amongst children or so it seems. Young viewers are able to enjoy such cartoons in a playful, make-believe way. But what about programmes such as *Coronation Street*, *Minder* or *The Professionals*, where the settings are contemporary, and the characters are human, and may resemble people we know. Under these circumstances, the distinction between what is real and made-up is more difficult to make. Indeed, even adults can be confused and taken in by some characters on television.

Anecdotal evidence is available to suggest that TV characters who appear on long-running series may become so familiar to viewers that they are thought to be real people. During the first five years of his appearance in the popular series *Marcus Welby M.D.*, actor Robert Young received over a quarter of a million letters from viewers, mostly asking for medical advice.[10] How did all these people think of Robert Young alias Marcus Welby, however? Did they assume that Robert Young, the actor, must have picked up a certain amount of medical knowledge whilst working on the series? Did they assume that the series probably employed a team of medical consultants who could answer their questions? Or did they actually believe that the character Marcus Welby was a real doctor? Whilst anecdotes of this sort do not constitute empirically acceptable proof of television's influence, they do serve to illustrate an important point. Even the more mature members of the public have many gaps in their knowledge about people, events and institutions in the real world with which they have had little direct experience, but about which something may be learned through watching fictional television.

Most viewers have never been in an operating room, a criminal courtroom, a police station or a jail, or a corporate boardroom. Much of what they 'know' about these diverse spheres of activity has been learned from television. Children, of course, have even less direct experience of life than adults, and consequently may be more easily taken in by the things they see on television.

However, the extent to which people – adults or children – are deceived by television depends to some degree on how specific are the aspects of programmes we are looking at. At a superficial level, the ability to distinguish between types of programmes and their settings is something that develops early on. Even quite young children are able to make crude distinctions between programmes featuring animated and human characters, and quickly come to understand that many of the fantastic heroes they see on television are not real people. Even these relatively easy character discriminations are nevertheless important. One researcher has found, for example, that among 5-year-olds, over half of those he questioned did not understand that TV characters are played by actors. At age 8, over two-thirds knew this, and by age 11 nearly all children appear to have learned this elementary fact.[11]

Considerable changes occur across childhood in the ideas young viewers hold about the reality of television programme content. Up to the age of 7 or 8, the distinction between fantasy and reality is often cloudy. By middle childhood, however, judgements about television's realism become much more refined. News is perceived differently from drama; commercials are distinguished from programmes and so on. But as cognitive sophistication improves, certain other perceptions develop. The news is categorised as depicting real-life events. But the critical viewer may come to consider ways in which TV news may be inaccurate, biased, misleading and in some ways 'unreal'. By way of contrast, drama programming is recognised as being fictional, but viewers may come to consider ways in which it nevertheless reflects aspects of reality.

Even before they have started school, children can make certain distinctions between which of their favourite programmes are 'real' or 'make-believe'. Children can identify cartoons as make-believe and news as real, but they may be confused about certain other shows.[12]

Distinguishing between different sorts of television characters improves with age: 4-year-olds even find it difficult to explain the differences between animated and puppet characters. At this early age, children are also uncertain about the mechanisms of television and this in turn affects their perception of what is real on television. One example of this confusion is their failure to understand how characters 'get inside TV'. One belief is that TV 'people are made smaller than us – they're lowered down by a rope'. Older children, aged 7–8 years, may be confused about how certain characters are made. They can, however, usually discriminate between human and animated characters.[13]

Children become more sophisticated about television programmes as they grow older. This development occurs at more than one level. Deciding about the realism of television may involve comparing television portrayals with real life. Another feature of this area of judgement, however, involves knowing how and why television programmes are put together. This is a subject we shall return to in more detail in Chapter 12 when we discuss how television viewing skills can be taught. For the present, though, we can look briefly at some examples of how children can get confused about how real television is, and the ages at which they begin to grow out of this confusion.

Accumulating evidence indicates that the knowledge that most fabricated television programmes are made up develops during elementary school years. One study found that from age 5 to 12 the knowledge that television characters were portrayed by actors (and were not real people) gradually improved. Among 5- to 6-year-olds, 58 per cent did not understand this at all. Among 8-year-olds, 45 per cent completely understood that characters were actors; another 26 per cent partially understood it and only 29 per cent did not understand it. Among 11- and 12-year-olds, 65 per cent had complete understanding. Thus, a major jump in knowledge occurred between the beginning and middle of elementary school, but, by the end of elementary school, about one-third of the boys still did not completely understand about actors.

Elsewhere the age of 8 has been found to be a crucial time when understanding suddenly improves. Children older than 8 seldom thought of television as offering a 'magic window' on the world. They understood something about the fabricated nature of programming. By the age of 8 children are generally aware that television programmes are made up. How completely they understand this varies, depending on the children studied and on what criteria are established for awareness.[15]

In one study, for example, children were given pairs of programmes and asked to say which of the pair was more real and why. The children aged 10 to 12 years were much more articulate than were those aged 6 to 8 years and gave more criteria as their reasons for their judgements. Younger children were more readily able to recognise the reality status of programmes which contained blatant violations or reality, but remained confused about the status of other programmes, such as fantasy drama. But even more difficulty was had with realistic programmes (news and sport), live programmes (talk shows and game shows) and comedy shows.[16]

In making reality–fantasy distinctions, younger children tend to focus on physical features of a programme as cues to its lack of reality, including the presence (or absence) of stunts, camera tricks, costumes, props and sets. Distinctions are also dependent on whether a presentation is acted, scripted, rehearsed, live or filmed. The degree to which the show is an acted performance is important here.[17]

Turning next to television versus real-life comparisons, three general strategies seem to be used. These include the category of 'actual', referring to whether or not television content exists in the real world. The second category is of the 'possible', which refers to content which could happen in the real world. And the third category is of the 'impossible', which consists of events which could not happen in the real world. Distinctions made in terms of what is actual are made by children of all ages. Distinctions made in terms of what is possible tend to be used more by younger children, while judgements made with reference to what is impossible have been observed to increase with age.[18]

Reality–fantasy discriminations are made frequently by reference to whether or not the televised content exists in the real world, with little apparent regard for its fictional status. For instance, the child's attention centres repeatedly on specific surface features of programming, such as the means by which programme portrayals violate physical reality. In the absence of such blatant features, the reality of television is often accepted. But eventually, these specific concerns with trickery lead to a more generalised realisation that television is not real life, but rather a representation of it; at the same time the nature of the television versus real-life comparisons change too. As children mature, they begin to consider more qualities in programmes, and make judgements about degrees of realism.

Children and adolescents can make distinctions between television and real life even though their real world experiences of certain objects or events may be limited. One study, for example, examined non-delinquent and delinquent adolescents' images of real-life and television police. Teenagers indicated the extent to which they felt each of thirty-six statements accurately described the way television or real-life police are, or operate. Six distinct patterns of perceptions emerged: three of actual and three of television police. Perceptions of actual police were diverse, ranging from highly favourable to openly hostile, with some mixed feelings in between. Perceptions of television police were relatively homogeneous and positive. Among both delinquent and non-delinquent adolescents there was widespread belief that television police were idealised dramatisations different from the real thing. Those youngsters who had favourable impressions of actual police tended to see greater similarity between actual and television versions than did those who held unfavourable impressions of actual police. However, delinquents did not on the whole see greater differences between actual and television police than did non-delinquents, despite their greater contact with the police in real life.[19]

Children's judgements about television characters and their actions

We have seen that as children grow older they come to follow the plots in televised dramas more effectively and learn to grasp fundamental distinctions between reality and fantasy content. Another aspect of television comprehension relates to the way viewers evaluate characters in television programmes. Changes in children's perceptions of television characters have been found to occur with age too. Although there is a tendency for children to ascribe more realism to specific characters with whom they are familiar than to the general category of 'people on TV', this perception tends to decrease with age.

A study of the dimensions used spontaneously by 8- to 12-year-old children to discriminate between pairs of popular television characters found four major dimensions: the humour of the characters; the strength of the characters; the attractiveness of the characters; and the activity level of the characters. 'How much like a real person' television characters were perceived to be did not emerge as an important dimension. The significance of the reality dimension seems to depend, however, on the characters that are selected for children's judgement.[20]

Recent evidence shows that a reality factor may in fact colour children's discriminations between television characters. It seems that as they grew older, children increasingly tend to organise pictures of television characters into discrete groups of human, animated and puppet characters. However, it is not until 9 to 10 years that children begin to realise that being alive and able to move autonomously are characteristics found only in human characters.[21] Prior to 10 years, children seem to have an incomplete understanding of the functioning of cartoon and puppet characters. Most children know, for example, that Tony the Tiger is not really alive, but they cannot necessarily explain how the character works. The finding that correct and clear identification of make-believe characters is not always obvious to young children carries important implications for the impact that television may have on these viewers. It cannot be assumed that children under 6, who do not yet have the mental ability to make clear distinctions between what is real and what is fantasy, will respond to television in the same way as more mature viewers.

What kinds of inferences do children make about characters and their actions? Television programmes portray varied persons, behaviours, roles, attitudes, situations and events. These portrayals provide examples of how to behave in different situations which children might on occasion emulate, and are also a source of knowledge about the world. Research has suggested, for example, that children may be influenced in their beliefs about different occupations, such as police work, doctors, lawyers and so on, by the way these things are shown on television. But the extent to which character portrayals do affect children's outlook on the world is determined to a significant extent by the ease or difficulty they have in understanding TV plots.[22]

Another important factor, however, is the way young viewers judge the characters themselves and their actions. If violent fighting or shooting is perpetrated by a character who clearly wishes to harm his victim and who is obviously punished for what he does, the character and his actions would, according to the norms of society, be judged as bad. On the other hand, violence for the purpose of freeing a hostage which earns the perpetrator a medal for bravery would be viewed much more positively.[23] This, then, is mainly true for adults, but to what extent is it true for children?

The motives or reasons for actions and their consequences for victims are potentially important modifiers of children's judgements about television portrayals. However, accurate judgements about an actor's moral character depend on being able to understand his or her reasons for behaving in a certain way.

In one experiment by a leading researcher in this field, Andrew Collins, children were shown edited versions of a TV action-adventure drama. The plot involved a man searching for his former wife to prevent her from testifying against him in a kidnapping case. He finds the house where she is hiding and shoots at her, but his attempt to kill her is thwarted by the arrival of police officers who arrest him and place him in handcuffs before leading him away.

Collins and his colleagues wanted to know how children of different ages would evaluate the moral character of the man. To do this, the programme was interrupted at different points and the children were required to say how good or bad they thought the character to be each time. The interesting finding to emerge was how soon children of different ages recognised the character to be essentially bad. Children aged 10 and over became aware of the character's badness quite early on in the story because of his early intentions to kill his wife. Children younger than 8 began to see the character as bad only when he actually tried to kill her. Even then, many younger children failed to give negative evaluations of the man. For most of the youngest viewers of 7 and 8, it was only at the point when the police handcuffed the man and took him away that they realised that maybe this person was bad – why else would he be arrested by police? What is even more significant, however, is that even after the programme had finished with the man arrested, some young children still did not see him as bad, having earlier thought of him in fairly positive terms.[24]

These findings show that very young viewers may not make accurate moral judgements about characters at all, or do so only following concrete demonstrations of how good or bad a character is. By the age of 10, however, children become more able to judge whether characters are good or bad on the basis of more subtle information about them.

Children's ability to follow and understand television is mainly dependent on age. As their understanding of the world in general develops, so too does their understanding of television. In the same way as they begin to make moral judgements about peer and adult behaviour in their own environment, similar judgements are also made about the behaviour of television characters. But is it children's 'real world' knowledge that is shaping these judgements of televised behaviour and beliefs or is television itself having some kind of influence on their developing perceptions as to what is good and bad in their own environment?

Chapter five

Does TV improve children's knowledge?

Under the ethos of public service broadcasting, television has been required not only to entertain, but also to educate and inform. Nowadays, from the security of their own homes, people are able to see graphic scenes of wars and disasters or the torments suffered by inhabitants of Third World countries as they struggle to survive. They are invited to journey visually through their own bodies via miniature cameras or survey the world beneath the sea or the insects in their own back gardens. Fifty years ago, before television was commonplace, only a few had some real-life experience of any of this, but now the majority are exposed to it daily without ever stepping outside their own front doors. Yet how much of this vast range of visual information is actually retained and understood, particularly by children, who may often take for granted television's ability to offer a window on the world.

Television is commonly cited by people as their major source of information about what's happening in the world. In public opinion surveys, samples often claim that they learn a great deal about the world from watching television, and that the news on television is more important to them in keeping informed than are any other sources.[1] As we saw in Chapter 2, children often claim that television provides various kinds of learning – both of factual knowledge and of how to handle other people and different social situations.

As we shall see, however, research on remembering of broadcast news has consistently indicated that much of what is presented seems to be quickly forgotten, particularly where children are concerned.[2] Yet there is no doubt that children do learn some things from television, both from programmes designed to entertain and from those whose main objective is to inform. The failure to learn consistently from television appears to have something to do with the way it is approached and used in the first place. If children decide to view for amusement or entertainment, much of what they watch will simply wash over them; little will stick. On the other hand, if they are motivated to find out about something through viewing, then learning is more likely to occur.

One body of evidence strongly suggests that how well viewers – young and old – are able to learn and remember from television can depend significantly on how the information is presented. Production practices routinely adopted by television news editors, for example, may result in programmes which present too much information, too quickly, and with built-in (often visual) distractions. Under these conditions, even interested viewers may flounder. Ultimately, though, whether or not children learn from television depends on a mixture of factors which relate to viewers' background knowledge and interests, reasons for watching television, degree of concentration and attention while viewing, and the way that programmes are produced.[3]

Learning from television news

Television news brings into children's homes a wealth of information about the world every day. Much of this information will concern people, places and events they have never seen or may never be likely to meet or experience first-hand. As we have already seen, television is not invariably a good or easy medium to learn from. Compared with other forms of communication, its ability to improve awareness and knowledge effectively often pales. It is not always easy to predict when or what children will learn from television.

Television drama is designed principally to entertain, though it can undoubtedly also tell us things about the world. Young audiences and old alike can learn various things about the world, about personal and social relationships, how to behave in different situations, what it might be like to work in a certain kind of job, how people live in far-away places, and so on. Some of this learning reflects truthfully the way the world really is, while some may not. Thus, television drama can influence viewers' beliefs about the world around them, though not always accurately or authentically.

Television news, on the other hand, is defined both by its producers and by its audiences as programming designed principally to inform. This is not to say that the news is not also found entertaining. Indeed it often tries to arouse and entertain. Despite its central aim to inform the public, however, research has shown that audiences often display poor memory for news on television. This happens consistently even though people subjectively feel that television news provides well for their news needs.

So, just how much does television news improve what children know about the world? Where it fails, can we identify the reasons why? Several different sources of evidence can be distinguished which shed some light on these questions. First, we can look at the role television news plays in the political socialisation of children. Second, we can examine the extent to which frequency of watching the news affects knowledge about recent or current news events. Third, we can test children's abilities to remember stories from individual television news broadcasts shortly after they have watched them.

TV news and political learning

Television is widely recognised by the adult public as their major source of news. Much of television news revolves around the affairs of governments and political activity. It is reasonable to assume, therefore, that television could play an important part in the political cultivation of young viewers.

Although the news does not feature among children's stated television favourites, as they grow older and approach teenage years, young viewers gradually tune in to the news more and more. One aspect of this development is children's political socialisation whereby youngsters acquire knowledge about their political environment and begin to form political opinions. Parents and school are known to have an influence over children's and adolescents' political opinion forming, but there is some indication too that the media can play an important role.[4]

Political awareness has been observed to emerge during elementary school years with children being able to articulate certain abstract emotional attachments and identification with political figures and institutions. At first these political allegiances are vague and ill-informed. During adolescence, however, they show signs of being founded in specific knowledge about politicians, government and the political process. Political party attachments can often be shaped by the family. Political knowledge, though, has been found to be related to children's and adolescents' use of the mass media and in particular to their interest in news and current affairs.[5]

Watching the news on television may play a part in the political education of young people and is testament to one kind of informational effect that television can have on them. While this effect may not always be powerful, nevertheless it is still there. The experts have not always agreed, however, about the significance of the role of television as a source of learning about politics. For some it is a primary influence, while for others its role is secondary to that of other sources.

One thing is for sure. Television has a tremendous potential for providing at least some information about government and political affairs. Such topics are covered nightly by news and current affairs programmes which are broadcast at times when millions of young viewers are watching. Those young viewers who take a special interest in watching these programmes might be expected to develop a greater knowledge about government and political leaders than those who do not pay much attention.

One early American study revealed that over half a sample of children said they received most of their information about the President and Vice-President from television; 30 per cent listed television as the most important source of information about Congress, and 21 per cent of information about the Supreme Court. However, newspapers and magazines were mentioned as far more important sources of information about elections, and about candidates and issues, with television running a fairly distant second.[6]

Further insights were provided by a study of 9- to 12-year-olds' reliance on newspapers and television for political information. The children were questioned about their identification with a political party, which party they would vote for, awareness of party interests, and laws and the role of government in making laws. Partisan identification and perceptions of party policy among children varied significantly with how much they watched television news or read newspapers. The more children tuned in to either of these news sources, the more they knew. Party voting choice was similarly related to both media. Political interest emerged as an important factor which mediated relationships between knowledge of legal processes and amount of watching television news or reading of newspapers. Increased use of these two news sources made a difference to knowledge of legal processes only among children who were already interested in these matters.[7]

In Britain, one study has yielded weak evidence that television news viewing is related to how much adolescents know about politics. Teenagers of 16 to 18 years were given questionnaires which measured five areas of political knowledge:

1 identification of party policies
2 identification of prominent political leaders
3 identification of local political leaders
4 knowledge of parliamentary and local political issues
5 knowledge of who was responsible for various public services.

They were also asked to indicate their interest in politics, economics and current affairs, and their use of television, radio and newspapers. Interest in politics emerged as the best indicator of political knowledge, while sex (boys were better than girls), heavier viewing of television news, and talking about politics with others emerged as weaker indicators.[8]

The best way to find out if television is having an influence on the developing political awareness of children is to study viewing and political knowledge growth over time with the same youngsters. One American piece of research studied children aged 5 to 10 years over a one-year period. The researchers administered questionnaires to the children on two occasions one year apart and asked the children whether they discussed news events with parents or friends, whether they had any interest in particular kinds of news topics and whether they ever tried to find out more about a news issue after seeing it reported in the news. The children were also asked whether they viewed evening network television newscasts for adults or the special news slots designed for their own age group and shown on Saturday mornings. (At the time of this study the CBS network in the United States produced specially designed two-minute sport news broadcasts for children every half hour during Saturday and Sunday mornings' children's entertainment programming.)

News and political knowledge levels, and the tendency to discuss news with others, were greater and more likely to occur among children who watched both more children's news and more adult news among 9- to 10-year-olds. Among younger children, greater news viewing was associated with better knowledge on the second, but not the first wave of interviews and also with interest in governmental affairs and discussion of the news with others.

The findings showed that more than half the children occasionally or frequently watched television news programming and that reported news viewing contributed to political knowledge, interest and information seeking. Looking at how these two things changed over time, it became apparent that the influence flowed from watching the news to becoming more politically aware. Young viewers became more knowledgeable about politics over time. There was no indication that children who were initially knowledgeable necessarily sought to watch television news more often.[9]

TV news and knowledge of recent events

Television news provides a daily supply of information about the world. How much does it improve children's knowledge about current and recent events? One way of finding this out is to examine correlations between how often they watch the news and the extent of their knowledge about events in the news.

In a series of studies since the beginning of the 1980s psychologist Ed Cairns has examined the role of television news broadcasts in providing knowledge about the 'Troubles' in Northern Ireland to younger viewers. This research has been interpreted to show differences in children's knowledge about current social and political problems in the province associated with television news viewing and indicated age-related differences in learning from the news among child audiences.

In embarking on their test study, Cairns and his colleagues hypothesised that even young children living in relatively peaceful areas of Northern Ireland who had not been directly exposed to violence were still aware of the violence going on in other parts of Northern Ireland. They went on to suggest that at least some of this knowledge was probably acquired by children from the news media, particularly from television news. Awareness of what was happening in Northern Ireland was assessed among children from Northern Ireland who were compared with two sets of children from Scotland, one of whom was exposed to Northern Irish television news broadcasts, while the other was not.[10]

From this study it was apparent that while Scottish children who had seen Northern Irish television news broadcasts were more aware of the violence and problems in Northern Ireland than were a control group of Scottish children who had seen none of these broadcasts, the children who revealed the greatest level of awareness were those actually living in Northern Ireland. Two possible explanations were offered for these results. First, although both Northern Irish children and some Scottish children had seen television news from Northern Ireland, the Northern Irish children were probably also exposed to other information sources (e.g. newspapers, family, friends) and hence had greater overall knowledge of events in the province.

Second, it could be that the Northern Irish children, because of their greater background knowledge about the 'Troubles', were able to absorb more information from television news programmes about this topic and thus increase their superiority. The latter explanation is akin to the knowledge-gap hypothesis whereby the already well-informed benefit more from exposure to the news than do the less well-informed, so that the gap in knowledge between the two groups widens.

Another study investigated the impact of television news viewing on Irish children's knowledge about the problems in Northern Ireland. Nearly 500 11-year-olds living in five different parts of Northern Ireland, some of which were closer to actual violence than others, were asked whether they watched television news either 'never, sometimes or frequently' and were also required to complete an eleven-item knowledge test. The latter consisted of 'items relating to what were felt to be relatively enduring features of the violence (for example, what the initials RUC and UDR stand for, where the Falls Road and Crossmaglen are, what a control zone and road block are and what the confidential telephone is used for)'. It emerged that boys were more knowledgeable than girls, children who lived closer to the violent areas knew more than those who lived further away, and those who claimed frequent news viewing knew more than those who claimed otherwise.[11]

The study falls down on a number of points, however, and solid evidence for a television influence here must be questioned. For instance, we do not know whether boys watched more news than girls or whether children living in violent areas watched more news than those living further away from the trouble spots. Nevertheless, other writers have suggested that at times of trouble, people do turn to the news media more often for information about the latest developments.

In a follow-up study nearly 600 children from the North and South of Ireland aged 8 years and 11 years were selected. Children in the North were from two distinct locations once again: those that had experienced relatively little violence and those that had experienced above average levels of violence. The news viewing and knowledge measures were the same as before.

Results showed main effects on knowledge for sex and age, but this time not for claimed television news viewing. There was, however, an interaction of television news viewing with age: 11-year-olds who reported greater viewing frequencies knew more. Claimed frequency of news viewing was not related to knowledge levels among the young children.[12]

There was also no attempt to measure the influences of other important factors. For example, to what extent were differences in knowledge in different areas affected by exposure to other media such as newspapers and radio, or by talking with family and friends? The relationships between reported television news viewing and knowledge about the 'Troubles' may indeed indicate that more knowledgeable children were also more active news seekers. But were they more active seekers of news not only through television, but also through radio, the press and elsewhere? We need to know about all this before we can be sure just what the separate effect of television was upon children's awareness.

Remembering what news programmes said

Some researchers have approached the problem of finding out how much viewers learn from television news by asking people to write down how much they can remember from a news bulletin shortly after watching it. This can be done in two different ways. One method is to contact people at home (usually by telephone or sometimes by sending interviewers to call on them) without prior warning just after the evening's news has been broadcast. They are then asked questions about the stories reported in the programme. The interviewer asks them to recall without any prompting all the stories they can remember and may then ask more detailed questions about particular stories. The second method is to bring people along to a central location where they are invited to watch either a live or specially prepared television news programme (usually the latter). Afterwards, they are tested for what they can remember about the programme.

Most of the research carried out with children has taken place either in classroom settings or some other central location. Interest has centred on how much they can remember from individual news programmes or from a series of recently televised programmes, how important their perceptions of the news are to their being able to remember it, the kind of news being presented, and the style in which it is produced.

In an American study carried out with children aged 8 to 13 years, Dan Drew and Byron Reeves were interested to find out more about particular psychological processes which might influence children's learning from a television news story. They wanted to test the assumption that a child's perceptions of a news programme would affect learning.[13]

The children were shown a ten-minute video-tape which contained a short news story surrounded either by cartoons or among other news material. Afterwards they were given a ten-item, multiple-choice quiz that asked factual questions about the news item. In addition they were asked to say whether they thought the function of the item was to inform or entertain, how much they believed the item was accurate and how much they liked the story.

Younger children remembered the item better when it was shown with other news, while older children (11+) did better when it was surrounded by cartoon material. Understanding that the story was designed to inform, liking the story and believing it were all positively related to learning.

Recall of television news varies with the type of story and the way in which it is presented. The presence of film footage in a news item can have a significant effect on how well it is remembered. Dan Drew and Stephen Reese found that memory and understanding among 10- to 16-year-olds were better for TV news items accompanied by film footage than when presented by a 'talking head' only.

Film had a particularly strong effect on understanding (as measured by in-depth recall accounts) among the oldest children. It was suggested that perhaps the film's ability to attract and hold attention enhanced learning. The visuals may have reinforced the verbal content of the news items, although we are not told the extent to which film and narratives were well matched.[14]

Another study has found that children vary in their reactions to and recall of violent news on television. In this, male and female teenagers were tested for recall of violent and non-violent news stories presented either audio-visually, in sound-track only, or as written transcripts. Males recalled significantly more than females, and print produced significantly better recall than audio-visual or sound-only presentation.

Recall of violent and non-violent news, however, varied according to both the way in which it was presented and with the sex of the respondents. When presented audio-visually as television news, males were more able to recall violent material than non-violent material; they also scored significantly higher than females on this aspect. On the other hand, females were much better at recalling non-violent material than violent material and scored significantly higher than males. However, when tested via sound-track only and written transcripts, there were no significant differences between the sexes and, in both instances, males and females were better at recalling violent content than non-violent.[15]

It would seem that something peculiar to the audio-visual presentation of these news stories caused male and female teenagers to learn from these stories differently. The important feature may have been the nature of the film footage accompanying the stories. It is possible that the females who took part in this study were more distracted by footage of street fighting, shootings and riots than were the males, and that the visuals disrupted females' learning of the story narrative. Males apparently were not affected in the same way by the violent footage and were relatively better able to learn the content of the stories despite it. Indeed, the evidence suggests that the violent items were actually more salient for male teenagers, because they remembered more from them than from the non-violent items. Violence may have been distressing for females, but amusing for males.

Is television a good learning medium?

Some writers have argued that television has severe limitations as an information medium, whereas others have demonstrated that its effectiveness in getting information across to the audience can depend significantly upon the reasons why people choose to watch television in the first place.

Research on children's learning from television, radio and print has indicated a number of factors inherent in the television medium and the way viewers approach television that affect learning from it, relative to how well they learn from other media. Television conveys dynamic visual images as a symbol system in addition to language and sounds or music, which are also conveyed by radio. Print, on the other hand, conveys information simply via the symbol system of language. Television's symbol system, therefore, is able to represent the shape and form of objects and events visually, whereas radio and print can present only verbal descriptions. According to one writer, the crucial difference underlying different patterns of learning the same narrative material, presented via different media, arises from the symbol systems presented by different media rather than from the media themselves. The symbol systems, not the media, vary in their ability to represent certain types of information. Through experience with the symbol systems which characterise different media, children come to acquire the requisite intellectual skills which enable them to learn more effectively from those media. Thus learning from media depends on sufficient development of sets of general skills and skills needed specifically to use particular media.[16]

Research with children has shown that structural differences between the media in the way they represent information can influence which content is conveyed most effectively by television, radio or print. Laurene Meringoff compared children's learning of an unfamiliar story either read to them from an illustrated book or presented as a comparable televised film. She looked at recall of story content and inferences about characters and events.

A subsequent experiment with young children compared story learning from audio-visual (television) and audio-only (radio) presentations of a common narrative sound-track. Recall of explicit story content was about the same from both media, but there were differences in the kinds of details recalled. Recognition of expressive language was facilitated by audio-only presentation, whereas picture sequencing was augmented by the audio-visual presentation. Once again, the use of general knowledge in forming inferences was more commonplace following audio-only (radio) presentation. The audio-visual (television) version enhanced inferences based on actions. In sum, the radio version promoted the use of verbal content, while in the television version, although verbal content was not totally ignored, more attention was given to visually presented material.[17]

Other recent work with youngsters has revealed that it is not only the symbol structures of the media and level of development of appropriate media-specific cognitive skills that mediate learning, but also the amount of mental effort typically invested in learning from different media. Children who saw the televised story remembered more story actions and relied more on visual content as a basis for inferences. Children who were read the story in picture book form recalled more story vocabulary and based more of their inferences on textual content and background knowledge. It was clear, in other words, that the structural differences in these media influenced which content was conveyed most effectively. The film's provision of more visual information may well have brought this content to the foreground of children's attention, since they apparently relied more on visually provided information in their responses to the programme. The less pronounced visual information offered in the book seemed to permit greater attention to the verbal text. Children who were read the story remembered more figurative language which (having no visual counterpart) relies solely on being heard.[18]

One prominent writer in this field, Jerome Singer, has argued that inherent in the power of television to attract viewers lie its limitations as an information medium. Fundamental to the appeal of television is its constant sensory bombardment in sound and in vision. But the fast pace at which television typically presents material is such that it leaves insufficient time for effective cognitive processing. According to Singer,

> *The [TV] set trains us merely to watch it.* It does not provide us as a rule with a psychological situation that permits us to process the information presented in a manner that will allow us the most efficient use of what we have seen.[19]

Singer refers to television commercials when illustrating how cognitive overload can occur when watching television. The parallel presentation of information in voice-overs, on film and in captions may be simply too much for us to deal with. To some extent, the same principle may apply in the context of learning from the news on television.

News programmes do not have the same objectives as advertisements, nor do they move as quickly in their presentation of information. However, there are certain significant similarities in so far as information may be presented via several channels – narrative, film footage, maps, graphics and captions – simultaneously or in rapid serial progression. The problem fundamental to television, and this includes television news, as an information medium, is that it constantly introduces new material before the viewer has been given a chance to grasp properly the visual and auditory material that has just been presented.

An Israeli researcher, Gavriel Salomon, reported a series of studies in which children's preconceptions concerning television and print were investigated in relation to levels of learning the same materials from each medium. In particular, Salomon wanted to know what the effect of knowing one's own ability and amount of effort required to process information from a particular medium would be on actual learning. If someone believes he or she is good at doing something, and that a particular task is very easy, then he or she may invest less effort in performing it, and the quality of performance may suffer as a consequence.[20]

In one study, Salomon presented 12-year-old children with a television film or the equivalent story in print. When asked about their ability with each medium, children generally believed themselves to be capable of learning more effectively from television than from print. Salomon also asked the children to explain success or failure in learning from each medium. He found that there were clear differences in the kinds of explanations they gave. Success in comprehending television was attributed by most children to the ease of the medium, whereas success in understanding print was attributed mainly to the readers' smartness. On the other hand, failure to comprehend television was blamed on the viewers' stupidity, while failure to comprehend print was seen to be a function of the medium's difficulty.

The children reported different amounts of effort with television and print. Less effort investment was reported by viewers than by readers. Comparing learning scores for each medium, there was no difference on simple memory, but print produced significantly better inference generation. It was the print group which reported investing more effort in comprehending the story that generated on average most inferences.

There were interactions also between perceived self efficacy and learning from different media. Those who believed they were good readers made more effort and learned more. However, those who believed they were good tele-viewers and that television was easy for them, invested less effort consequently and learned less.

In a further study, comparisons were made between more and less able children and their learning from television. More than ninety 12-year-olds were questioned about the amount of effort they generally expended in watching television and in reading, and about how worthwhile they thought effort is for each medium. They were then asked to estimate their own abilities to generate inferences and remember from television and from print. Next the children were divided into three groups to watch television or read an easy or difficult passage based on the same film sound-track. Afterwards, recall and inference generation, along with effort expenditure, were tested.

Results showed that children reported more effort expenditure in reading the difficult text than in reading the easy text or watching television. Ability corre-lated higher with information processing with the difficult text than from the easy text or television film. Ability was associated also with perceptions of how worthwhile it would be investing effort in reading or viewing. More able children thought it more worthwhile investing effort in the difficult text than in the easy text or television film. In terms of learning, high-ability children performed best in the two print groups, and least well in the television group, while low-ability children performed best with television and worst with the difficult text. It would seem that the more able children perceive television to be less demanding than the less intelligent ones, and report less effort investment in viewing than their less able peers. Abler children look down on television. Another interesting result was that children's belief in their ability to remember details correlated neg-atively with reported investment of mental effort – and in turn with actual learning. The conclusion one is led to draw from these findings is that since abler children enter the viewing situation with the preconception that television is an undemanding medium, they are inclined not to try very hard to process its contents, and hence don't.[21]

Are these preconceptions sufficient to explain the shallower processing of material from television than from print? Singer, whom we have already referred to above, suggested a range of inherent characteristics of television itself and the way it presents information which may also be significant factors. Television's pace is fast, facts are often crowded together, and its pictorial, mosaic-like qualities impede information uptake. Salomon accepts that television can be processed shallowly and still be enjoyed, unlike print. But this does not mean that television cannot be processed deeply if the preconceptual context of the viewer has been adjusted appropriately. If information from television is not processed effectively because viewers do not believe the medium itself demands or is worth much careful attention or cognitive effort, then perhaps its educational or informational benefits can be enhanced by requiring viewers to invest more energy into their viewing.

In a third study reported by Salomon an attempt was made experimentally to change children's perceptions of the task to be accomplished by watching a television programme. Children from the same age-group as the previous studies were divided into groups who either watched a television programme or read the text of the show. These groups were further subdivided into those who were told that the material they were presented with was 'for fun' (low demand), and those who were told to see how much they could learn from it (high demand).

As expected, the high-demand instruction produced reports of greater cognitive effort than the low-demand condition. In addition to this, however, it had certain important effects on learning. In reading, the instruction had little effect; apparently effort is high when reading regardless of pretext. Task demands, however, had especially strong effects on learning from television. High demand produced better learning from television than did low demand. Furthermore, the instruction worked particularly well for more able children. More intelligent children learned considerably more than less intelligent children when told to make more effort.[22]

Children themselves then are aware of television's potential to enhance knowledge and provide information about the world even though they regard gaining knowledge via television as less intellectually demanding than gaining knowledge through print. However, children also believe that television, particularly through its dramatic representations of characters and situations, offers other kinds of knowledge which is of particular relevance to them. As can be seen from Greenberg's research, cited in Chapter 3, one of the reasons given by children for watching television is so as to learn more about themselves and how they should interact both with their peers and adults. But does television have this effect? To what extent is the medium able to teach children about social roles?

Chapter six

Does TV teach children about social roles?

In the next few chapters we turn our attention to television's influences upon children as they grow up and learn the ways of the world. Children have to learn how to behave in different social situations. Society requires its citizens to follow certain norms or conventions and to adopt appropriate and accepted social roles. In other words, as they grow and develop, children become socialised. During the early years of their lives, children are required to and do learn an enormous amount about living in the world with other people. Much of this learning comes from watching and listening to parents, brothers and sisters, peer groups, teachers and other adults. Today, however, television is another prevalent potential source of social learning. Characters on television may provide role models whom children may strive to emulate. Even if they do not directly copy their favourite characters, children may acquire certain values, attitudes or rules from them. A fundamental question about television, therefore, is whether it contributes to children's social development and to their learning of social roles and conventions.

So far we have established that television is a pervasive medium which is readily available to nearly all children. The vast majority of children watch television every day and on average they may spend three to four hours daily in front of a set. Although they may have difficulties early on, children soon learn to understand and follow programmes, become able to articulate refined opinions about what they watch, and make mature judgements about what is real and what is not.

Television is used primarily for entertainment but it is also a source of information. It can tell us things about the world which we were not previously aware of and it can serve to reinforce what we already believe and know. It imparts information *explicitly* through regular news broadcasts and sets out to teach us things through its educative documentaries and magazines. But television also offers *implicit* messages that are present within all programme areas whether they are educational, informative or designed purely as entertainment. For example, if news programmes or documentaries tend to place greater emphasis on one view of a world event or social problem, then this might well have an effect on how viewers perceive the issue, particularly if they are lacking in prior knowledge. Television may also have a more subtle educational or cultivational effect through its drama and entertainment-oriented programming. Events are played out in these programmes which, though fabricated, may nevertheless touch upon circumstances or experiences which are familiar to us. It may thus provide valuable lessons in how to deal with life's problems through its fictional enactments of them.

Television and sex-role perceptions

Research has established that children know what sex they are by between 1 $\frac{1}{2}$ and 3 years of age.[1] The sex of a person is more than simply a biological gender classification. What sex we are embodies a cluster of conceptions and beliefs about how we are or how we ought to be in the way we display our own character and personality and in the way we behave with other people.

Society holds certain expectations of men and of women, and these are not always the same in respect of each sex. Thus certain characteristics are designated as mainly female and others as mainly male. This is not to say that there can never be any cross-over between the sexes of a particular personality trait or pattern of behaviour. Rather what is referred to here is a classification of convenience, which offers for the sake of simplicity a system of socially conditioned stereotypes which are attached to each sex.

Sex stereotypes can limit the roles which males and females are encouraged or even permitted to play in life. Their development in the minds of children is a learning process. It is one aspect of social learning which is geared to produce individuals who as adults conform to social norms. What is the significance of television in the shaping of these ideas about sexuality? This is a subject to which we now turn.

Studies of television's influence on sex stereotyping among children have produced mixed results. To assume that television can impact upon a passively receptive child audience with messages about sex stereotyping, thus moulding innocent young viewers' conceptions of gender, is largely accepted as an over-simplistic picture of what really goes on. Viewers exhibit a degree of activity in selecting what to watch on television, what to pay attention to, and what to remember of the things they see on the screen. Even children respond in a selective fashion to particular characters and events on television, and their perceptions, memories and understanding of what they have seen may often be mediated by dispositions they bring with them to the viewing situation.

What is the evidence? In a small number of surveys, significant links have been reported between personal or parental estimates of children's television viewing and their sex-role perceptions which have been interpreted as evidence for a television influence.[2] Youngsters who were categorised as heavy viewers were found to hold stronger beliefs than did lighter viewers in what the researchers defined as being a stereotyped direction. Much of this work, however, failed to produce precise measures of what young viewers actually watched.

One researcher conducted interviews with children of both sexes between the ages of 3 and 6, asking them what they would like to be when they grow up. As well as specific questions about television viewing habits, each child was asked, 'What do you want to be when you grow up?' Then they were required to imagine what they would be if they were a member of the opposite sex. Thus, boys were asked, 'If you were a girl, what would you be when you grow up?' Finally, the children were engaged in a game called 'The OK Picture Game' in which they were shown several pictures, some of which were quite ordinary scenes of situations and others of which depicted something unusual or out of place, such as a five-legged cat. The interviewer explained to the children that the object of the game was to see whether a picture was 'OK' or not. Among several 'dummy' pictures were three scenes in which traditional sex roles had been reversed – a father feeding the baby, a man pouring coffee for a woman, and a female telephone-line repair person.

Results on career aspirations indicated a strong relationship between sex and envisaged future occupations for both children's own sex and for that of the opposite sex. Boys tended to nominate traditionally 'masculine' professions such as policeman, sports star or cowboy; girls preferred quieter occupations such as nursing. While the actual jobs nominated by girls and boys were different, the tendency to stereotype career aspirations was virtually the same for both sexes. Over 70 per cent of the boys and 73 per cent of the girls chose stereotypical careers for themselves. Even when asked what they would be if they were a member of the opposite sex, in nearly all cases, these youngsters selected what is normally regarded as appropriate for that sex.[3]

Responses to pictures indicate that sex-typing increased as images moved from child-care to husband–wife roles to occupation. The children's beliefs reflected the increasing post-war trend of husbands helping around the house. However, regardless of the growing women's liberation movement, children still showed strong sex-typing with respect to occupational roles; whilst young children's sex-role perceptions measured here indicated strong stereotyping of ideas about the sexes, to what extent are they affected by television portrayals?

The researcher responsible for this study claims that sex stereotyping of career aspirations was more likely to occur among heavier viewers of television, but she presents no data to back up this assertion. Furthermore, her sample was small and unrepresentative of this age-band and her findings would need to be replicated with other groups of children before they can be confidently accepted.

In a subsequent piece of research children aged 4 to 12 were interviewed about their viewing, along with their parents, and then given a projective measure of sex stereotyping. The latter was a paper and pencil test which examined children's choice of sex-typed toys. A clear-cut relationship emerged between amount of reported television viewing done by children and the type of toys they selected. The heaviest viewers were found to be the ones who selected toys in the most stereotyped way.[4]

The conclusion of the study was that children learn about traditional sex roles from television. A number of critical questions remain unanswered, however. Why were boys and older children more traditional in their attitudes? Was it their traditional attitudes that made some children heavier television viewers in the first place? What role did parents play, not only in teaching children about sex roles, but also in helping them to interpret what was seen on television? How accurate was parental monitoring of actual viewing among the youngest children? Was the sample of forty boys and forty girls representative of their age groups? Was the projective test a valid measure of children's sex-role development?

Further evidence has emerged of positive relationships between increased viewing of television and more stereotyped beliefs about the sexes. This study examined variations in sex-role prejudice as a function of television viewing, demographic characteristics and family background of children among 155 North American children of average age 9½ years. In general it was found that these children were not strongly stereotyped in their sex-role perceptions, but that where stereotyping did occur it was most evident among girls with lower IQs, who had mothers with higher educational attainment and who watched great amounts of television. The same results did not emerge among boys.[5]

The studies above all provide a 'snapshot' of links between reported television viewing and sex stereotypes at one point in time. A different approach was adopted by Michael Morgan who wanted to try and find out if there was a meaningful link between adolescents' sex-role attitudes and television viewing over time. He obtained information from a large sample of teenagers about their amount of television viewing, acceptance of sex-role stereotypes and educational and occupational aspirations over a period of two years. The results support the view that television cultivates certain sex-role views, although the effects are limited to girls. The heavier TV viewers among the girls became more likely over time to think that women are less ambitious than men and are happiest among children. No such change was noted among boys in relation to the amount of television they said they watched. Among girls, also, the link between TV viewing and sex-role stereotypes was stronger among the middle classes. Both lower-class girls and boys were generally more sexist regardless of viewing levels.

Morgan also reported, again for girls only, a relationship between amount of television viewing in the first year of measurement and subsequent educational aspirations. Interestingly, however, the heavier viewers were the ones who two years later set their sights higher. This result, although predicted by Morgan on the basis of television's over-representation of professional women, runs contrary to the traditional influences reported by most studies.

Although on balance the tone of Morgan's interpretation of his findings points to a sex-role stereotyping effect of regular television watching, in fact careful observation of the details of Morgan's study reveals that his findings are complex and difficult to explain. Correlations between television viewing and sex-role perceptions were made at and across two points in time and were compared not only between boys and girls but also between three (high, medium and low) IQ groups. Television viewing was significantly related to sexism only among medium IQ boys and high IQ girls. No explanation is provided for the result among the boys, whilst the correlations among the girls were interpreted as evidence for television's influence, on the assumption that girls with high IQs are less likely to be sexist in the first place. Unfortunately, the small size of his correlations does not provide strong evidence on which confidently to assume an effect of television.[6]

Tannis MacBeth Williams' Canadian study (already outlined in Chapter 1) investigated the effects of the introduction of television on an essentially television naive community, and also examined children's sex-role perceptions. Children in the three communities, labelled Notel, Unitel and Multitel were administered scales to measure their sex-role attitudes both before and two years after television reception was introduced to Notel. A set of Peer Scales asked children to rate how appropriate or frequent certain behaviours are for boys and girls their own age, and a set of Parent Scales asked children to rate how frequently their own mother and father perform certain tasks.

At the outset, children in the television-receiving towns were found to be much more stereotyped on peer ratings than were those children from the town with no television reception. At the two-year follow-up point, children living in Notel were found to have become significantly more stereotyped in their attitudes towards the sexes. This change was restricted to the perception of peers, however; no similar change was observed with regard to perception of parents. The researchers concluded that in the longer term television has the potential to shape children's sex-role attitudes and recommended that more women should be presented on television. Special attention should be given to the way women are presented. In Notel also, boys developed stronger stereotyped attitudes than did girls over time after the introduction of television. It would appear then that if television was broadcasting sex-stereotyped messages these were being absorbed more especially by boys.[7]

In Britain, a recent survey explored children's perceptions of whether on TV different occupational activities were seen to be done principally by males ('boys or men') or by females ('girls or women'). The children were 334 members of a national UK viewing panel, and were aged between 5 and 12. The children were then asked about their own occupational aspirations and an attempt was made by the researchers to link what the children saw on TV with their personal ambitions.[8]

First of all, which occupations shown on TV are perceived to be male or female? From a list of fourteen, some jobs clearly emerged as 'male' and others as 'female'. For instance, 'serving customers in a shop', 'attending to patients in a hospital', 'taking care of baby children' and 'typing in an office' were perceived to be things which were done by girls or women on TV. These were much less often perceived to be done by male TV characters.

On the other hand, 'working a big machine in an office', 'piloting an aeroplane', 'laying bricks to build a house', 'manning a fire engine and putting out a fire' and 'repairing TVs and electric machines' were the occupational domains of male TV characters. There were, in addition, several occupations including 'being in charge of curing a sick animal' and 'driving a police car' which were seen as both male and female occupations. This was especially true in the case of driving a police car and may imply something about the impact on children of programmes like *Cagney and Lacey*, *CATS Eyes* and *Juliet Bravo*.

Girls were more likely to notice female activities, while boys were more attuned to male activities. Thus, girls were much more likely than boys to have noticed female characters in typist jobs and driving a police car. Boys meanwhile were more likely than girls to have noticed male characters serving in a shop and working as pilots, builders, firemen and computer operators.

Another interesting finding emerged. Those activities classified as female were commonly seen also to have been performed by male TV characters, among both boys and girls. 'Male' activities, however, were rarely seen as carried out by female characters.

Subsequently, when children were asked which occupations they would like to do, three more from the entertainment industry were added to the list. All three – 'be in a TV serial', 'work the camera in a TV studio' and 'be a singer in a pop group' – were relatively popular choices. Girls were much more likely than boys to want to be soap stars or pop singers, however. Boys were more inclined to want to be camera operators.

Were there any links between jobs boys or girls perceived their own sex to be shown doing on TV and their own aspirations? The results showed that there were some connections between the two. Thus, the kinds of things females were shown to do on TV corresponded well with the kinds of things girls said they wanted to do in the future. Similarly, the kinds of things males were associated with on TV were largely the things boys wanted to do. Neither boys nor girls were particularly inclined to choose to do the things TV was perceived to associate with the opposite sex.

Countering the stereotypes through television

Successful demonstrations have been carried out with television as an effective agent of counter-stereotyping. In a recent book called *Positive Images*, Jerome Johnston and James Ettema reported on an American project in which television was used to improve children's sex-role attitudes.[9] This project was funded to the extent of $4 million by the National Institute of Education and marked the successful collaboration of researchers, educationalists and TV producers in the production of an entertaining and instructive TV series called *Freestyle*. The main idea of this series was to expand career awareness among children in the 9 to 12 years age range through a number of short stories in which child characters, especially girls, were seen in non-traditional sex roles. Based on attitude questionnaires administered before and after viewing thirteen episodes of the series, *Freestyle* was shown to be successful in making boys more accepting of girls engaging in mechanical activities, football and basketball, whilst girls who saw the series became more interested in these things. Both boys and girls became more approving of men and women who have non-traditional jobs: for example, women as mechanics, lorry drivers or engineers, and men as nurses or secretaries. Their perceptions of appropriate male and female family roles – responsibility for cooking and home repair – also became less stereotyped.

Attempts to study the impact of televised examples of counter-stereotyping on children in Britain have been limited. Kevin Durkin reported two experimental studies, one with primary school children and the other with secondary school children. Both attempted to facilitate changes in the sex-role beliefs of young viewers using a single programme in which examples of non-stereotypic behaviour were depicted.[10]

The first experiment with fifty-two primary school children used an edition of a programme called *Rainbow*. This programme had an introductory story and subsequent sketches, cartoons and song and dance sequences amplifying the theme. The story was about a conventional family consisting of the father, mother, son and daughter, who suffer an unfortunate event in that the father is made redundant. The mother goes out to work instead and the father is left to take responsibility for household chores and looking after the children.

The children were randomly split up into three groups. One group saw *Rainbow*, one saw a programme about the weather, and a third group saw no programme at all. The youngsters' sex-role beliefs were measured both before and after viewing the programme by sixteen questions concerning stereotypically male occupational roles (e.g. bus driver, doctor, farm worker), stereotypically female occupational roles (e.g. shop assistant, secretary, nurse), stereotypically male domestic roles (e.g. putting up shelves, cleaning the car), and stereo-typically female domestic roles (e.g. cooking, ironing, shopping). The children were asked to say whether a man, a woman or both could perform these roles. The test was administered for the first time about one week before the programme was viewed, and a second time within a day of viewing.

Both boys and girls in the *Rainbow* group changed their views substantially. The *Rainbow* programme produced a short-term shift of opinion away from stereotyping. The programme seemed particularly effective in modifying children's beliefs about domestic roles. Durkin suggests that this may be because it, to some extent, alerted them to actual as opposed to stereotypical behaviour. Perhaps many of these children already had fathers who helped with the dishes and shopping. After viewing, the children who watched *Rainbow* may have recalled these things more readily. The programme produced less change in beliefs about occupational roles, however. And this may have been because, for these children, such roles were still too far distant from their own experience and concerns for already well-established stereotyping to be changed by just one television programme.

In his second experiment, Durkin attempted to modify adolescents' career beliefs with specially prepared educational films. A total of ninety-nine children aged 12 and 13 years participated in this exercise; they were divided into four groups. One group saw a film introducing traditional career opportunities; a second group saw a non-traditional opportunities film without any explicit attention being given in it to alternative careers for each sex (implicit counter-stereotype); a third group was shown a non-traditional opportunities film in which men and women discussed their occupations more openly (explicit counter-stereotype); and a fourth group saw no film.

The traditional film showed a male doctor, a female nurse, a male plumber and a female secretary. The counter-stereotype films showed the same four occupations, but the actors were interviewed in pairs, one male and one female for each occupation. The difference between the implicit and explicit films was that in the latter more emphasis was placed on the reasons why particular actors had chosen a job not normally pursued by their sex.

Children in each group were given a list of twelve occupations consisting of four stereotypically male jobs, four stereotypically female jobs, and four 'neutral' jobs. They were asked to indicate in each case whether an occupation was 'just men's work', 'just women's work' or somewhere in between. The general finding was that children tended to rate male jobs as male, female jobs as female, and neutral jobs as neutral. There were very few differences between groups and therefore very little effect of experimental treatment. Even though the films were designed to offer career guidance, they seemed to have very little impact on children's existing stereotyped beliefs about occupations.

Television and race-role perceptions

Research into the effects of ethnic minority (mainly black) portrayals on television has investigated their impact on white children's perceptions of and attitudes towards ethnic groups and on black children's perceptions of themselves. In terms of the methods of research, these divide between, first of all, surveys in which self-report data were collected from children about their viewing habits (in particular their watching of programmes known to contain ethnic minority characters) and their attitudes towards ethnic groups and, second, controlled experiments in which selected groups of children were shown a single episode or edition of a programme or a series of programmes containing relevant character portrayals and tested for reactions or changes in their attitudes contingent upon such viewing.

Effects on white children

Historically, the effects of television on young viewers' perceptions of race can be traced back to studies of motion pictures in the 1930s. This early work gave the first indication that film portrayals could affect children's and teenagers' attitudes towards minority groups. Evidence emerged from the USA that

Hollywood-made films could alter white children's attitudes towards Blacks, Germans and Chinese. For example, the major silent production *Birth of a Nation* was found to produce more negative stereotypes about Blacks among those youngsters who had seen the film.[11]

Turning to television, much of the research on the impact of ethnic minority portrayals in programmes dates from 1970 onwards. A division can be made here in terms of the types of programmes whose impact was examined as well as in terms of the research methodology, i.e. survey or controlled experiment. Some studies focused on the impact of educationally oriented programmes produced especially to cultivate and encourage the development of positive racial attitudes. These tended to control the viewing situations and type of material participating children watched. Other studies attempted to find out if commercially made, popular entertainment programmes could affect ethnic or racial minority perceptions.

Research with educational programming

In the United States, the 1970s saw the production and introduction to television of a number of educational programmes. Some of these included, among their educational objectives, the cultivation of positive, multi-ethnic attitudes among young children. Prior to these television series, evidence had already begun to emerge that television was an important source of knowledge about nationalities and ethnic groups. White American children, for example, reported obtaining most of their information about other nationalities (e.g. Africans, Chinese, Eurasians and Indians) from their parents and television. With increased age there was greater self-reported reliance on television as the information source about foreigners.[12]

We have already mentioned *Sesame Street* in an earlier chapter; among its educational objectives was included an aim to produce in children a more informed and balanced perception of ethnic minorities. The series was found to have had some impact, though this took time to occur. White children who were regular viewers of *Sesame Street* for two years did exhibit improved positive racial attitudes towards black and Hispanic people. Children who had viewed the series for only one year, however, showed no real shifts in their attitudes. Apparently, sustained viewing for fairly long periods is necessary before television can produce positive attitudes towards ethnic minority groups.[13]

A study with the Canadian version of *Sesame Street* investigated the effects of two types of inserts which showed ethnic minority children, either Oriental or Indian, in one of two settings. The children were shown either in an ethnic, non-integrated setting or in a racially integrated setting. The other type of insert featured a Canadian boy who was identifiable or not identifiable as French Canadian by whether or not he spoke French. White English-Canadian pre-schoolers were shown one presentation of both types of inserts in a nursery school setting. In each case, after viewing the youngsters showed a strong preference for playing with minority children as opposed to Whites. This preference, as measured by means of photograph selection, was sharply contrasted with those selections of a control group of white children who did not see the racial integration segments, who preferred a white playmate. Similarly, there was greater preference for the French-Canadian boy over an English-Canadian, whether or not his cultural identity was evident. In this study, ethnic or segregated settings and integrated settings were equally effective in inducing positive attitude change towards people of other races. Further, only limited exposure was necessary to produce attitude change.[14]

Research on other educationally oriented television programmes has indicated further positive effects on young children's ethnic minority perceptions and attitudes. One educational series called *Vegetable Soup* was produced for pre-school and elementary age children. This series was designed specifically to try to ameliorate some of the negative effects of racial isolation on children. The series featured live and animated characters, which included Euro-Americans, Afro-Americans, Asian-Americans, native Americans and Latino-Americans in a variety of settings, roles and activities.[15] An evaluation study indicated that it did alter white children's attitudes towards other racial groups. Boys and girls between 6 and 10 years of age were shown sixteen half-hour programmes over an eight-week period in school. Those who watched the series were more likely than age mates who had not seen it to endorse statements indicating greater acceptance of children of different racial groups, including Blacks, and increased friendliness towards different groups.[16]

A further study produced evidence that educational television can influence white children's attitudes about diverse ethnic and national matters. A television series produced in the United States called *Big Blue Marble* was designed, among other things, to alter children's views about children from other cultures and parts of the world.[17]

Big Blue Marble showed how children in other lands live and grow up. A study with a sample of 9- to 11-year-old white US children found that after viewing four episodes of the series, white children became more likely to perceive foreign children as healthier, happier and better off, more likely to question whether US conditions were highly superior to those in other countries, and less likely to assume the cognitive superiority of American children.

The influence of popular entertainment programmes

Specially produced educational programmes are designed to influence children's attitudes. In some cases, as we have seen, they do work. In addition to these programmes, however, young audiences are exposed to portrayals of ethnic minorities in popular entertainment programmes, which are not explicitly produced to change racial attitudes. Nevertheless, youngsters who watch these portrayals may learn from them certain things about the characteristics and habits of ethnic minority groups. The extent to which particular programmes which contain such portrayals have a specific influence can be difficult to measure. There are many sources of influence on children's beliefs about the world and the people who live in it. Television is only one such source of influence and may be difficult to disentangle from all the others.

It does seem that children are aware of the presence of black actors and actresses on television. Research with 9- and 10-year-old white children in the United States, for instance, has indicated that more than four out of ten could name at least one black television character that they would like to be like. Furthermore, at the time that this research was done in the early 1970s, five shows featuring black characters (*Mod Squad, Julia, Flip Wilson, Bill Cosby* and *Mannix*) were mentioned among the white children's ten favourite television programmes. The most frequently mentioned source of information about Blacks was television, and this source was most important for rural Whites who had almost no other sources of contact or interaction with Blacks.[18]

Additionally, television exposure to black people seemed to have more impact than personal contacts in the neighbourhood or at school. So those white children with higher levels of exposure to Blacks through television were more likely to cite black shows among their favourites and to name black characters as identification figures than those with lower levels of exposure. However, exposure to television Blacks did not seem to influence the racial attitudes of the white children in this study. With the exception of a sharply negative subgroup of urban white youngsters, most Whites in this study felt that Blacks and Whites were about the same on most personality attributes. Neither level of television exposure nor place of residence was related to attitudes towards Blacks in general or towards television Blacks.

Popular cartoons have been found to have some effect on racial perceptions. One study of cartoons that featured black characters in either the numerical majority or minority, in which racial minority characters were portrayed in either a positive or negative fashion, showed that the racial attitudes of white children between 6 and 8 years of age could be altered after just one such cartoon. Attitude change was measured by the frequency with which children associated positive or negative characteristics with black or white stimuli. Positive portrayals of black characters produced more positive attitudes towards Blacks and conversely negative portrayals produced less favourable attitudes. Further, regardless of characterisation, black people presented in the numerical minority produced more positive attitude change than did black people in the numerical majority. The study suggests that integrated settings were more effective in producing positive attitude change than segregated or predominantly black settings. Similar findings have emerged from studies of other programmes featuring Blacks depicted either in a favourable or unfavourable light.[19]

The extent to which white children are influenced by TV in their perceptions of races may depend on how much direct contact they have with other races. American research has revealed, for instance, that the greater the contact white children have with black people in real life, the less real they judge TV portrayals of Blacks to be.

Long-term effects of TV

Much of the evidence discussed above has derived from research which measured the effects of television on ethnic minority beliefs only in the short term. In the longer term, just how powerful are television's effects on what people believe about other races? In general, the perceived reality of the racial attitudes presented in *All in the Family* and *Sanford and Son* was neutral. However, subjects rated *All in the Family* more realistic in its portrayals of Whites' racial attitudes than they did *Sanford and Son* in expressing Blacks' racial attitudes.[20]

Young viewers' own racial attitudes may affect their perceptions of black characters on television. One study found, for example, that Whites who were antagonistic to Blacks were more likely to report that there were more Blacks appearing on television compared to more favourably disposed Whites. It was more highly probable that highly antagonistic Whites would report that television was more likely to be fair in the presentation of Blacks than would Whites with more favourable attitudes.[21]

Effects of black portrayals on Whites

A British study focused on adolescents and their parents and divided sources of knowledge about Blacks into two: (1) situational sources involving personal experience and (2) media sources.[22] It was assumed that either the media may reflect ideas and images which are already commonplace among the viewing public or they may cultivate new ideas and impressions which may not necessarily mirror those which exist in reality. Groups from areas with both high and low immigrant population densities were tested.

To begin with, adolescents were asked what they knew about 'coloured people living in Britain today'. Respondents were free to answer in their own way. Personal experience was the commonest information source mentioned followed by various mass media. Mentions of personal experience were more common among youngsters living in areas with a high density of immigrants, while media sources were mentioned more frequently by those living in areas with relatively few immigrants. Those youngsters naming media sources most often were also the most heavy users of media as evidenced by independent measures of media use.

In examining attitudes towards Blacks no evidence emerged that the mass media made much difference. Ethnic attitudes appeared to be influenced more by personal experience, although the mass media were cited as sources of ideas about the problems caused by coloured people more frequently than as sources of knowledge about good things about the black immigrant.

What about the extent to which viewers felt deprived in their own lives when comparing their own position with that of images of the rich often depicted on television? Would such dissatisfied individuals in turn hold more hostile attitudes towards Blacks? A substantial proportion of those people who had seen images of wealth portrayed on television felt more deprived in consequence. Among those who said that they did, there was a weak tendency to hold more prejudiced attitudes towards Blacks.

An American study of longer-term effects among young viewers of television portrayals of Blacks on their beliefs about the traits associated with black people was carried out by Charles Atkin and his colleagues.[23] While a basic prediction is that young people who watch programmes featuring Blacks may remember those portrayals or aspects of them, the extent to which their beliefs about black people in actuality are influenced is mediated by a range of important social-psychological variables which include

1 direct contact with Blacks and the extent to which TV portrayals are perceived to be consistent with real world knowledge
2 motivation to watch television – for relaxation or for information
3 identification with characters on television – strong identification may lead to viewers extracting more information from portrayals and perhaps to stronger influence.

There is evidence that the presumed influence of television on the basis of what appears on the screen may not always match its actual influence. Descriptions of content do not always reflect the meanings viewers perceive selectively in that content. In the sphere of ethnic portrayals and racial prejudice, there have been a number of studies of the top-rated US television programme *All in the Family*. In addition to providing mass entertainment, a secondary objective of this programme was to combat bigotry by poking fun at it and helping viewers gain insight into their own prejudices. However, the selective perception process seems to prevail with this type of satirical content. Several researchers have reported that authoritarian prejudiced individuals tend to accept the racial slurs of the bigoted character, Archie Bunker. Less prejudiced members of the audience meanwhile perceive Archie as a foolish, narrow-minded bigot and interpret his comments as satire. Thus, there is a tendency for selective perception to distort the intended message towards the predispositions of the viewers, resulting in reinforcement of prior prejudices.

The Atkin study was carried out with 316 white children aged 9–13 years recruited from two inner-city areas where Whites had varying opportunities for direct contact with black youths and adults. The following measures were obtained:

1 extent of watching programmes featuring Blacks
2 motivation to learn about Blacks from television
3 perceived reality of black portrayals on television

4 identification with black characters on television
5 comparisons of black and white television characters
6 beliefs about actual attributes of Blacks
7 beliefs about actual differences between Blacks and Whites
8 beliefs about how many Blacks were in the population
9 beliefs about extent to which knowledge about Blacks gained from
   television.

Results showed that effects of televising black portrayals on white viewers appear to be limited and selectively processed. About one in four reported that most of the things they knew about Blacks came from television. The effect of sheer exposure to television programmes with black characters on beliefs about traits of black people was minimal. The only real effect was that greater viewing of these programmes apparently led children to perceive Blacks as funny. Since most black characters appeared in comedy roles, this was not surprising. In the case of beliefs about dissimilarities between real-life Whites and Blacks, there was limited evidence that amount of television viewing had a direct influence. It was young viewers' perceptions of distinctions between TV portrayals of Whites and Blacks that made the most important contribution.

The largest direct impact of television occurred on beliefs about the frequency of Blacks in society and subjective learning. The more Blacks on the television were seen, the higher the estimate about prevalence of Blacks in the real world, and the stronger the feeling that knowledge about Blacks was acquired from television.

The overriding result that effects on beliefs depend on children's existing perceptions and experiences both of Blacks and television indicated that television's role may be to reinforce prior dispositions rather than cause dramatic changes. This suggests the important role that parents and schools play in shaping the process of learning from television, since these sources directly influence attitudes that the viewer brings to the set.

Effects of black portrayals on black audiences

Much of the psychological literature on black people's personality development indicates that a large percentage of black adults and children are more likely to reject black models and images than they are to accept or highly value them.[24] This rejection of black stimuli may be so intense that black children will racially mis-identify themselves at a rate between 5 per cent and 54 per cent. Research into how Blacks perceive themselves finds that most Blacks experience a negative or decreased sense of esteem because of their race, although this has improved somewhat in recent times.[25]

What impact do portrayals of Blacks on television have? Will young black viewers identify with possible non-stereotypic role models of their race? If black portrayals support negative stereotypes that already exist about Blacks, will exposure to such undesirable role models increase low self-esteem and magnify negative attitudes towards Blacks?

Black children have been found to hold up white TV characters as more attractive role models than black TV characters. Southern black children in the United States, who had yet to start school, were found in one study to imitate white TV models more readily than black ones. Even when the black character was seen to be rewarded for his behaviour, he was barely imitated more than a white character who had been punished.[26]

There is further evidence to suggest that young black viewers regard Whites as more competent than Blacks. In one situation, black children watched a television film of a group of black and white peers choosing toys to play with. After viewing, the black viewers were given the same toys to pick from. All of the black children selected toys chosen by the white children in the film. This imitation of white choices occurred even when the toys selected were smaller or inferior in quality to toys selected by Blacks in the film.[27]

Elsewhere the imitation of television Blacks by black children has been measured in terms of their willingness to report black shows and characters as favourites. Black children aged 9–11 years were found to watch shows featuring Blacks more often than their white counterparts. For example, 61 per cent of Blacks watched nine or more shows featuring Blacks, compared to 21 per cent of Whites. When asked to name three television characters they would most like to be like, 75 per cent of the black children named at least one black character compared to 43 per cent of white respondents.[28]

Although some of the evidence concerning the influence of television in forming children's perceptions of social roles still seems open to question, the medium's ability to reinforce both positive and negative social attitudes cannot be ignored. If television has the potential to encourage stereotypical views of social groups through its character portrayals, can the actions of these characters have some kind of an effect on the viewer's subsequent action and behaviour? Does television wield some kind of influence on social conduct? It is this question that we turn our attention to next, particularly in terms of anti-social conduct and violence.

Chapter seven

Does TV influence aggressive behaviour?

Over the years, more funding and research effort has been invested in the study of television violence than in any other aspect of television output. Despite all this, there is still considerable disagreement among researchers about the existence of links between violence on the screen and aggressive behaviour among those who watch it.

Nevertheless, evidence that has been published of the possible harmful side-effects of viewing television violence, especially where children are concerned, and the widespread public concern accompanying it have led to calls for stricter controls on the depiction of violence in programmes. In the United States, for example, the setting up and organisation of consumer action groups to lobby against the showing of violence on television has almost become a growth industry in itself.

The National Coalition on Television Violence (NCTV) is one such group that is dedicated to the removal of violence from all popular entertainment programming. According to the NCTV's Managing Editor, Ruth Clayton, writing in the Coalition's March–April 1984 Newsletter, television viewers are cajoled by the networks to consider the use of physical force with intent to harm, maim or kill a person enjoyable viewing. The group employs its own team of part-time monitors to record occurrences of physical violence in peak-time entertainment programmes on the major US TV networks. Every few months NCTV publishes its latest statistics on the volume of violence shown by each network and presents a league table of the worst offending programmes.

Is there too much violence on television? It is often claimed that there is. This claim is usually accompanied by the call for tighter controls over the showing of violence on TV. But does this question on its own really mean very much? When talking about TV violence, perhaps we should also be asking 'violence for whom?'

Calls for the control of violence on the screen necessitate some consideration of what is meant by violence in the first place. How should violent content be classified or defined in order that it may be monitored effectively and, if necessary, limited in the extent and form of its occurrence? It is easy enough publicly to condemn the depiction of violence on TV, but far less easy to arrive at a monitoring system which takes full account of the values and tastes of the people who matter – the audience. We all have some idea of what *we* mean by violence. But what one person sees as violent may not be seen in the same way by someone else.

A common method of quantifying TV violence has been to count up incidents in programmes defined by the researchers themselves as violent. But since violence is not the same for everyone, there are problems with this approach. Viewers have their own scales for deciding the seriousness of incidents and their opinions do not always agree with researchers' categories of violence.

We can, nevertheless, begin by looking at estimates of how much violence there is on British television as derived from traditional methods of content analysis, focusing especially on those programmes children are likely to watch. After this we will look at what viewers, young ones especially, mean by violence on TV.

Violence on television

The basic method used by researchers to quantify the amount of violence on television uses simple counting techniques. Violence is defined objectively by researchers who then code samples of television programmes for any incidents which match their own violence definitions. A number of one-off studies carried out in the United States during the 1950s and 1960s established this perspective with television.[1] These studies fail to provide a coherent analysis of trends across the period, however, mainly because they used different definitions of violence or different indices of the amount of violence in programmes. Most were, nevertheless, interpreted to show that the occurrence of violence on popular entertainment programming broadcast by the majority US networks was quite commonplace.

The most comprehensive analysis of TV violence so far, and certainly the longest running, has been that directed by Professor George Gerbner and his colleagues at the Annenberg School of Communications, University of Pennsylvania. Using a technique founded on a simple, normative definition of violence, this research project has monitored samples of network prime-time and weekend daytime programming for all the major American networks since 1967.[2] Violence is defined as 'the overt expression of physical force (with or without a weapon) against self or other, compelling action against one's will on pain of being hurt or killed, or actually hurting or killing'. Further specifications were made that the incidents must be plausible and credible, but that no idle threats should be included. However, violent accidents or natural catastrophes, whose inclusion in dramatic plots was reasoned by Gerbner to be technically non-accidental, were included. This analysis of the violence profile of American network television has indicated that violent incidents are prevalent in prime-time entertainment-oriented drama. More importantly, it provided the model for British research in this field.

Violence on British television

Three major studies of violence on British television have been carried out since 1970. James Halloran and Paul Croll of the Mass Communication Research Centre, Leicester, analysed broadcast material of BBC1 and one ITV region (Midlands) during one week of April 1971. Using the framework developed by Gerbner, they coded violent incidents occurring in fictional drama programmes and news, current affairs and documentaries. At around the same time, the BBC's Audience Research Department undertook a more extensive analysis of TV over a six-month period and analysed content from dramatic fiction, news and current affairs, documentaries and light entertainment programmes. Although broadly the same type of study, the BBC's analysis was not precisely the same as that conducted by the Leicester group.[3]

Each of these British investigations indicated that, although a common feature of programming, violence was not as prevalent on British television as on American television. In fictional drama, the only category of programming in which direct comparisons between American and British findings were possible, Halloran and Croll found that nearly 56 per cent of programmes coded contained violence – compared with a reported 80 per cent of fictional programmes on American television at that time. In nearly 48 per cent of fictional programmes, a major character was involved in violence either as aggressor or victim. The rate of violence on British television drama was 2.8 incidents per programme or just over four incidents an hour, again substantially less than an average rate of over seven incidents per hour on comparable American television.

In their more extensive analysis of British television content, BBC researchers found a somewhat greater prevalence of violence in fictional drama in terms of the number of programmes containing at least one major violent incident (63 per cent), but somewhat less violence in terms of the rate at which violent incidents per programme – just over two per hour – were recorded.

The prevalence and rate of violent incidents were also found in both studies to vary considerably across different forms of drama programme. Thus, Halloran and Croll noted that the most violent type of programme in the fiction category was the cartoon. All cartoons coded by them contained some violence and the rate of incidents per hour in such shows was nearly thirty-four. None of the cartoon incidents averaged over four per hour. This contrasted with plays, of which 50 per cent were violent, but even then, with an average incident rate of fewer than one per hour, they were unlikely to be very violent programme by programme. After cartoons, the most violent programmes coded by Halloran and Croll were crime, western and action-adventure shows. All programmes in these categories contained violence at an average rate of nearly eight incidents per hour.

Turning to the BBC's analysis of the prevalence of violence for different programme forms or 'themes', once again agreement with Halloran and Croll was not complete. Feature films contained at least one major violent incident in

86 per cent of cases, which compares quite well with Halloran and Croll's 80 per cent figure, whereas the category of programmes labelled as 'TV series' by BBC researchers, which consisted largely of crime-detective, western and action-dramas, contained violence in only 75 per cent of cases, as contrasted with *all* such programmes monitored by the Leicester researchers. Inconsistencies across the violence measures produced by these two studies for the same areas of television content become even more pronounced when consideration is given to mean rates of violent incidents per programme type. The BBC team coded an average of just over three incidents per hour for feature films, one per hour fewer than Halloran and Croll. But even more significantly, they coded 2.2 incidents per hour for 'TV series', a little over 25 per cent of the average rate of incidents per hour recorded for the crime, western, action-drama categories by the Leicester team. Even when examining particular themes or particular series, BBC violent rate statistics remained lower than those reported by Halloran and Croll. Thus, the BBC reported that westerns contained a higher rate of violent incidents than any other type of TV series, but at 3.9 incidents per programme, this was still only about half the rate reported by Halloran and Croll for crime-western-action categories.

A more recent study of the portrayal of violence on British television was commissioned by the BBC from the Aston University Communication Research Group, under the direction of Dr Guy Cumberbatch. The research analysed all television programmes (excluding advertisements and Open University programmes) transmitted in four separate weeks on all four channels between May and September 1986. This covered 1,412 hours of television – 930 BBC programmes and 1,146 ITV/Channel 4 programmes.

Once again, 'violence' was defined before counting began. The definition of violence used in this study was 'any action of physical force with or without a weapon against oneself or another person, animal or inanimate object, whether carried through or merely attempted and whether the action caused injury or not'. Both intentional and accidental violence were included. Violent accidents and catastrophes were also covered but acts of nature were included only when violence to victims was shown. Verbal abuse and threats were coded separately. The study reported on the frequency of violence, the pattern of violence and how levels of violence had changed over time. Out of 2,078 programmes monitored, 30 per cent contained some violence. The overall frequency of violence was 1.14 acts per programme or 1.68 acts per hour. The average violent act took twenty-five seconds, thus violence occupies just 1 per cent of all television time. However, when boxing and wrestling were excluded, these figures changed to thirteen seconds per act and 0.5 per cent of all television time. If a viewer watched four hours of television a day, he/she would be likely on average to see 6.72 violent acts as defined by the study. Top of the list for violent acts were spy, fantasy, cartoon, war, detective, crime and thriller programmes, and at the bottom of the list came quiz, game and chat shows, along with sport (non-contact). The research found that programmes were more likely to contain violence after 9.00

pm than before. During family viewing time prior to 9.00 pm, when the concentration of children in the audience is greatest, the extent to which violence occurs in programmes on average is much less.

In looking at children's television, the analysis showed that with the exception of cartoons, violence was rare in children's programmes. Cartoons are another and more difficult matter, especially since there is some argument over whether cartoon violence should actually be regarded as different from or comparable with other forms of portrayed violence on television. In terms of a strict mechanical count of acts per hour, cartoons are notably violent, with American cartoons being twice as likely to be violent as British ones. If cartoon violence is to be treated as more than a joke, then cartoons do number amongst the most violent programmes on television. As we shall see in the next section, however, viewers themselves do not take cartoons seriously in this respect.

Perceptions of TV violence

Research into programme content indicates that violence is commonplace on television. But how salient is it for viewers? Viewers can be highly discriminating when it comes to portrayals of violence. They do not invariably read into television content the same meanings as do researchers. Merely knowing how often certain pre-defined incidents occur in programmes does not tell us how significant these features are for viewers. Thus, viewers' perceptions of how violent television is may not accord with objective counts of programme incidents.

One BBC study showed that when viewers were asked to fill out a questionnaire about specific programmes shortly after they had been broadcast, in which reactions to violence and other aspects of the programmes were probed, whether or not a particular programme was perceived as violent did not depend on how many 'violent' incidents it contained. Nor was there any strong relationship between perceiving a programme as violent and verbally reported emotional arousal. Assessment of violence as unjustified, however, was associated with negative evaluations of the programme.[4]

Realism was an important element in viewers' perceptions of televised violence. Real-life violent incidents reported in the news or shown in documentaries were generally rated as more violent than violence presented in fictional settings. These exploratory findings were subsequently corroborated in a later study in which viewers' perception of violence as portrayed in a range of fictional programmes was investigated. From this research, it emerged that familiarity of surroundings is one of the most powerful factors influencing viewers' perception of television violence. The closer to everyday life the violence is portrayed as being in terms of time and place, the more serious it is judged to be.

Children's perceptions of TV violence

Are children's perceptions of TV violence similar to those of adults or are they more in line with the researchers', who have based their analyses strictly on number of incidents irrespective of context? Van der Voort conducted a study of children's perception of TV violence at three schools on Holland.[5] In all, 314 children were shown full-length realistic crime drama (*Starsky and Hutch* and *Charlie's Angels*), two adventure series (*Dick Turpin* and *The Incredible Hulk*) and fantasy cartoons (*Scooby Doo*, *Tom and Jerry*, *Popeye* and *The Pink Panther*). Immediately after showing each programme a post-exposure questionnaire was filled in measuring ten perception variables:

1 readiness to see violence
2 approval of violent actions seen in the programme
3 enjoyment of the violence seen
4 evaluation of the programme
5 emotional responsiveness
6 absorption in the programme
7 detachment while watching
8 identification with the programme's chief characters
9 perceived reality of the programme
10 comprehension and retention of programme content.

Van der Voort investigated whether programmes perceived to be realistic were also more absorbing for children who would thereby respond to them with more emotion and less detachment than they showed towards programmes perceived to be more fantastic. Thus, *Starsky and Hutch* and *Charlie's Angels* were perceived to be realistic, while *The Incredible Hulk*, *Dick Turpin* and cartoons were seen as fantastic. Realistic programmes were watched with more involvement, more emotion and less detachment. The two crime drama series mentioned above were regarded as containing the most violence of any of the programmes the children were shown.

Van der Voort found in fact that 9- to 12-year-olds' judgements of the amount of violence programmes contain differ little from those of adults. He makes the important point, however, that children's violence ratings do differ from those of content analysts who analyse the amount of violence a programme contains by means of the systematic observation of programmes recorded on video-tape. Programmes that are extremely violent according to 'objective' content analysis can be seen by children as 'hardly containing any violence'. Thus, although content analyses have identified cartoons as being among the most violent of television programmes in terms of numbers of objectively identified incidents per hour or per show, such programmes tend to be seen by children as containing hardly any violence at all.

On the basis of the above findings, both with adults and children, it is clear that viewers classify programme content differently from the descriptive counts of objectively defined programme violence where overly narrow definitions of violence are usually employed. In reflecting the attitudes and perceptions of the audience, research into the amount of violence on television ought therefore to include at least some subjective input from viewers. This would provide an indication of which types of programmes or portrayals viewers themselves regard as violent and with what degree of seriousness.

The effects of TV violence

Does TV violence cause social violence? There are two things we need to consider here. First, what kinds of effects are we talking about? Second, how are the effects measured and to what extent can we believe the evidence?

Mechanisms of effect?

We will consider four kinds of effects here. In each case they refer to a psychological mechanism or process through which TV violence is hypothesised to produce changes in the attitudes or behaviour of viewers. A fifth mechanism, known as catharsis, is discussed in the next chapter, which deals with the prosocial effects of television on children's behaviour.

1 Arousal
2 Disinhibition
3 Imitation
4 Desensitisation.

Arousal

The arousal hypothesis suggests that watching violent television programmes can arouse viewers and make them more excited. This kind of effect is not restricted to violent content; sexual or humorous content can have the same effect. The emotional arousal itself is conceived as being a non-specific physiological response; it is defined by the individual in terms of the type of material he or she happens to be watching.[6] Thus, according to the hypothesis, if viewers are watching a highly amusing comedy they are likely to interpret their arousal as amusement. But if they are watching a programme containing violence they may interpret their arousal as anger.

Disinhibition

According to this hypothesis, watching violence on television may legitimise the use of violence by the viewer in real life by undermining social sanctions against behaving violently, which normally work to inhibit such behaviour. Research carried out under contrived laboratory conditions has supported this hypothesis and shown that viewers may behave in a more aggressive manner after watching film violence and especially if they are already in a bad mood before they watch it.[7] As we shall see later, however, there are problems with laboratory research of this kind which throw question marks over the validity of this evidence.

Imitation

This is the type of effect which has, over the years, probably attracted more publicity and attention than most. This hypothesis assumes that viewers, most especially very young ones, are inclined to learn from behaviours they see performed by TV characters, and copy such actions themselves. It is hypothesised, for example, that children may learn that violence is a useful and appropriate way of overcoming one's problems. Alternatively, young viewers may copy their heroes' behaviours to become more like them.[8]

In specific laboratory settings, research findings have indicated that children can be encouraged to behave in more aggressive ways following exposure to violent behaviour on film or TV. This effect has usually been attributed to 'observational learning' in which children imitate the behaviours of the models they observe.[9] The actual importance of imitation effects cannot be determined by laboratory experiments alone, however. It is essential to find out and establish that there are actual linkages between normal everyday viewing experiences and enhanced propensities to behave in a violent way.

Desensitisation

According to this hypothesis, repeated viewing of violence on TV leads to a reduction in emotional response to violence on the screen and to an increased acceptance of violence in real life. The argument runs that young viewers become increasingly used to violence in programmes if they watch a lot of this sort of television. As a consequence, demand grows for more and more extreme forms of fictional violence as that which viewers become accustomed to seeing loses its 'kick' and hence its appeal.

Researchers have expressed concern that exposure to large amounts of film violence may desensitise children to real-life violence. Although the mechanism through which desensitisation might occur is unclear, it is possible that watching violence may increase the child's tolerance for real-life violence either by implying that such behaviour is normal or by making real-life violence seem trivial by comparison. Furthermore, desensitisation might occur through reduced emotional response to violence after viewing film violence.

Just a few attempts have been made to provide practical demonstrations of a desensitising effect of televised violence on children. These have investigated either the effect of TV violence on young viewers' own disposition to act responsibly, by trying to stop what they believe to be a real fight, or the degree to which they show an emotional response to violence.

Two studies, for example, looked at whether watching televised violence would make any difference to the response of 8-year-old children who witnessed a real fight between two other children in a playroom. Would they be any more or less likely than children who had watched a non-violent programme excerpt to warn an adult about what was happening? In any event, the youngsters who viewed violence were less likely to behave responsibly and seek the help of an adult.[10]

Further research has shown that children who are relatively heavy viewers (25+ hours of viewing on average per week) were much less responsive to TV violence, in terms of physical measures of emotional arousal, than were relatively light viewers (fewer than 4 hours per week).[11]

Research methods

We now turn to consider how the effects of TV violence have been measured. A common argument levelled against the broadcasters is that advertisers would not spend vast sums of money on commercials if they did not believe that television can affect consumer behaviour. Yet broadcasters still claim that television violence has no effect on the social behaviour of viewers. Is there not an inconsistency in this argument? But is there really a conflict here? Television advertisements are different from programmes. They are messages designed to get across to the audience information about a particular product. The effect on buying behaviour is not invariably direct and does not act equally on all viewers. The main aim of television advertisements, as with advertising through any medium, is to rouse awareness of an item's existence, especially among that segment of the population that is most likely to be in the market to buy. There is an element of persuasion contained within most adverts, of course, but the main aim is to say to those people who may already be interested in buying from a particular product or service range: here is one example of the thing you want to buy which you might wish to try first.

Television programmes, on the other hand, are not designed to persuade or to sell objects or ideas. This is not to say that ideas are not learned from them – because research tells us that indeed they are. But any 'effects' of programmes are incidental and by their very nature, therefore, are much less likely to occur. Furthermore, it has been established that whether viewers are affected by programmes, together with the shape any influence takes, depends on how they approach television in the first place. By and large, viewers learn from television when they want to; otherwise, they do not.

There have been many studies of TV violence, but these can be condensed down to a handful of basic research methods, each of which has crucial design limitations often sufficient to cast doubt on the validity of the findings. Most of the work done so far can be broken down into four categories:

1 laboratory experiments
2 field experiments
3 correlational surveys
4 longitudinal panel studies.

Laboratory experiments

These are designed to demonstrate a causal relationship between watching a violent event on TV and increased viewer aggressiveness. Typically, however, these studies test only small unrepresentative groups of people under highly contrived unnatural viewing conditions. Their measures of TV viewing and aggression tend to be so far removed from normal everyday behaviour that whether laboratory findings have any meaning in the outside world is something which can be debated quite strongly.

It is worth outlining the nature of some of this research. Through laboratory experiments researchers have tried to demonstrate empirically that television violence can have a variety of different kinds of effects. These include encouraging children to imitate examples of violence they see in programmes, reducing socially learned inhibitions which normally act to discourage children from behaving aggressively in everyday life, and increased desensitisation to violence in real life consequent upon continued and regular exposure to violence on television.

A series of experiments by Albert Bandura and his associates in the 1960s addressed the imitation issue. Bandura believed that children could learn anti-social behaviour through observation. In other words, by watching favourite television characters behave violently on screen, young viewers could identify with these actors and their actions and might under appropriate circumstances be inclined to mimic them. A demonstration of this effect was provided through an experimental design in which children were shown a character on film behaving in an aggressive manner towards a large plastic 'Bobo' doll before being placed in a playroom with lots of toys including the doll. Other children were put in the playroom having either seen the same actor not behaving violently, or having seen no film at all. While observing the children playing, Bandura and his colleagues noted higher levels of imitative aggressive behaviours (towards the 'Bobo' doll) among children who had seen the violent example than among other children. In a variation of the original experiment, Bandura found that if the film character was seen to be rewarded for his behaviour, he was more likely to be copied than if he had been punished or if nothing had happened to him.[12]

Research subsequently showed that social sanctions and prior experience in the play situation were among a number of factors which could affect the nature and extent of mimicry. If an adult, watching with the child, praised the film actor's behaviour, the child was more likely to imitate it than if the actor was criticised for behaving the way he did. Criticism could reduce imitation. If the children had been given an opportunity to play in the room full of toys before watching the film, thus establishing their own forms of play, the actor had less influence on their behaviour than if they had been given no chance to play with the toys beforehand.[13]

In addition to imitation, there is some concern that television violence may have adverse effects on children's social behaviour by weakening socially learned inhibitions against behaving aggressively. The leading protagonist to have carried laboratory experiments designed to prove the existence of this type of effect is Leonard Berkowitz. Although nearly all Berkowitz's studies were carried out with college students, the principles addressed are believed to apply to younger viewers too.[14]

The nature of this research was usually to take male American college students and to place them in a contrived situation in the laboratory where they are first of all either intimidated and thus angered by an accomplice of the experimenter, or treated in an innocuous fashion. Then they are given the opportunity to watch either a violent or non-violent film clip, or no clip at all. Finally, each participant is given a chance to get even with their antagonist. The technique here was to enable participants to deliver electric shocks to the other person every time they made a mistake on a bogus learning task. The findings usually revealed that angered individuals who watched a violent film clip expressed more aggression than did either non-angered participants or those who had been angered but watched a non-violent clip.

Evidence of desensitisation effects has emerged from experiments in which children are shown either a violent or non-violent clip from a television programme and are subsequently put in a situation where they have to monitor other children younger than themselves and warn the experimenter if those children start to misbehave themselves at all. Children shown a violent programme sequence tend to take longer to give a warning about the violence or misbehaviour of other children compared with similar children who have not watched any television violence. These results are interpreted as showing that watching television violence may produce a greater tolerance of real-life violence among those who watch it.[15]

The main problem with these experimental studies is their artificiality. They are unrepresentative of reality in their settings, their samples and in their measures of behavioural aggression. The validity of the electric shock procedure, for example, as an indicator of aggression in real life must be seriously doubted. Further, the norms governing what is acceptable or unacceptable behaviour in the laboratory differ from those in the outside world. The participant is invited to deliver an electric shock to another person and complies because he feels that this is what the experimenter expects of him. The distressful consequences that the participant's action may have for the victim are perceptually reduced through a process of devolved responsibility for what happens on to the experimenter, and there is no threat of punishment or retaliation contingent upon the participant's 'anti-social' behaviour. Indeed, the question of whether the participant actually perceives his behaviour as deviant or anti-social is not investigated, and yet for most people (children included) this is an important factor affecting whether or not they behave violently in real life.[16]

Experimental studies have been interpreted to provide a clear demonstration of a link between viewing film violence and aggressive behaviour among children. Furthermore, because the children are randomly assigned to film view-ing conditions and because the experimenter can hold constant all factors except which film was seen, causal conclusions can be drawn. These studies do not simply show an associative link between viewing violence and aggressive behaviour but from them we can also conclude that viewing the violent films may have caused the increase in aggressive behaviour in that particular situation. The ability to draw causal connections is an important advantage of laboratory studies. In more naturalistic studies, it is often impossible to distinguish whether the connection between viewing violence and aggressive behaviour means that children who watch TV violence become more aggressive or that aggressive children choose to watch violent shows, or some combination of both. However, the advantages the experimental study gains in terms of control are lost when applied to the real world. For instance, a number of factors differ in the experimental study from the everyday life of children:

1 The films are very short, about three minutes long instead of the half-hour or hour-long shows children usually watch on television.
2 Aggressive behaviour is measured immediately after viewing, thus only the immediate rather than long-term effects are studied.
3 The situation in which aggression occurs is very permissive and any realistic consequences of behaving aggressively, such as peer retaliation or adult sanctions, are absent.
4 The aggressive behaviour measured is often unrealistic consisting of aggression against inanimate objects or pressing a lever to hurt someone. Thus, although we can be quite certain about what occurs in the laboratory, we are left with a great deal of uncertainty concerning how much the process demonstrated in the laboratory accurately reflects what happens in children's lives.

Field experiments

To avoid some of the problems associated with the laboratory study, while retaining some of its advantages, social scientists have conducted field experi-ments. In these studies, children are randomly assigned to view violent or non-violent television programming for a period of a few days to a few weeks. Measures of aggressive behaviour, fantasy or attitudes are taken before, during and after the period of controlled viewing. In order to ensure control over actual viewing, children in group or institutional settings have been studied. The two most common of these settings have been nursery schools and residential schools or institutions for adolescent boys. With one exception, all of these studies have confirmed the results of the laboratory studies; in general, children who view violent TV are more aggressive than children who view non-violent TV.

Two particular studies have indicated this kind of link among pre-school children. In one study, the researchers found that the children who watched a ten-minute aggressive cartoon for eleven days were more aggressive during a free-play situation than were children who had watched non-aggressive cartoons. In another study, pre-school children were shown either violent, neutral or pro-social television for ten to twenty minutes a day for four weeks. The researchers found increased levels of aggressiveness during play only among those children who were initially more aggressive anyway and who were then shown a diet of violent cartoons.[17]

The field experiments involving adolescent boys have either taken place in residential boarding schools or in institutions for delinquent teenage boys. Using several measures of physical and verbal aggression, these studies have found an increase in some measures of aggression in boys watching violent films, and an increase in other measures of aggression only among those boys initially high in aggression who viewed violent shows.[18]

The field experiment has some of the advantages of the laboratory study, in particular the random assignment of viewers to viewing conditions. It also avoids some of the disadvantages of laboratory studies in that real TV shows are used, they are viewed in a natural setting, and aggression occurs in a situation where naturally occurring consequences are present.

There are, however, limitations to most field studies. The situation cannot be as well controlled as in a laboratory and thus the researcher is not as certain that the only difference between groups is the kind of TV viewed. One limitation is that often subjects cannot always be assigned to viewing conditions completely at random. If the residential setting involves natural group living conditions such as cottages or dormitories, the researcher must sometimes assign groups rather than individuals to viewing conditions. To the extent that boys are not assigned randomly to these existing groups, then they are not assigned randomly to viewing conditions.

The individuals studied are often not representative of children in general. This is particularly true of the studies of adolescent boys in residential living settings. These boys may be different in important ways (for example, the delinquent boys are probably more aggressive) from adolescent boys living at home. Furthermore, we know nothing from these studies of the effect on adolescent girls. Equally, the field study environments, when the viewing and the aggression occur, are not representative of the living situation of most adolescent boys. While problems of sampling and environmental validity are less serious with the pre-school studies, there is the problem of lack of control over the total viewing situation since the children's home viewing is not controlled during the study.

Even with these limitations, however, the results of the field studies confirm the findings of the laboratory studies, replicating the basic finding that an increase in violent viewing is related to an increase in aggressive behaviour in a more naturalistic setting.

Correlational surveys

These improve on experimental studies in terms of the representativeness of samples, but often fall down in the accuracy of their measures of exposure to TV violence. The basic approach in correlational research is to obtain a measure of viewing violent TV and to relate this to a measure or group of measures of aggressiveness. The ultimate goal is to demonstrate a causal relation; the first step is to find that some relation exists. Viewers often have to identify or recall from lists of programme titles which ones they like best or watch most often. Occasionally, more effective diary measures are used, but even then assumptions are made about the probable violent content of programme viewers say they have seen, which are not backed up by any better evidence. If some doubt exists about amounts of violence watched on television, there must also be doubts about the evidence offered on the supposed effects of this conduct. In any case, correlation surveys are unable to demonstrate causal relations. They can simply show where degrees of statistical association exist between certain correlations of attitudes or behaviours and patterns of TV watching. And even then, the small size of most of the correlations indicates some very weak associations indeed.

In contrast to the experimental designs, the correlational survey does not assign people to groups at random, but rather uses already existing groups of people who differ in their exposure to television or to violent content. Thus, what the naturalistic study loses in terms of control and thereby the ability to make causal conclusions, it makes up through its usefulness as a means of assessing effects in real life.

Consequently, the results of naturalistic studies are more mixed than those of field experiments or laboratory studies. Two early studies did not find a relationship between presence or absence of TV in the home and teacher reports of aggressive behaviour or scores on an aggression scale – although in the latter case there was a modest link with aggressiveness among 15-year-old boys who watched a lot of TV and read less.

Among researchers who have looked at the relationship between self-reports of favourite shows and self-report or peer ratings of aggression, some have found that children who prefer violent programmes were themselves rated as more aggressive, in other cases as less aggressive or that no relationship as such emerged at all. The most consistent results from naturalistic studies have been those in which overall amount of viewing violent TV was related to certain measures of aggression. Two studies in particular have reported a positive association between amount of violent TV viewing and self-reports of aggressive behaviour.[19]

Longitudinal panel studies

These represent perhaps the best kind of studies of TV effects. They can test causal hypotheses and they usually employ sound sampling methods. The aim of this type of investigation is to discover relationships which may exist or develop over time between TV viewing and social attitudes and behaviour. In this respect, such research addresses the notions of the cumulative influence of television violence. This view posits that the link between watching television and personal levels of aggressiveness should increase with age and repeated exposure to televised violence.

So far, however, the evidence from these studies has been equivocal. Some researchers have claimed to have found a strong link between watching of TV violence-containing programmes in early childhood and the subsequent development of aggressive tendencies among children and adolescents in later years.[20] Other researchers using similar procedures have concluded differently.[21]

In the United Kingdom, a major investigation of the impact of television violence on the behaviour of adolescent boys was carried out by William Belson.[22] This study used a simulated panel survey. In other words, the respondents were not actually studied across separate points in time, but were questioned retrospectively at a single point about their habits over previous years. Detailed and lengthy interviews with these teenage boys revealed a relationship between certain aspects of their claimed viewing behaviour and self-reported attitudes and dispositions towards the use of violence in their lives. In particular, the more the boys claimed to watch particular types of dramatic television content – classified by Belson as containing violence – the more likely they were to report having used aggression themselves under different circumstances. Belson's results have not been universally accepted and critics have questioned the validity of the biographical information obtained from his young respondents about not only their current viewing habits and behaviour, but also those they tried to recall from ten years earlier. The study does indicate usefully that certain types of programming may have a more significant impact than other types on anti-social behaviour among young viewers, and that it is not sufficient to examine only the overall amount of viewing that is done.

In an attempt to make causal inferences from naturalistic studies, one study which used panels of youngsters interviewed on more than one occasion found that, for boys, the amount of TV viewing at age 8 tended to be more strongly correlated with peer ratings of aggression two years later than with peer ratings at 8. Furthermore, there was no relationship between early aggression and later TV viewing. The authors infer from this pattern of conditions that the earlier TV viewing caused the later aggression.

Another major panel survey with children was sponsored by the National Broadcasting Company in the United States. Some 3,200 elementary school children and teenagers participated in this research. The primary age children were surveyed on six occasions and the teenagers on five occasions over a three-year period (May 1970 through December 1973).[23]

The aim of the research was to find out if there were links, either at any one point in time or over time, between the character of television viewing and the propensity of aggressive tendencies among the children and teenagers under study. Among the primary school children, evidence about verbal and physical acts of aggression was obtained from school friends, while the teenagers reported on themselves. Television viewing was measured by giving respondents checklists of programmes available on the major networks which had been pre-classified for their violent content. Thus, not only did the researchers obtain some indication about general viewing patterns but also more specific information about levels of exposure among these young viewers to violent programmes.

During the analysis phase, the researchers assessed linkages between aggressive behaviour and levels of claimed viewing of different types of programming among different subgroups of children as well as among children as a whole. Only small statistical associations were found in any of these cases. Further analyses showed that, compared with the influence of family background, social environment and school performance, the significance of television viewing as an indicator of aggressiveness was very weak. This led the authors to conclude that television viewing was not a factor in the development of aggressive behaviours among the children and teenagers in their sample.

In Canadian research by Tannis Macbeth Williams which we discussed in Chapter 1, unobtrusive observations of children's behaviour were used in addition to teacher and peer ratings of aggression in a community where television had recently been introduced for the first time. We may recall that in this study the impact of television on the local population of young people was examined in three towns which at the outset either had no television reception (Notel), only one channel available (Unitel) or several channels available (Multitel).[24]

The major finding of the study was that the aggressive behaviour in the playground of grade school-aged children (aged 6–11) increased in Notel over the two-year period while playground aggression in Unitel and Multitel showed no increase. This pattern of increased aggression was true for both physical and verbal aggression; girls and boys; longitudinal (children aged 6–7 prior to TV reception and 8–9 two years after) and cross-sectional (children of same age at each testing) samples; children initially high or low in aggression; and for children who were either heavy or light viewers. In conclusion, the evidence in support of the hypothesis that viewing violence leads to an increase in aggressive behaviour is very strong.

Conclusion

Television violence continues to feature prominently in public debates about the regulation and impact of the world's most prevalent mass medium. Much of the focus of concern has been on the reactions of children to violent depictions in programmes. We do not argue with the sincerity and significance of this public anxiety. Children's minds and social consciousness are malleable and immature in many ways. Young viewers may be susceptible to subtle influences, often unintended, of television, which most adults are immune to. Whatever might be considered as appropriate viewing fare for grown-ups may therefore not invariably be suitable for children, who may take what is shown the wrong way.

What is questionable then is not the significance of the issue, but the validity and reliability of the research evidence about television violence. Television is accused of showing too much violence. When measuring violence on television, however, researchers often begin by setting up an 'objective' definition of violence which does not necessarily reflect the public's perception. Physical incidents or body counts provide a measure of something, but not necessarily of what ordinary viewers would themselves consider to be violence.

For viewers, and this applies to children as well, context is important. Viewers can and do discriminate between types of programmes and the way in which different programmes depict events. These perceptual discriminations are significant mediators of how viewers respond to television. They affect programme preferences, evaluations of how tasteful or offensive programmes are thought to be, and behavioural reactions to programmes.

We have seen that, in the end, anxieties about television violence rest on the supposed harmful effects it may have on viewers, particularly on the young and impressionable. There have been many studies of the influence of television violence (although the actual number is often grossly overstated) but these can be condensed to a handful of basic research methods – laboratory experiments, field experiments, correlational surveys and longitudinal panel studies. In each case, the methods have shortcomings, which are sufficient to cast some doubt on the validity of their findings. This is not to say that all the research is useless, rather the point is made as a note of caution to be borne in mind when interpreting what research results really show.

The debate about television violence will continue both in the public and academic spheres. The question of whether or not there is too much violence in programmes is a subjective one as much as it is a scientific one; the answer lies to a large extent in prevailing public taste and opinion. Values change constantly and are reflected in what is deemed to be acceptable viewing fare. On the question of whether or not television violence has any direct effects on viewers, the answer is neither simple nor straightforward. Much depends on the type of effect to which reference is being made and on the method used to measure television's impact. From the range of research which has been completed so far, it has become apparent that the measurement of television's effects, and of factors that mediate those effects, is highly complex. Often, researchers have relied upon methodologies that inadequately represent real world television viewing experiences and upon conceptual frameworks that omit important contributory variables. Although some progress has been made in eliminating the nature of certain types of television influence, we are still a long way from knowing fully the extent and character of television's influence on children's aggressive behaviour.

Chapter eight

Does TV encourage good behaviour?

Concern about possible anti-social influences of television far outweighs the consideration given to any other area of children's involvement with television. How far is the perception of the box in the corner as a 'one eyed monster' justified? The possibilities that television's examples of bad behaviour provide models to be copied by susceptible young viewers cannot be treated lightly. But the assumption, which commonly seems to prevail, that television has been demonstrably proved to have a bad influence, over-simplifies both what 'the box' brings into the home and how children get involved with it.

Television programmes contain many examples of good behaviour, of people acting kindly and with generosity. It is equally logical to assume that these portrayals provide models for children to copy too. In this chapter, therefore, we turn to the question of whether television encourages good behaviour among children. Although not as voluminous as the work on television violence, an important body of research exists which indicates a variety of ways in which television can or might, under certain circumstances, have soundly beneficial and desirable effects on children.

The notion of catharsis

One pro-social possibility, which runs counter to much established thinking on the subject, is that watching violence on television serves to provide an outlet for pent-up aggressive drives. According to the catharsis hypothesis, originally proposed by Aristotle, accumulated aggressive urges are supposedly drained after watching violence, with the result that the individual behaves less aggressively. In its strongest form, the hypothesis holds that anyone can purge their aggressive impulses through vicarious cathartic experiences. This form of the catharsis hypothesis is currently in general disfavour after passing through successive periods of uncritical acceptance and controversy. As we shall see, however, a weaker form of the hypothesis has been proposed and some evidence has emerged which suggests that for some people catharsis may be possible as a response to TV violence.[1]

Rather than thinking of catharsis as a process which can occur in anybody, increasingly researchers have suggested that if such a discharge of hostile feeling can occur at all, it is probably restricted to certain types of personality. It has come to be theoretically conceived as a dimension of human skill or competence involving the ability to fantasise, daydream or use one's imagination.[2] These mental faculties are not equally well developed in all people. There is some evidence, though, which we look at later in this chapter, that children with lively imaginations are better at shifting their mood from one of anger to one of more positive emotional feeling, thus reducing the likelihood of overt expression of aggression. Furthermore, such children are better equipped to get rid of their hostilities through films or television programmes with which they become emotionally carried away.[3]

Much of the evidence for catharsis as linked with the way people respond to televised portrayals of violence has derived from the work of Seymour Feshbach. In the 1950s and 1960s his work provided several early demonstrations that individuals can harmlessly discharge their aggressive impulses either through fantasising about violence or through watching fictional portrayals of violence under controlled laboratory conditions.[4] Later, at the beginning of the 1970s, Feshbach and his colleague Jerome Singer reported a reduction of aggressive tendencies among teenage boys under more natural conditions after they had been encouraged to watch mainly violent television programmes.[5]

Over 600 teenage boys from three private residential schools for middle-class boys and four residential treatment homes for boys lacking in proper home care had their viewing diets manipulated over a six-week spell. During this period, some boys were shown a minimum of six hours per week of primarily violent programming, while other boys were shown primarily non-violent programmes. Additional hours of viewing were allowed so long as they involved the assigned programme types. A behaviour rating scale was completed daily by a member of the staff familiar with the boys' activities throughout the experiment.

The teenagers who watched mainly non-violent programmes exhibited higher levels of physical aggression against their peers than did those who watched mainly violent programmes. Thus, the boys who saw mainly non-violent programmes had twice as many fights as the other boys and were more likely to provoke fights.

The study has not been received without criticism and an attempt by another researchers to replicate its findings under similar conditions failed. Problems with it stem from the unknown amount of violence there may have been in non-violent programmes, something that was not checked. Programmes which other researchers have labelled as violent, such as cartoons, found their way into the non-violent diet. It is not known either how attentively the children in each condition actually watched television. Finally, there were complaints among some teenage boys in the non-violent diet condition because they were not permitted to watch some of their favourite programmes. The frustration caused by being deprived of programmes they liked and would normally be able to watch may have contributed towards these boys' increased aggressiveness.

While there may be problems with the interpretation of Feshbach's results and a question mark hangs over the validity of the strong form of the catharsis hypothesis, there has recently been some discussion of a more idiosyncratic way in which catharsis might work. It could be that catharsis is more likely to occur among certain types of people than others.[6]

In place of the simplistic catharsis framework based on the 'hydraulic' model of aggression as a reservoir of psychic energy which can be purged via fantasy – a non-specific vicarious activity available to all individuals – there is an alternative conception that views fantasy as a dimension of human skill or competence. This imaginative capacity may be manifested among children as skills in creativity, daydreaming or fantasy play behaviour. Thus, the practised young daydreamer can turn to fantasy activity in dealing with frustrating problems or situations, whereas the less experienced daydreamer may be unable to do this and is limited to the direct expression of anger through aggression. It is known that youngsters who are adept at fantasising can reduce their aggressive feelings not only through vicarious involvement in fantasy portrayals of aggression, but also by daydreaming about non-violent, imaginative themes such as being successful at school, going out on dates and so on.

A series of interesting experiments by Grant Noble in the 1970s showed that children's reaction to televised or film violence was not invariably to become more aggressive in their subsequent play or interactions with other children; sometimes violent portrayals encouraged them to play more imaginatively and less destructively.[7] The type of violence made a difference. Highly stylised, fictional portrayals of violence subsequently encouraged children to be friendlier and less hostile towards each other, while more realistic portrayals of violence, especially where the victim was seen, resulted in increased aggressive tendencies.

Realistic violence, such as that contained in a televised wrestling match, made both aggressive and non-aggressive boys more aggressive afterwards when they played with other children. Stylised violence as shown in a western, however, produced more imaginative play among boys already known to be prone to aggression. At the same time it also made relatively well-behaved boys more boisterous with other children, though less so than did watching wrestling.

Individual differences in imaginative play behaviour and in the ability to fantasise or daydream may underlie differences among children in their responses to TV violence. Youngsters who are particularly skilled as day dreamers may be able to reinterpret their aggressive feelings and use their fantasies to shift their mood from one of anger to a more positive, pleasant emotion, thus reducing the likelihood that they will show any overt expression of aggression.

One researcher has tested this idea by comparing the reactions of children who were either skilled or not adept at fantasising in their reactions to violent and non-violent film material with one another.[8] In a manipulation of how children felt, two accomplices of the researcher were employed to annoy the children by interrupting them while they were building a toy. Next, the children saw either a film containing violence, or a non-violent film, or no film at all. Finally, the children were placed in a room of toys, some of which they could have played with in an aggressive fashion. Their behaviour at play was observed, unknown to them, for a further ten minutes, during which they were scored for any aggressiveness they displayed.

Children who were skilled daydreamers exhibited significantly less aggressiveness at play after being given an opportunity to watch either violent or non-violent film material, than when they had watched nothing. Among youngsters who were not adept at daydreaming, none of the film material, regardless of whether it was violent or non-violent, made any difference to their behaviour.

Children who were high fantasisers seemed to be able to reduce any anger they had while generally improving the way they felt while watching violent and non-violent film sequences. For some children at least, fictional violence can have positive effects. This research throws some doubt on the popular view that violence on television and in motion pictures is harmful to all children, even if they view a great deal. It seems that in the case of some youngsters, particularly those who have highly developed imaginations, the effects of these materials might even be beneficial. Violent as well as non-violent television programmes may provide a means through which some children can reduce their angry feelings. It should be noted that so far such beneficial effects of viewing media violence seem to apply only to those children who are active and regular fantasisers. Children with low levels of fantasy activity are unable to deal with their aggressive feelings in this way and may actually become more prone to react aggressively following exposure to film violence. Thus, the same television programme could have beneficial or harmful results depending upon youngsters' abilities to use it in active and positive ways to improve how they feel.

What is required at this stage are developments in several new directions, and perhaps the following ideas may provide some useful indicators: (1) experimental research showing the extent to which individuals differ in fantasising capabilities; (2) closer examination of relationships between fantasising or imaginativeness and reactions to various kinds of TV content; (3) collection of data to show what proportion of youngsters have sufficient fantasising abilities to use television dramatisations in a constructive way to control their negative emotional and behavioural tendencies.

Can television teach good behaviour?

A growing body of evidence indicates that televised examples of good behaviour can encourage children to behave better. Research has shown that young viewers can learn how to behave in a more socially acceptable or desirable fashion through watching not only specially produced educational programmes, but also examples of good behaviour contained in more popular establishment programmes produced for the mass audience.[9] The evidence for pro-social effects of television can be grouped into four types:

1 laboratory studies with prepared television or film materials
2 laboratory studies with broadcast materials specially produced for social skills teaching purposes
3 laboratory studies with programme materials from popular TV series
4 field studies relating amount of viewing of pro-social television content to strength of pro-social behaviour tendencies.

Using these various techniques, researchers have investigated the potential of television to affect children's levels of displayed generosity and unselfishness, their friendliness and deferred gratification in contrast to wanting immediate rewards for anything they do.

Research with prepared materials

Specially prepared film and television materials have been found to influence several different types of children's self-control behaviour, including courage, delay of gratification and adherence to rules. Controlled study has also been made of television's ability to affect charitable behaviour among young viewers.[10] Several researchers have demonstrated the therapeutic potential of television material, particularly with regard to helping children overcome fears. Showing pre-school children, who were initially afraid of dogs, a series of films that depicted other children approaching and playing with a dog resulted in substantial decreases in their fear of dogs. The same effect failed to occur following exposure to films of Disneyland. Similarly, successful film examples have been reported to help cure children's fear of the dentist.[11]

Further important work has shown that specially prepared television material can help lonely, self-conscious children to make friends more readily. Thus, youngsters who have difficulty getting on with other children can be encouraged to take a step back while watching fictional scenarios in which examples are portrayed of how to mix with others in various social situations.[12]

Brief television portrayals have been used to influence children's self-control regarding delay of gratification and the impact of symbolic models on viewers' adherence to rules. For instance, children have been found to be more willing to wait for a valued reward after watching a video-taped sequence of an adult modelling delay of gratification in the same way and explaining why he has done so.[13] In another study, children were shown a child on television of their own age conforming to an explicitly stated rule while playing a game. These children were less likely themselves to deviate from this rule than were other children who had not seen the television example.[14]

Another example of self-control has been examined in studies which were carried out to see if television programming could influence children's 'resistance to temptation'.[15] The typical situation involved observations of 7- and 8-year-old boys playing with toys in a games-room. While left on their own in this room they were forbidden to touch or to play with one particularly attractive toy. On average, around six minutes and forty seconds would go by before a boy in this situation would touch the toy. However, if the boy had watched a TV programme showing another boy of around the same age playing with similar toys, though not going near the forbidden toy, the average boy would wait nearly eight minutes before transgressing. If, on the other hand, the boy in the programme was seen to play with the toy, young viewers were apt to touch it subsequently within three minutes of being left in the games-room. These effects were found still to be present one month later.

The way in which television's portrayal of good behaviour or bad behaviour can influence children to behave similarly may depend on whether youngsters watch on their own or with someone else of their own age. One American study examined 5-year-old boys' reactions to either a short film depicting a male character behaving in an aggressive manner towards a person costumed as a clown and compared this with their reactions following a film in which the same character acted in a friendly, helpful manner towards the clown. Each child saw only one of these films. However, in some cases, these young boys watched on their own, while in others they watched with a companion.[16]

Afterwards, when the film had finished, the boys were taken to a playroom which was located in the experimenter's 'own trailer'. Here, they were introduced to the clown figure in person and left to talk and play with him for a short period, during which the experimenter went away. The children were at this time monitored unobtrusively by hidden observers.

These observations revealed that children who had watched the aggressive film depiction were significantly more likely than those who had seen the other version to play with the clown more 'aggressively', that is, they made more hostile comments, played shooting games, hit the clown with a mallet and, when in pairs, were more aggressive towards each other. These effects were more pronounced among boys who had watched the film in pairs. In contrast, boys who watched the friendly version were in turn more likely to behave in a constructive, friendly way towards the clown. Viewing in pairs with a companion made no substantial difference to the friendly film's effects.

Children's charitable behaviour may be influenced by televised examples of people making donations. One demonstration of this type of effect emerged from a series of controlled experimental studies with 6- to 9-year-old children. These youngsters were shown a specially constructed video-tape film showing a character playing a bowling game and winning gift certificates.

In a different version of the film the bowler could either give some of his certificates to a charity or kept them all for himself. In addition, sometimes he also preached the merits of giving to charity. After watching this film, children were placed in a similar situation and were observed to see how much they would give their winnings to charity. The results were that children who saw the video-tape in which the character gave to charity were more likely to make donations them- selves than were those who saw the character behave selfishly. The bowler's actions spoke louder than his words, since preaching about giving to charity made little difference to how the children behaved.[17] Children's charitable behaviours may be short-lived, however. Although televised examples of generosity can encourage children to be more giving, this effect may have worn off within a week or two.[18]

Television may influence children's friendliness and affectionate behaviour. Demonstrations of this effect have been made in laboratory settings and under more natural viewing conditions. In a controlled viewing environment with specially prepared television material, nursery school children have been observed to express greater affection towards a toy clown after watching an adult TV character do likewise on screen. However, this copy-cat behaviour was more likely to occur among boys only if the affectionate character was male; a female character showing affection had no effect. The study suggests that at this early age children already select to follow appropriate models for them and perceived similarity of TV characters (in this case being of the same sex) can be important.[19]

Research with broadcast materials

A number of special television productions have emerged from major television companies, especially in the United States, but also in the United Kingdom and Sweden, which have been designed to enhance the social maturity and responsibility of young viewers. One of the most notable examples of this type of production is *Sesame Street*. This series was primarily aimed at teaching disadvantaged children living in urban ghettos a variety of social and mental skills which they would need in school. Its appeal, however, has been extensive and it has attracted a far wider and more heterogeneous audience than that for which it was originally intended. While it is undoubtedly a very successful programme in terms of popularity with audiences around the world, what evidence is there that *Sesame Street* and similar types of programmes have pro-social effects upon young viewers?

There is some evidence that children as young as 4 and certainly those aged 7 years are able to identify and remember the co-operative and helping behaviours emphasised by certain segments of the show. Another programme, *Mister Rogers' Neighbourhood*, which has also been made to improve children's social awareness and social skills, has been found to have similar effects.[20] For instance, children aged 4, who were shown four episodes of the series depicting characters attempting to understand and help a stranger, were better able to behave in more helpful and co-operative ways than were children who saw different programmes.[21]

Some educational programmes appear to be better than others at encouraging children to behave in a more friendly manner towards their peers. Among children aged between 3 and 5, for example, American researchers found that watching *Mister Rogers' Neighbourhood* produced much friendlier dispositions both among children and between the children and adults over a period of several days. Watching *Sesame Street* had the same impact, but only among those children who tended to be poorly behind in the first place.[22]

Research with popular drama materials

There is growing evidence then that appropriate, specially manufactured television programmes or film clips can influence children's altruistic tendencies, in the short term and under contrived conditions. However, these studies have used a comparatively narrow range of television and film materials. Even those experiments which used actual broadcast material from network television generally featured only carefully selected clips from educationally oriented programmes. Their results may not, therefore, be generalisable to the portrayals found in existing, action-oriented television dramas which usually attract the largest audiences among children as well as adults and are often of the type found at the centre of the television violence controversy. Although fast-moving sequences typical of many action-adventure shows on television may contain examples of aggressive behaviour which could conceivably be imitated, does the occurrence of pro-social behaviours in this type of fictional context also provide salient imitation cues? The answer, at least for contrived viewing conditions in research, appears to be 'yes'.

Television dramas depicting pro-social behaviours can encourage children to behave unselfishly. One study with 5- and 6-year-olds had the children divided up to watch one of three unedited programmes – an episode of *Lassie* in which a small boy risked his life to save an endangered puppy; an episode of *Lassie* that featured dogs in a positive light but portrayed no example of a human helping a dog; and an episode of *The Brady Bunch*, a family situation comedy. After viewing, children were first introduced to a situation engineered so that they were faced with a choice between persisting at a button game, or breaking off from the game to push another button that would bring assistance to (fictional) puppies in distress, thereby reducing the number of points they could win. The illusion of a troubled puppy was created by asking the children to monitor a kennel by earphones and to press the button signalling the attendant that the dogs might be in distress if the child heard barking over the earphones. Children who saw the dramatic example of a boy helping a dog in the *Lassie* episode chose to help puppies in distress more quickly and for a considerably longer period of time than children in either of the other two conditions.[23]

From a practical point of view these results imply that it is possible to produce television shows featuring action and adventure which have appeal for child and family audiences and at the same time have socially desirable, as opposed to anti-social, influences upon viewer behaviour. However, it should perhaps be carefully noted that throughout these experiments the helping behaviour portrayed in the television episode and the behaviour required of the child in the post-viewing situation were very similar in nature. Can pro-social content occurring in popular television series have more general effects upon dissimilar as well as related viewer behaviours?

Several pieces of research from the United States and Australia have explored this question. These have shown that popular television programmes can provide examples of sociable effects which may generalise to good behaviour other than those shown in the programmes.

One study with Australian pre-school children examined the effects of a specially controlled diet of television on the youngsters' social behaviour. The experiment used a selection of episodes from television series including *Lassie, I Love Lucy, The Brady Bunch* and *Father Knows Best.*[24] First of all, these programmes were content-analysed and classified in terms of the amount of 'pro-social' behaviour they depicted. On this basis they were divided into two sorts: 'pro-social' and 'neutral'.

The children were assigned to watch either 'pro-social' or 'neutral' programmes for half an hour each day, five days a week for four weeks. They were tested one week before and again one week after conclusion of the special viewing diet on measures of sociability. Regular watching of pro-social programmes was found to be associated with an increase in helpfulness among boys and in co-operative behaviour among boys and girls. The precise behaviours measured were quite different from anything depicted in any of the programmes. This indicated that when young children watch standard television programmes in which the main characters display concern and consideration for others, their own consideration may increase.

Another study showed children either an episode of *The Waltons* or a television film in which people were not very helpful towards each other. Children who saw *The Waltons* were more likely to help an experimenter who dropped an armful of books than did those who watched the other film. This effect did not generalise across other situations, however. Thus, the results provide only some evidence that ordinary broadcast material can enhance the goodness in people.[25]

Field studies of pro-social TV effects

What happens outside the laboratory, though? Do programmes such as *The Waltons* have an effect on how children behave towards each other in their everyday lives? One way of finding this out has been to monitor children's viewing habits and social activity and conduct over time in natural surroundings. One survey in which this was done obtained from children information about the programmes they watched and classified their viewing diets in terms of the number of programmes they watched which contained either anti-social or pro-social behaviour examples. Thus, each programme watched was coded in terms of how much anti-social or pro-social content it usually carried. Children's own behaviours were rated through self-reports and teacher reports. Findings revealed that the less TV they watched in total, and that if they watched a lot of programmes with high levels of pro-social content, the more likely they were to behave in a pro-social manner.[26]

In a comparison of the relative influence of pro-social versus violence viewing, correlations obtained between viewing habits and pro-social behaviour were lower than those obtained between viewing habits and aggressive behaviour. However, there are several reasons for this which point to limitations in the current state of research in this field and offer a number of potential lines of enquiry for future research.

First of all, children learn quite early that they should help or share, and thus television's pro-social content only reiterates what they already know. Aggressive behaviour, on the other hand, is generally punished in a child's home and school environment, and seeing it performed with frequent success on television contrasts with its treatment in reality. It may be useful for future studies to find out the extent to which children of various ages clearly differentiate pro-social and anti-social behaviours and their outcomes in reality and in television's fictional drama, and to obtain measures of the relative salience and attractiveness of these behaviours for the child.

A second point also concerns the manner in which pro-social and anti-social or aggressive behaviours are presented on television. Pro-social behaviours are very often subtle and verbally mediated, whereas aggressive behaviours are blatant and physical. Because young children learn better from simple direct and active presentation, they may be more likely to learn from violent than from pro-social portrayals customarily shown on television. At present, no evidence is available to show that these differential portrayal characteristics produce differences in perception and learning of pro-social versus violent content.

Finally, content analysis has shown that televised pro-social behaviours are predominantly performed by female and non-white characters rather than by white males who are also the most successful and powerful character type on television drama. Thus, the relative influence of pro-social and violent behaviours may be compounded with the types of characters who normally portray them. It is important for future research to assess the relative amounts of pro-social and violent behaviours performed by specific leading characters. If it is to be assumed that their preferential production treatment makes their presence more noticeable then their actions may provide sources of learning and behavioural influence for young viewers.

Recently, there has been some indication that the pattern may be changing somewhat in a positive way. Barbara Lee, formerly of the CBS television network in the United States, has reported findings from an analysis of pro-social portrayals on American prime-time network television entertainment programming. Over 1,000 pro-social incidents were recorded from 235 entertainment programmes.[27] The portrayal of helpful and altruistic, affectionate and co-operative behaviours was prevalent, though more frequently occurring in some types of programmes (e.g. action-adventure). Pro-social behaviours were usually depicted as successful in working out whatever conflicts existed and easing people's problems. In over half (56 per cent) of the incidents, the pro-social behaviour was intended to resolve an immediate problem or conflict. In eight out of ten of these cases, it was rated as being wholly or partially successful in problem-resolution. Most of the good behaviours observed occurred among those who were relatives or friends. This accounted for three out of four pro-social content incidents.

Conclusion

In this chapter we have discussed the pro-social potential of television. Despite widespread criticism of television for promoting anti-social behaviour and under-mining the moral fabric of society, there is evidence that it may provide a channel through which hostile impulses can be harmlessly dispersed. Furthermore, televised examples of good behaviour can encourage children to behave in friendlier and more thoughtful ways towards others.

We began the chapter where the previous one had left off – with the subject of TV violence. The catharsis hypothesis proposes that, through watching televised violence, youngsters may discharge their aggressive urges harmlessly and be less likely to behave aggressively with others. We dismissed a major US field study of boys in public institutions which examined and claimed to produce evidence in support of the catharsis hypothesis. Close scrutiny of this study by others resulted in doubts being cast on its major conclusions. An attempted replication failed to yield consistent findings. However, interest in the notion of catharsis encouraged further research and a modified hypothesis.

In a weaker form of the original idea, it has been proposed that catharsis can occur but that it is dependent on the ability to fantasise or daydream. Children who daydream vividly seem to be better able to discharge their aggressive urges through media portrayals of violence. The type of violence is important too. Obvious fictional portrayals seem to offer better possibilities for the harmless reduction of aggressive feelings amongst young daydreamers than realistic portrayals of violence. Imaginative fantasising is a cognitive skill and although it is more evident in some children than others, it can be improved through appropriate training. This would seem to offer a route through which young viewers can be equipped with the ability to use their experiences with televised violence in a socially beneficial and constructive way.

In addition to taking advantage of vicarious involvement with television violence to provide a means of improving the child's mood, another way in which television can have a beneficial impact on children is through the portrayal of kindness, generosity, being helpful and socially responsible. These portrayals have been shown to exert both short-term and longer-term influences on similar behaviours among children. Television can have such socially desirable effects not simply through its educational programmes, but also when pro-social portray-als feature in its entertainment and drama productions made for non-popular consumption.

Although research on the pro-social effects of television still has a long way to go, the early signs are that this area of television content has important social behavioural influences which need to be examined in greater depth. Through both specially designed campaigns and educational fare as well as through its fictional entertainment output, television can play a positive role in helping to build cultivated and socially responsible young people. It is possible that pro-social content may counteract anti-social content to some extent, and finding out which pro-social television material is most effective in this respect may provide valuable alternative programme content control guidelines to simply cutting violence.

Chapter nine

Does TV advertising affect children?

Advertising: why the concern?

On many television networks around the world a not insubstantial proportion of TV airtime is filled by advertisements. Controls over advertising on television are more rigid in some countries than others. For example, rules governing the amount of advertising content in each broadcast hour, and the frequency with which advertising breaks can occur during a single programme, place more restrictions on television advertising in Britain than is found in the United States. Even so, the number of advertising breaks during the course of each day's programming, especially during peak-time, on British television is sufficient to merit empirical consideration and exploration relating to the impact this material has on the audience.

In the United States, anxieties over the influence of television advertising, especially on children, have resulted in parental movements on a national scale which have voiced their concern at the highest levels.[1] On an intuitive level, at least, this concern of parents for the mental and behavioural welfare of their youngsters, who may be exposed to thousands of commercials during their young lives, should not be regarded as trivial or unwarranted. Very often, the standards of production of television advertisements are equal to or even better than those in programmes and consequently their impact on the attention of the television audience should not be under-rated or ignored. Furthermore, the faces and voices prevalent on television advertisements are often the same as those seen and heard in other contexts on popular television shows. One ought not to be too surprised, therefore, if young children confuse programmes and advertisements.

Given these similarities between programming and advertising, how difficult is it for children to distinguish between the two and how susceptible are they, therefore, to commercial appeals broadcast on television? The answer to this question is not certain because research in this field lags behind that on effects of other types of television content such as violence or sex – at least in the academic sphere. There is, of course, ample research conducted by advertising agencies and others involved in the advertising industry. This proprietary research rarely surfaces outside the agencies responsible for conducting it and seldom enters into discussion about the efficacy of television advertising. Although increasing numbers of academic studies have emerged during the 1970s and 1980s, our knowledge of the ways children are affected cognitively, emotionally and behaviourally by commercial messages on television is still limited.

Many parents and critics fear that children are particularly susceptible to commercial appeals because young viewers lack the necessary cognitive skills to defend themselves against what are often highly attractive and skilfully worded persuasive messages.[2] Other undesirable consequences of television commercials listed by their critics are that they lead youngsters to pressure parents into purchasing products unnecessarily and thereby often create conflict within the family, and that the number and nature of televised commercials to which children are exposed before they leave school are such that they are likely to be socialised into over-materialistic ways.

The first published work in the area of advertising was an American study carried out with 400 children aged 6–12 years, who were asked to list as many products advertised on television as they could remember. They were given fifteen minutes to do this. Even the youngest could recall some products, with children generally producing an average of twenty. The three most recalled products were detergents, beer and cigarettes, which were not directly advertised to children.[3]

A few years later, a book called *The Hidden Persuaders* emerged which painted a picture of people – the innocents – being manipulated by advertisers who used sophisticated selling techniques to persuade people to buy things they do not really need anyway. This was a highly rhetorical statement about the impact of advertising but not effectively backed up with hard evidence. Nevertheless it set the scene for future thinking about advertising.[4]

Children's reactions to advertising

Many early instances of advertising adopted a very simplistic understanding of the way advertising works. Where children are concerned, for instance, there is assumed to be a straightforward cause-and-effect relationship between the advertised message and the behaviour it recommends. In other words, on watching an advertisement on television children may be directly encouraged to go out and buy the advertised or attempt to persuade someone else – a parent perhaps – to buy it for them. This view of the influence of advertising fails to take into account the full complexities of the process, however. It ignores children's ability to process and evaluate advertisements, just as they do with programmes, prior to deciding whether or not to believe the commercial appeal or to act upon it.

Lately concern has grown about children's susceptibility to more subtle messages in advertisements. The IBA, which regulates advertising on television in the UK, judged a recent commercial for Levi's 501 jeans as too sexy to be shown during children's programmes or on Saturday afternoons. According to one writer, what is happening in the pursuit of selling is that the barriers are being shifted to a point many will find unacceptable.[5]

The first advertisement in the Levi's campaign, Nick Kamen's launderette commercial, was marked with a touch more humour than sex. The next, however, used a 14-year-old girl, shown after parting from her boyfriend, lying on her back dressed in T-shirt and knickers, suggestively pulling on the Levi's he had left her. The latest has a muscular stranger coming downstairs in an American midwestern boarding house, dressed only in shirt and underpants. He smoulders at the owner's daughter as the father looks on with suspicion; he sighs as he pulls on his Levi's taken from the fridge and then rides off into the desert leaving an obviously aroused woman behind him.

The advertisement is extremely well made – but to what end? It is not just increasingly explicit sex that advertisers are using; it is a whole range of immoral practices from attempted murder to squeezing a man out of his job. Two more examples illustrate this point.

In the commercial for Pirelli, again a beautifully crafted little piece of drama, the male protagonist sets out in his car – but the woman in his life has tampered with the brakes; thanks to Pirelli tyres he survives.

Or there's the bought woman in the Volkswagen offering. This time the mistress walks out; symbolically she throws away a succession of expensive gifts including the expensive fur. But she keeps the keys to the Volkswagen Golf.

The concern among some writers is that while using 'immorality' to sell goods, the advertisers are also selling the immorality itself. Another worry is that audiences will grow accustomed to this style of advertising and be less aware of its gradual influence upon them. To what extent is this alarmist viewpoint substantiated by what is known about the effect of advertising on children – and with what children themselves know and understand and have to say about advertisements?

Increasingly, research has revealed that children exhibit a growing sophistication about advertising during their formative years. Although early on in life they may have no proper understanding of the dishonest character of advertisements and their purposes compared with programmes, this soon changes. Research has shown that advertising does not directly influence its audience. The potential impact of the message can be determined by a whole range of other factors. In this chapter we shall examine the nature and extent of television advertising's influence on children. We can begin by examining some of the substantiated facts about children's experience with television advertising and then explore what children themselves think about television commercials.

Making sense of advertising

Although advertising is designed ultimately to manipulate consumer behaviour, this influence is mediated by what people think about advertising *per se* as well as about specific advertisements. Before a commercial can change people's minds about what to buy or encourage them to favour one brand over another, its message must be taken in and examined. Viewers must pay attention to their TV sets for this to happen. They must pay sufficient attention that they are able to remember the commercial or the elements of it that the advertiser hopes will make their product more appealing. The influence process also depends, however, on what viewers know about the aims of advertising and on how much they believe what advertisements tell them.

Thus, in the context of the impact of television advertising upon children, several important questions need to be considered.

1 Are children aware of advertisements as distinct from programmes?
2 Do children understand what advertisements are about?
3 Do children remember and believe what advertisements tell them?
4 Are children likely to respond to advertising by wanting the things advertised for themselves?

Children's distinctive awareness of TV advertising

Before advertising can affect young viewers, it must impinge upon their consciousness in some way. Although there has in the past been concern about the effects of subliminal advertising, solid support for the efficacy of this sort of advertising from research has failed to materialise. In any case, the use of subliminal images or messages in TV advertising in the UK is outlawed.

Even though presented in a normal, perceptible way, children may not necessarily notice advertisements. If they look away from the screen for a minute or two, the message may easily be missed. Another problem, especially with very young viewers, is that they simply may fail to make the distinction between programmes and advertisements. The two may run together as an indistinguishable montage of images and voices.

Children's attention to TV advertising can be measured in a variety of ways. Children can be asked directly whether they watch and remember advertisements, or parents can be questioned about their children's reactions to TV ads. A more objective method used by some researchers has been to make their own direct observations of children's attention to the screen during ad breaks. The latter have the advantage that they monitor children continuously while watching television and that running logs are kept by independent observers of levels of attention during actual viewing. Evidence derived from the reports of children or their parents may lack the same degree of measuring because it relies heavily on the often fallible memories and dubious vigilance of respondents when required to monitor their own or others' viewing behaviours.

Parents, for example, have been found to provide higher estimates of children's attention to TV adverts than independent, continuous observations typically viewed. Both types of evidence, however, have indicated an increase in attention to screen during ad breaks with age. Thus, when, in one American study, sixty-five mothers were invited to report on the home viewing of their children (aged 5 to 12 years) they indicated lower levels of attention among younger than among older ones.[6]

Younger children also tended to pay less attention throughout the advertisements as compared with older children. Children aged 5–8 years were at full attention 67 per cent of advertisement viewing time, and 9- to 12-year-olds averaged full attention 75 per cent of the viewing time. Older children's attention when a series of advertisements was presented in a block tended to drop towards the end. Older children tended to make more critical comments about adverts they saw than did younger children.

In an observational study in which researchers placed video cameras in family homes, somewhat lower levels of attention to television advertisements were found. They found that children up to 10 years old whom they observed watched adverts only 40 per cent of the time they were on-air, while 11- to 19-year-olds watched them 55 per cent of the time they were on.[7]

Even direct observations of children's television viewing by trained monitors do not always produce the same impressions of young viewers' attention to the screen. Much depends on the setting in which viewing takes place. For example, observations made of children's viewing in schools have found higher levels of attention to advertisements than ones made in home viewing contexts.

Another indication of children's awareness of advertising is their ability to recognise or recall it. As with their level of attention to ad breaks, children's memory for advertisements changes with age. As they get older, children become better at remembering adverts and are able to recall more about different TV ads.

It would appear that there is a major change in the type of information retained from advertisements between the ages of 5–6 and 8–9 years. Younger children tend to recall single elements from the commercial whereas older children tend to recall more product and commercial plot line information. Recognition (measured by selection from a range of alternatives) seems to be uniformly poor, ranging from a level slightly above chance for 5- to 6-year-olds to an average level of 70 per cent for 8- to 9-year-olds (based on a chance recognition score of 33 per cent). There can be a high degree of variability across children, however.[8]

Despite generally low recognition and recall scores, young children seem to find certain features of advertisements more salient than others. In particular, commercial slogans, jingles or unusual, humorous elements may stand out far more than brand names.[9]

Children's understanding of TV advertising

There are two principal issues concerning children's understanding of TV advertising. The first concerns their understanding of what TV advertising is about. What is the purpose of advertising? How does it differ from programming in its aims? A second important feature of children's understanding relates to how much they are able to follow and interpret the appeals made by adverts for the commodities being advertised.

For children to understand the purpose of TV advertising, however, they must be capable of making a series of important discriminations. They must be able

1 to distinguish advertisements as separate from programmes
2 to recognise a sponsor as the source of the commercial message
3 to perceive the idea of an intended audience for the message
4 to understand the 'symbolic' nature of products, character, and contextual representation in commercials
5 to discriminate by example between products as advertised and products as experienced.

When interviewed or questioned in general terms about TV advertising, children's ability to describe the differences between advertisements and programmes has been found to improve considerably with age. Usually, very young children below 8 years old express a certain amount of confusion when asked to define the nature of television commercials. Older children, on the other hand, are able to distinguish between programme and commercial material on the basis of an overall understanding of each message's meaning.[10]

To measure children's awareness of TV advertisements as distinct entities from programmes without relying purely on youngsters' personal accounts, some researchers have monitored changes in children's levels of visual attention whilst they are actually watching television. One consistent finding is a tendency often for children to exhibit a drop in visual attention to the screen during an advertising break compared with their amount of looking at the screen while watching prior programming. In addition, children's looking at the screen may continue to decline across the ad break and over the course of subsequent breaks in a programme. Age differences are once again very apparent.[11]

The smallest decreases in attention tend to occur among the youngest viewers (5- to 7-year-olds) who displayed higher and more stable levels of visual attention to both advertisements and programmes than do older children. Young and immature children may exhibit a higher degree of stability in their visual attention to programmes and advertisements, whereas older children show a higher degree of differentiation in when they look attentively at the screen.[12]

In one illustration of children's patterns of looking at television across different kinds of material, one group of researchers showed groups of 6-, 8- and 10-year-old children a fifteen-minute television programme in which was embedded a commercial break consisting of two advertisements. While viewing this material the children themselves were video-taped and their attention to the programme and the advertisements was assessed. Attention dropped during the time the first advertisement appeared and decreased even further during the course of the second advertisement. This effect occurred whether the advertisements were presented in the context of a live-action or an animated programme and was observed over eight different types of advertisements, indicating that it was unlikely that the drop in attention was specific to particular kinds of advertising or programme content.[13]

Studies which use children's visual attention to the television screen as a measure of their ability to discriminate between programmes and advertisements can be difficult to interpret. Attention to an advertisement or a programme may shift because of differences in certain physical features, such as the kinds of images being shown, the background music and so on. This does not necessarily mean that children are making a conceptual distinction between an 'advertisement' and a 'programme' and thus choose mentally to switch off when the ad break occurs.[14] The children's attention may shift according to how interesting or boring they find what they are watching and not just because they know what is coming next (i.e. an ad break) and therefore do not need to watch.

Although shifts in amount of looking do occur among children when watching programmes and advertisements, these may signify little more than superficial perceptual responses to these two types of material and may not confidently be interpreted to represent a deeper, conceptual differentiation between advertising and programming.[15] A more precise measure of children's understanding of television advertising is needed which explores what they actually assimilate from individual commercials.

What do children remember from TV adverts?

From the perspective of the advertiser, a successful advertising campaign is a memorable one because the opportunity to buy a product following its appearance on a television advertisement is usually delayed. Therefore, it is the information which the viewer has stored and is subsequently able to retrieve from memory about the advertised brand that will influence the decision whether or not to choose that brand rather than others from the same product category. However, measures of children's memory for advertising content may also provide an indication of how children come to understand the nature and purpose of advertisements as distinct from programmes.

It seems that although there is generally no intent among young viewers to seek information from television commercials to use in a purchase decision, except perhaps at Christmas time when they may be looking for gift ideas, children may nevertheless use information which they have already learned from commercials when asking parents for specific products at a later date.[16] Advertising may also influence a child to buy a particular attractive or highly valued attribute than other brands of the same type. Children may remember certain aspects of TV adverts better than others. Furthermore, it seems that the better children are able to retain and understand factual and emotional appeals made about products by advertisements, the more they distinguish adverts from surrounding programmes.[17]

Researchers can sometimes underestimate children's understanding of television, however, especially when they use techniques which are insensitive to the subtleties of what children pick up from what they watch. One illustration of this is the way children are tested for what they can remember about adverts. Recall measures may not always be sufficient to tap memory (and therefore perhaps comprehension) performance of children on television commercials. When asked to recall freely younger children may not always understand what is required of them and inevitably lack the skill to articulate their thoughts as clearly as older children. Instead, recognition scores may be a more sensitive means of measuring memory, especially among very young viewers. Fortunately, using recall, one study found that 8-year-olds showed considerably better overall memory for the product appeals contained in commercials than 3- to 4-year-olds. But when recognition measures were used, this difference was substantially reduced as the percentage of younger viewers remembering the commercial product elements increased substantially.[18] Another study provided children aged between 4 and 10 years with photographs of animated presenter characters from either programmes or food commercials and asked them to identify the characters. On the basis of recognition scores, it was found that even children as young as 4 years could distinguish between animated characters as they appeared in programmes or in commercials and could also link those characters from food commercials to their respective products.[19]

The selling purpose of TV advertising

An important aspect of children's understanding of TV advertising is the ability to recognise the selling motive of adverts. There is consistent evidence that younger children who do not understand the persuasive intent of commercials are more likely to perceive them as truthful messages, whereas older children who can discern persuasive intent tend to express sceptical attitudes towards commercials. Results of various survey studies indicate that below the age of 6, the vast majority of children cannot readily explain the selling purpose of advertising. Between the ages of about 5 and 9 years, the majority of children come to be able to recognise and explain the selling intent of advertising.[20]

In a British survey, when children were asked 'What is the main reason they have advertisements on TV?' eight out of ten (80 per cent) replied that it is because the advertisers want to sell you something, while around one in eight (12 per cent) thought it is because they want you to know something. Fewer than one in ten (8 per cent) did not know. These responses did not differ by age or by social class, but they did differ by sex. The girls in the study were even more likely (84 per cent) than the boys (75 per cent) to indicate that the main purpose of advertisements was to sell something; the boys were more likely to indicate that they did not know the main purpose.[21]

Children's verbal replies to questions about what television advertisements are and why they are shown have thus revealed significant improvements in understanding. In all such studies, however, the apparent growth in understanding has to be weighed against the relative abilities of younger and older children to articulate the differences between programmes and advertisements, regardless of whether or not they actually make the distinction in their own minds.

Research in which understanding of the purposes of television advertisements has not relied on the children's verbal abilities, but in which children merely have to point at pictures in order to indicate what the character in a commercial wanted them to do, has revealed that although the grasp of concepts improves with age, children as young as 3 years of age have exhibited some understanding of selling intent.[22]

Children's trust in TV advertising

Whilst understanding of the nature of TV advertisements appears to improve as children get older, belief in the truthfulness of advertising appeals tends to decline. Before they begin school, there is widespread belief among young viewers that TV adverts tell the truth all the time, while few believe this at age 8 and hardly any still do at age 12.[23]

At the same time, children's attempts to influence parents to buy advertised products seen on television show a marked decline. In general, it seems that as children grow older they understand more completely the selling motive under-lying television advertising and become less responsive to commercial appeals. Older children make more numerous and more refined judgements about television commercials and develop a cognitive mechanism against persuasion.

A survey of British children's views about TV advertising asked a national sample of more than 500 4- to 13-year-olds if they thought that advertisements on television tell the truth. Only a few (6 per cent) thought that advertisements 'always' tell the truth, while rather more (15 per cent) thought that they 'quite often' are truthful. Most (60 per cent) felt that advertisements tell the truth 'sometimes'. Nearly one in five (18 per cent) thought that it is not common for advertisements to tell the truth, while a small number (2 per cent) felt that advertisements were never truthful. Perceived truth in advertising was not found to differ by the sex or social class of children, but age did make a difference. The youngest children were most likely to believe that advertisements told the truth, while older children became more sceptical.

Attention to advertisements would seem to vary across children. Around one in three (31 per cent) said that when advertisements come on they watch them all, while even more (37 per cent) said they watch most. Relatively fewer claim to be less attentive; fewer than one in five in each case said they watch around half the advertisements in a break (15 per cent) or watch just a few (18 per cent). None of the children said that they did not watch any. Responses to this question did not differ by age or social class, but there was a significant, although not large, difference between boys and girls. The girls reported greater attention to advertising than did the boys, a phenomenon which other research indicates carries over to adulthood.

Furthermore, amount of exposure to advertising was positively related to the perceived truthfulness of advertising; those who said they paid more attention to advertisements were also more likely to say they believed more of the advertisements. And those who said they were more attentive were also more likely either to give positive or negative opinions about advertising.[24]

Do children want what they see advertised on TV?

Television advertising is designed to influence consumer behaviour either by encouraging consumers principally to switch from one brand to another or to remain loyal to the one they currently buy. To some extent, advertising may also be concerned with creating markets for new brands. When looking at possible influences of TV advertising on children, it is important to make certain crucial distinctions between them and adult consumers. Children do not always have the means to buy many advertised items. Although children today have more personal disposable income than at any time hitherto, they are often reliant on parents to buy things for them. This situation commonly changes with age. As they get into their teens, young consumers have money of their own to spend – either from part-time jobs or pocket money. They also have more freedom and independence to go out on their own than during earlier years. Thus new opportunities to spend open up to them. To some extent, therefore, advertisements may probably direct themselves at youngsters who have their own money to spend. Alternatively, advertising may operate through encouraging children to approach their parents with requests to purchase items.

The extent to which children ask their parents to buy them things they have seen advertised on TV can vary across items. There is no firm evidence that children necessarily become generally less demanding as they get older, however. It has been observed that requests for some toys advertised in the pre-Christmas period became less frequent, but this may simply reflect a declining interest in toys anyway as children grow older.[25] Requests for TV-advertised products which are relevant to children of all ages, such as snack foods and soft drinks, tend not to decline with age.

In Britain, one survey, referred to earlier, found, on asking a national sample of children whether they had ever asked their parents to buy them something they had seen in an advertisement on television, that 85 per cent said that they had, while just 15 per cent claimed not to have done. Asking for something they had seen advertised on television was done equally by boys and girls. However, there were differences by age and social class. For the age groups, there was a drop-off in such requests among older children: 97 per cent of 4- to 5-year-olds, 94 per cent of 6- to 7-year-olds, 86 per cent of 8- to 9-year-olds and 71 per cent of 10- to 13-year-olds claimed to have made such requests of their parents. For the social classes, there was a substantial lessening of such requests reported among the higher social classes. Requests were reported by 81 per cent of children from ABC1 households, by 84 per cent of C2 households and by 92 per cent of DE households. Some 66 per cent claimed that their parents had bought them something advertised on television after they had requested it. The rate of buying did not differ by sex, age or social class.

Those children who did report that their parents had bought something were asked what it was, and then their responses were grouped into several major product categories, constructed on the basis of the responses received. The distribution, by category, of items purchased was food/cereal (15 per cent), toys/dolls (44 per cent), toys/others (28 per cent) and all others (13 per cent). What was bought for the children did not differ by sex (note: Transformers were considered a male doll), or by social class, but did differ by age. By age, the results are linear, that is, they increase or decrease consistently across the four age groups, with the following results: the oldest were more likely to have received a cereal purchase (21 per cent) by comparison with the youngest (7 per cent). The youngest were more likely to have received a toy/doll purchase (51 per cent vs. 11 per cent) and a toy/other purchase (31 per cent vs. 21 per cent). The oldest were more likely to have received some other purchase (15 per cent vs. 6 per cent).[26]

To what extent do parents acquiesce to children's requests? From the same survey, most of the children reported that they had asked their parents to buy them something they had seen advertised on television; a sizeable majority of those making the request were granted it. The children were asked to identify one such product. In all, the children identified 161 different products that had been purchased at their request. Three different products dominated these purchases: My Little Pony was cited by forty-eight youngsters (9 per cent of all the youngsters in the survey); Transformers were cited by forty-four; and Barbie products by thirty.

No other single product was cited by as many as twenty of the youngsters. However, twenty-six of them responded to the question with the generic term 'toys'. Eighty-nine children each cited one specific product, and thirty-two products each were cited by two children. The dominance of toys as the item requested from parents is apparent already; it is further emphasised by the fact that the next four most-mentioned products of parental-induced purchase were also toys – Care Bears (fifteen), Star Wars (thirteen), Cindy (twelve) and He-Man (twelve). A majority of the children specifically attributed a toy purchase requested by them of their parents to a television advertisement.

Is there a behavioural effect of TV advertising?

Reports by children that they ask parents to buy them items advertised on TV or from parents that their children make such requests provide subjective evidence of an impact of TV advertising in young people's consumer behaviour. It is difficult to check the reliability of this evidence, however, since it is dependent on the ability of respondents to provide accurate accounts from memory that such advertising-related behaviours occur.

A more objective way of assessing the effects of TV advertising on consumerism is to examine links between research exposure to this advertising and the level or nature of consumption for particular commodities. In relation to young people, one area that has come in for close scrutiny in recent years is the role of advertising in alcoholic drinks consumption. Increased concerns about excessive drinking amongst young people and particularly about under-age drinking have led to calls for more stringent controls over alcohol advertising.

There is evidence that alcoholic drinks adverts are among the most popular advertisements on TV. This has led some critics to argue that advertising plays a significant part in encouraging children and teenagers to experiment with drink. A number of published studies, which include large-scale surveys and controlled experiments, have attempted to produce evidence to clarify whether or not this influence occurs.

One American survey of teenagers aged 13 to 17 used questionnaires which respondents had to complete themselves and which asked them about their use of various mass media, their personality profiles, family background, alcohol consumption patterns and attitudes towards drinking. Virtually no effects of exposure to televised alcohol advertising on level of consumption emerged for the sample as a whole. However, certain orientations or predispositions to advertising were shown to make a difference to advertising influences.

Teenagers who were highly motivated to attend to advertising, because they thought they could learn something from it about how to behave in social situations, were found to be influenced by exposure to alcoholic drinks advertisements. Likewise, among teenagers who attended to advertisements as a means of vicariously participating in desired activities and life-styles, there was a statistically significant effect of advertising on consumption.[27]

There are some important caveats to consider, however. First, even under those conditions in which a significant advertising effect was found, the magnitude of the effect was largely trivial. In no case was more than 1.5 per cent of the net variance in consumption associated with advertising exposure. Second, the fact that particular orientations or attitudes to advertising facilitate even the minimal advertising effects found in this research points to the role of parents in socialising children towards media use and consumption behaviour. Developing 'resistance' to commercial persuasions in adopting particular orientations towards advertising is part of the process by which children learn rational consumption attitudes and behaviours from their parents.

A further study examined relationships between attention to advertisements for alcohol on television and in magazines among teenagers in Michigan, California, New York and Georgia and found that drinkers aged 12–16 or those who intended to drink when older were more likely to have seen beer, wine and spirits commercials. The researchers asked their respondents to say whether or not they drank alcohol and, if so, how often. The youngest, who were well below the legal drinking age, were asked if they intended to begin drinking when they were older. Other questions focused on parental and peer attitudes towards drinking as perceived by respondents themselves. Results showed that peer influence was the best indicator of spirits drinking. High-exposure advertising on television, as measured by claimed viewing of television for prime-time and sports programmes when most alcohol advertising occurs, was associated with greater consumption of beer and wine than was low exposure to such advertising on television. A similar finding emerged for spirits drinking in relation to liquor advertising in magazines. For the subset of adolescents who had not yet begun drinking, those heavily exposed to advertising were more likely to indicate that they planned to drink in the future.[28]

In summary, the study found that the relationship between exposure to advertisements and liquor drinking amongst these American teenagers was strongly positive, while there was a moderate association for beer and a fairly weak association for wine. Peer influence appeared to play a bigger role in beer and wine drinking, while the contribution of advertising was more powerfully related to both beer and spirits drinking than was parental influence.

There were certain limitations to the design of this study – many admitted by the authors – which make the interpretation of the findings problematic. It is possible, for example, that the association between exposure to advertising and drinking might be explained by common antecedent variables. Certain unmeasured personality characteristics or attitude variables could be important, and underlie both frequency of drinking and amount of viewing of television. Second, the direction of causality is not established by this study. While alcohol advertisements may stimulate drinking, it could also be true that heavy drinkers are motivated to attend to advertising for drinks more carefully. The authors point out that adolescents are more likely to see advertisements for alcohol before they start drinking than the other way round. This assertion does not take into account the possible early examples of, and introduction to, drinking by parents or other relatives in the home environment, though, which may presage attention to alcohol commercials. A stronger point is that adolescents who had not yet started drinking were more likely to say they would if they had been heavily exposed to advertisements.

Although relationships between exposure to advertising and the consumption of alcoholic drinks have not been conclusively demonstrated by correlational surveys among young people, other evidence has suggested that the impact of advertising on children's or teenagers' propensities to drink may operate in a much more subtle fashion. Youngsters may, for example, be influenced by advertising through its images of drinking and the personal benefits and social advantages supposedly associated with it. Do media images of alcohol affect the perception and attitudes of those exposed? Are values, attitudes, beliefs and other perceptions created by media images?

A group of researchers at the University of Strathclyde held hour-long discussions with groups of children, totalling 150 in all, about advertisements (including ones for alcoholic drinks) they had seen. These discussions dealt with a number of issues concerning advertising and examined advertisements youngsters like or disliked. The children were aged 10 to 16 years.[29]

The findings suggest that advertisements for alcoholic drinks become increasingly salient and attractive over the years 10 to 14. Although 10-year-olds rarely mentioned advertisements for alcoholic drinks when talking about favourite television advertisements, older children tended to do so at the very beginning of this phase of the discussion. The children's perceptions of the characteristics of drinkers changed as they grew older, tending to become less 'moralistic', more positive and more differentiated as they approached their mid-teens.

There were also consistent developmental trends in their descriptions of liked and disliked qualities of advertisements and of the symbolism in commercials for alcoholic drinks. Whereas the 10-year-olds' comments tended to be tied to what is specifically shown in commercials, the older children tended to go beyond this and alluded to much more complex imagery, much in the same way that adults do. For example, the 14- and 16-year-olds tended to see lager and beer commercials as promoting masculinity, sociability and working-class values. Certain of the more stylish and sophisticated alcoholic drinks advertisements (e.g. Bezique and Martini) were perceived to present attractive qualities – especially to teenage girls.

These observations raise an important question about the way in which advertisements may indirectly influence under-age potential drinkers. Much of the controversy about whether advertising for alcoholic drinks should be more strongly controlled revolves around the issue of whether it influences volume sales or whether, as the industry claims, it reflects brand-switching strategies. Despite the claim that the target market at which these advertisements are aimed consists of young adult drinkers, the finding that they also contain attractive images which appeal to younger teenagers carries implications for a possible role they might play in the development of positive attitudes towards alcoholic drinks and drinking behaviour.

Conclusion

Children, though confused about the distinction at first, soon become able to separate in their own minds advertisements from programmes. Although unclear about the purpose of television advertisements in their very early years, they are already beginning to understand the aim of advertising, in crude terms at least, by the time they reach middle primary school. And as their understanding grows, so too does their cynicism about advertising. Nevertheless, TV commercials are often well-liked and remembered, and they may in some instances provide a source of ideas for inspiration for items children would like to acquire for themselves.

Children often claim that they have at some time asked parents to buy them something they have seen advertised on television. These items tend to be the sorts of things we would expect children to be interested in – for instance, toys and certain types of food. Parents confirm that children make such requests, though it is less certain just how often they give in to this pressure from their offspring.

Despite the evidence of these subjective reports, investigation of an impact of advertising on particular kinds of consumerism through more objective measures has produced less convincing evidence that children are powerfully and directly influenced by television advertising. Research into the effects of alcoholic drinks advertising on young people's drinking propensities has revealed only uncertain, or at best very weak, direct impact. Some researchers have suggested that television advertising can influence children and teenagers indirectly through more subtle mechanisms. The attractive imagery of advertising associates positive and appealing attributes with products which are highly valued by young people. These attributes in turn enhance the perceived attractiveness and desirability of the product, increasing the likelihood that young consumers will wish to buy it. This is an interesting theory which could well hold true to some extent where certain products are concerned.

Critics of advertising worry that such subtle influences make young people more avaricious. However, the growth of children's critical awareness during the pre- and early teenage years produces a powerful inoculation against the direct impact of advertising. Furthermore, much of the objective cause–effect research indicates that advertising works to offset the brand share of an item compared with its competitors in the same product category amongst individuals who are already in the market for that type of product.

Chapter ten

Does TV affect school performance?

We began this book by highlighting some of the general concerns that are continuously expressed about the *effects* of television on the young. Much of the criticism is inevitably directed at the effect the medium may well be imposing on children's educational development.

For children to achieve their full potential at school, two factors come into play. They need not only to develop the basic skills, such as reading, writing and numeracy, to perform the tasks expected of them but also the motivation to want to acquire those skills. Television has been accused of hindering both of these two things – but what is the true picture?

Television and motivation

First, can television affect motivation? And if so, is it to do with the amount of viewing or types of programmes viewed, and does the child's own personality and home environment interact with either of these?

One suggestion is that watching television has become such a popular pastime that many children have little time left over to practise and acquire one of the most essential of the basic skills – *reading* – and because television offers them a daily fare of differing narrative discourses, they lack the incentive to learn in the first place. In other words, television comes to displace reading.

One explanation of this displacement effect is that television replaces reading because both activities satisfy similar needs, and television offers the most attractive package. Thus, during the pre-television era, children (and adults) sought diversion or excitement through reading light fiction, thereby practising their reading skills – even comic books provide some reading practice. In contrast, television provides entertainment with a minimum of effort on the child's part. The hours that used to be spent reading are now taken up by television viewing. But how true is this statement? What is the real relationship between the amount of television viewing and reading habits?

Research has indicated that the amount of time children devote on average to viewing television tends to increase steadily during primary school years until it reaches a peak of between three and five hours daily by the age of 12.

Furthermore, as television comes to play an increasingly prominent part in the life of the child, the amount of time spent reading seems to decrease.

Early studies conducted during periods when television was just being introduced in various parts of the world generally reported significant displacements of comic book reading[1] and book reading.[2] But many of these studies also included intelligence testing as part of the research and there is some indication that IQ and not television viewing could account for differences in reading levels.

Hilde Himmelweit and her colleagues observed that the impact of the introduction of television in the United Kingdom on book reading was most marked for children of average intelligence. Brighter pupils were not affected much, while the less intelligent read little anyway. With time, television seemed to stimulate an interest in book reading – particularly of books whose stories had been televised or which were linked in some way to television programmes.[3] Wilbur Schramm and his co-writers made a similar study of media usage among children in a number of North American communities including towns with and without television. They concluded that the reading of books, newspapers and quality magazines is not affected by television, but the reading of comics and pulp magazines is reduced with the introduction of television.[4]

A third study in Australia also produced similar results. John Murray and Susan Kippax studied 5- to 12-year-olds in three Australian communities: No-TV (no television), Low-TV (one channel – the public channel with a mandate to provide educational programming for use in the schools), and High-TV (the public channel and a commercial channel).[5]

Their research produced the findings shown in Table 10.1, based on reported estimates given by the children themselves.

Table 10.1 Children's reading levels in communites with and without television

	Books (per week)	Comics (per week)
No-TV children read	1.08	5.84
Low-TV children read	1.61	3.91
High-TV children read	1.85	2.76

Source: Murray and Kippax, 1978

It seems that although High-TV children spent less time reading, it was their *comic* reading that was significantly reduced when compared with the No-TV group. In fact , their reading of books, which could be described as 'quality' reading, proved to be higher than both of the other two groups.

Much of the research so far, then, is inconclusive, when considering the amount of television watched and its likelihood either to encourage or to discourage good reading habits. Some studies, however, have attempted to examine the relationship in more detail in taking account of children's programme preferences and how this might interact with their attitudes and ability to learn.

For example, a Japanese study examined 10- to 11-year-olds' analytical abilities and thinking styles in relation to programme preferences. Children who preferred informational programmes were deemed to be more analytical and reflective in their thought process, approaching problems in a considered and logical manner. Those who preferred fictional entertainment were categorised as impulsive, that is they were more likely to tackle problems in a random, intuitive fashion. In fact, when the same children were tested a year later it was also found that this preference for commercial programming was related to an increase in impulsivity, particularly amongst girls. However, it is possible that these children were predisposed to become more impulsive anyway and there is no indication as to whether other causal factors such as home environment, parental rearing practices and so on were taken into account.[6]

Nevertheless, these results have been supported by more recent findings in the United States. A group of American researchers looked at relationships between television viewing preferences and reading habits among children in the same age-range as the Japanese sample.[7] Information concerning the youngsters' behaviours at home and in school was obtained from parents and teachers. Among these children, those who spent more time reading tended to be the ones with higher IQs and highly educated fathers, but who also watched fewer fantasy, violent-action programmes such as *The Incredible Hulk, The Six Million Dollar Man,* and *Wonder Woman.* Children who were rated by their teachers as the most imaginative also tended to be those who viewed fewer of these fantasy, all-action shows. Even among children who were only moderate viewers of television anyway, reading habits were influenced by the types of television programmes watched. Regular viewing of action-adventure shows and also of game and variety shows usually meant less time spent reading. And it seems that television's more realistic, and often violent, adult action-dramas are not to blame here. Very few of these children watched what the writers called 'hard-core' violent programmes, such as *Starsky and Hutch* or *Hawaii Five-O.* Instead, it seems that programmes featuring fantasy, super-human characters and fast-moving action sequences, which children generally find highly enjoyable, have come to replace adventure books, comics and other popular children's reading matter as a source of entertainment and satisfaction of their fantasy needs. This is not to say that there is no cause for concern, though; after all, *passive* viewing of fantasy television content does not stimulate the active, imaginative, mental processes essential for advanced intellectual growth.

Television's cognitive development and the acquisition of skills

If passive viewing does not stimulate children's imagination, can it actually harm the development of their creative, analytical and linguistic abilities?

Reading, for instance, requires and encourages mental effort on the part of the reader to examine carefully the context in which it is used or to consult a dictionary to find out its meaning. Further, difficult or discriminating passages may encourage the reader to draw upon his or her own experiences, memories or fantasies to add meaning to the written material. According to some experts, however, most commercial television programmes essentially train children passively to sit and watch rather than actively to think and do. The cognitive growth of the child depends very much on how often and to what extent his or her imagination is exercised.[8]

Make-believe play is one of the most important ways in wi..ch pre-school children learn about their environment. It can help children to develop a large vocabulary, it may play a role in development of sequencing or ordering of events, and it may foster concentration. Children can mimic the utterances or behaviours of fantasy television characters, but popular programmes broadcast on the public and commercial networks rarely offer the opportunity for the child to engage in the kind of creative imaginative play that is essential for advanced cognitive development. For one thing, the pace of commercial television programming may be too rapid for children effectively to assimilate the words, ideas and images it contains.

A further concern is that regular viewing of television may have an adverse effect on the intelligence of the young viewer. There is certainly ample evidence that child TV watchers exhibit lower intelligence scores compared with non-watchers,[9] which has resulted in the charge that viewing television lowers the IQ. But on taking a closer look at some of the studies, it soon becomes clear that these kinds of accusations are based on over-simplified interpretations of the results. For example, correlations between children's scores on intelligence tests and their reported TV viewing do not prove a causal connection. In fact, extensive research in ten communities in the USA and Canada revealed that high intelligence was positively related to regular viewing up to the age of 11, and it is not until after this age that the opposite effect occurs. In this particular study, the brighter children, who were motivated to do well academically as well as participate in a wide range of leisure activities, tended to reduce their viewing by the time they reached mid-teens. However, the duller ones, who also displayed less interest in both school and alternative pursuits, had increased their viewing.[10]

This particular finding has not yet been fully explained. One hypothesis could be that most TV programmes are matched to the interests and abilities of bright, younger children, who then outgrow them. At the same time, the less bright youngsters become more dependent on television for both stimulation and enter-tainment as it seems to offer material at an intellectual level with which they can cope.

Further evidence has emerged from another American study by Michael Morgan and Larry Gross, who examined relationships between amount of tele-vision viewing and intelligence and reading comprehension scores for over 600 children, aged between 11 and 14 years, at a New Jersey public school.[11] Among this sample, children with lower IQs again tended to watch more television than those with higher IQs. But while children with lower IQs also exhibited poorer reading skills, when the effect of IQ difference was controlled, a significant negative relationship still remained between amount of viewing and reading performance. Although suggestive, these latter results are not unequivocal because there are still two possible explanations for the observed relationship. It is possible that television viewing impedes development of reading skills; but it could equally be the case that children with reading problems turn to television as an alternative source of gratification and amusement.

Two further studies which took account of other environmental factors in conjunction with television are also worth considering. The first examined the development of reading skills by means of a TV diary kept for the child by the parent and information about parental disciplinary practices and household routines.[12] Good reading comprehension among middle-class children by the time they reached 7 or 8 years of age was predicted best not only by fewer hours of television watching during pre-school years, but also by a more orderly household routine with more hours of sleep, the self-description of mothers as resourceful and curious about the world, and the use of democratic rather than authoritarian parental disciplinary practices. Among working-class children, however, television viewing during pre-school years was associated with better school performance along with having a mother who reports herself as curious and imaginative. Television emerged, therefore, as just one out of a number of features of the home environment that are important to the child's reading development.

The second study concerned itself with the development of children's writing skills, seen by educationalists as a natural progression from reading. A sample of 11- to 15-year-olds, 102 in total, were asked about their viewing habits and preferences, parental restrictions in relation to these, their reading habits and their after-school activities.[13] Parents were also given a questionnaire asking similar questions to confirm children's answers. Writing ability, in terms of skills and creativity, was then tested by asking each child to write a story about an imagined situation. Each piece of work was then scored for grammar, spelling, punctuation, sentence construction and idea development.

According to the results, writing ability correlated significantly and positively with the number of books read per month, parents' level of education and parental interest. Degree of parental interest was judged by use of a scale which combined items concerning restrictions of viewing by parents, whether the parent read to the child when the child was younger and whether the parent watched and used programmes with the child. Writing ability correlated both significantly and negatively with television viewing hours. In other words, the more TV the children said they watched, the worse their writing ability. This still held true irrespective of the number of books they said they needed or the degree of parental encouragement, although these were also powerful predictors of writing ability. Of course, this study does not establish the direction of causality. The question still remains: does television viewing cause poor writing skills or do poor writing as well as reading skills cause children to watch more television anyway?

Up to this point, this chapter has sought to examine the possible detrimental effect of television on children's education. Obviously, many other studies could have been cited but the overall picture remains the same; there still seems no definite proof that television alone can hinder children's scholastic achievement. But what about television's potential for *improving* school performance? It is to this question that we turn our attention next.

Television as an instrument of education

Although educational television is not used by many schools as an integral component of the curriculum, other programmes designated as 'educative' have also been produced for home consumption. In the United Kingdom perhaps the most well known of these have been *Play School*, recently replaced by *Play Bus* and aimed at the pre-school child, with *Blue Peter* for the older viewer. Both of these attempt to provide information for children in an entertaining manner. In the United States one of the most active and productive groups involved in the development and production of both educational and educative television has been the Children's Television Workshop. This group has produced a number of children's television series on which experienced television producers, educationalists and researchers work together to create programmes designed to achieve specific goals with carefully identified target child audiences. A great deal of effort is expended in formative research and consultation to ensure that the educational messages get across. Feedback is obtained regularly from young viewers both to pilot programmes and during the production of the actual series itself, as a running check on what children find appealing and what is being understood or misunderstood.[14] In this way, appropriate changes can be made wherever necessary. Two of the most successful programmes, *Sesame Street* and *The Electric Company*, have been produced specifically for younger viewers.

Sesame Street

One of the best-known productions to grow out of this 'marriage' of the creative programme-making process, research feedback from the audience and consultation with professionals in education is *Sesame Street*. At the outset the aim of the programme was to help prepare children for school, and in particular to provide special assistance to children from disadvantaged homes and neighbourhoods. It was intended that the show would not simply teach young children factual knowledge, but also enhance their abilities to think for themselves.

These global objectives were to be achieved through a range of specific functions served by each programme. Tuition would be provided in the recognition and use of letters, numbers and geometric forms. Mental processes concerned with ordering, classifying and identifying relationships between objects and events were to be exercised. Information was provided about natural environmental phenomena in the world; social skills training and understanding of the need for social rules were also given some attention.

Before the first series went on-air, a staff of formative researchers spent eighteen months pre-testing elements and segments designed to be included in *Sesame Street*. This procedure continued to form an essential part of the production process. The research effort invested in the design of *Sesame Street* has been matched by that concerned with assessing the impact of the series. During the first two years that the series was broadcast, learning from the programme was assessed by the Educational Testing Service (ETS). Achievement in eight areas of cognitive development stressed by the programme was evaluated: body parts, letters, forms, numbers, relational terms, sorting, classification and puzzles. In later years, as the programme came to stress pro-social and affective dimensions more frequently, other tests have been derived to evaluate their impact.[15]

An early publication reported the ETS research from the first year of *Sesame Street* on 943 children, 731 of whom were classified as disadvantaged. Improvements in relevant abilities, skills and areas of knowledge were found to be directly related to the extent to which children viewed the programme, with younger children achieving more than older ones. There were also family differences between children who responded well to the programme and those who did not. Parents of high learners were more likely than parents of low learners to be educated and to talk to their children about *Sesame Street*. The parents of low learners tended to be less optimistic about their children's schools and teachers, but all high–low learner comparisons had insufficient numbers of subjects for conclusive interpretation. Nevertheless, the general conclusion after the first year was that the series had had an educational impact for other areas of cognitive development contained within the programme.[16]

More detailed research was carried out at the end of the second year of transmission with similar results.[17] This second wave of assessment also revealed that children viewing for the second year performed better on more difficult tasks than first-time viewers. This finding seems to support the educational viewpoint that children need constant repetition and to be able to build on existing knowledge to understand new concepts. The second-year viewers also displayed significantly more positive attitudes towards school and race of others than did viewers who had seen only the first season and summer of *Sesame Street*. Teachers who were unaware which pupils had seen the show prior to entering school ranked viewers higher than non-viewers on seven criteria, with attitude towards school and peer relationships reflecting statistically significant differences. Other writers were not so convinced as to *Sesame Street*'s ability to teach children unaided. There was some indication, for instance, that viewing alone was not sufficient to produce widespread significant changes, but needed to be reinforced by encouragement to watch and to think about what was seen.

Sesame Street has been broadcast in the original English language version in more than forty countries outside the United States, including Canada, the Caribbean, Europe, Africa, the Far East, and Australia and New Zealand. Many countries enter co-production arrangements for *Sesame Street*, and foreign language adaptations are produced locally and tailored to individual cultural requirements. Such arrangements have been made with Spain, Holland, Germany, France, Latin America, Brazil, Kuwait, Sweden and Israel.

The first foreign language versions with local adaptations were in 1972: *Plaza Sesamo* in Mexico City and *Vola Sesamo* in Brazil. *Plaza Sesamo* was the occasion of extensive carefully controlled examination of viewers' cognitive achievement. In many ways the findings replicated those of the American studies with regular viewers scoring significantly higher than non-viewers in all the areas examined. Education gains to impressive levels have also been measured among viewers of *Sesame Street* in other countries, for example in Chile and in Israel. In Israel, co-watching by mothers increased enjoyment and learning; in Chile, heavy viewers of the show did better on almost all tests.[18]

Sesame Street was the first mass audience educational programme and still maintains the largest number of young viewers. Each week in the United States in 1980–81 *Sesame Street* reached 78 per cent of all 2- to 5-year-olds within range of its signal, with its signal coverage estimated as 92 per cent of all US television households. *Sesame Street* was the flagship of the 'education by entertainment' or 'learning can be fun' perspective, the facilitator and product of a rare synthesis of art and science to serve the cause of education, and the pioneer in the use of a child-oriented magazine format with a variety of special production techniques to educate (e.g. animation, word balloons, and the Muppets).[19]

The Electric Company

The Electric Company (TEC) was designed by the Children's Television Workshop to increase reading skills among primary school children (aged 6 to 10 years). The reading skills emphasised were symbol and sound analysis and meaning. The show had a magazine format and a variety of entertaining and attention-grabbing production techniques.

Formative research for *The Electric Company* provided a number of innovative techniques and critical insights about learning from television. Pre-production research measured the appeal of characters by eliciting children's responses to photographs in identifying the main characters, and by asking them to describe the role of the character in the programme, and rank characters on appeal by means of sorting photographs. The children were also asked to tell why they liked or disliked characters in attempts to distinguish between reactions to programmes and photographs.

Appealing attributes or production techniques were identified through observations of young viewers' eye contact with the television screen while particular segments of the programme were being shown. This was done using a time-lapse camera technique. Formative testing was employed to improve the ability of segments to encourage children to read aloud from the screen. A coding system was devised to describe all programme segments by defining attributes related to appeal (type of humour, theme, characters) and to comprehension (e.g. manner of presenting print, pace, density, or instructional content).

Each of these elements was further broken into components (e.g. humour included sight gags, incongruity, puns, whimsy, parody). Comprehension was evaluated using eye movement recording, a stop tape technique, free verbal reports, test analytic procedures, and group observation. Eye movement recording determined whether the viewer was attending to relevant aspects of the segments. Some elements that were found to be positively related to visual attention were integration of print with action, dynamic presentation of print, and animated format, while negative elements were print in the lower quarter of the screen, distracting action and rapid presentation of segment material.[20]

The stop tape technique was the most frequently used method of comprehension testing for *The Electric Company*. Children were shown individual *Electric Company* programme elements, and the presentation was interrupted at pre-determined points to question the viewers about what had happened, had not happened, or would happen. The group observation technique operated under the assumption that comprehension is related to viewers' active participation, relating spontaneous verbal responses to the show to programme attributes.

After the second season, Children's Television Workshop monitored and video-taped visual, verbal and behavioural classroom responses to programming transmitted from Children's Television Workshop (CTW), which remotely controlled the pan, zoom and focus of the camera in the classroom. Through a transmitter, CTW staff members asked children questions before and after the showing. With the programme viewed by the children superimposed in a corner of the CTW monitor, a continuous record of both stimuli and responses was available.[21] It was subsequently reported that the programme produced significant positive effects on reading among children in grades one to four (aged 5–9), with the largest improvements among first-graders. Overall, gains for viewers over non-viewers were noted for seventeen of the nineteen reading skills tested. Children who viewed for the first season only displayed similar reading gains to those who also watched for the second season. For those who watched for the two seasons, it seemed that seeing both series was only a little better than seeing one. No differences in effects were noted for viewing in black and white versus colour. No effects were found either for amount of home viewing, attitudes of children towards school or reading, attitudes of teachers towards children or reading performance of children. However, some parents, in particular those of first-grade viewers, appeared to reveal positive attitudes towards the educational benefits of the programme and seemed more confident that their children were achieving at average levels or above in reading than the parents of non-viewers of similar ages.[22]

It seems then that both of these American programmes appear to have promoted gains in educational ability amongst young children. However, as made evident by the *Sesame Street* research, it is doubtful if significant learning occurs from solitary viewing of an individual programme. The children who achieved most appeared to be those who received encouragement from an adult, enabling them to discuss what they had seen, thus reinforcing the educational 'message' contained within the programme.

The UK experience

In the UK a similar picture emerges, although research on individual series such as *Sesame Street* has been far more limited. A study of the use of educational programmes in the 1980s, with particular reference to the programme *Look and Read*, also points to the need for some kind of adult reinforcement if children are to achieve positive learning from television. In this particular study, teachers who stated their commitment to the programme and maximised the educational opportunities it offered reported significant gains in reading ability. They pointed out that educational television appeared to be most successful if children themselves perceived that the content of the programme and the follow-up work was particularly real and relevant to them. In this study, successful planning by teachers frequently gained a corresponding response from the pupils; that is, they became more willing to observe, criticise and query if the teachers displayed a similar attitude towards broadcast material.

Look and Read aims to help 7- to 8-year-olds, still at the 'emergent' reading stage, to become more skilled at both the process of reading and abstracting meaning from the text. Like *Sesame Street*, it uses cartoon figures and songs to emphasise specific language points, but as a later pilot study carried out in the mid-1980s revealed, it was rare for a child to grasp the 'message' unaided, even though some teachers involved in the study were convinced that the phonic information had been understood.[23]

Part of the problem in the UK seems to be that although the producers of educational programmes publish booklets advising teachers of the kinds of follow-up work that can be carried out in schools, the take-up of this advice is limited. For educational television, as it is used in schools in the UK, to be effective, teachers need to be committed to its use and incorporate it as an integral part of the curriculum. Teachers are rarely given advice in the use of educational television either during their initial training or by subsequent in-service training provision; instead they are expected to adopt and adapt individual programmes to suit their children's needs as best they can. It is not surprising, then, that teachers rarely admit to their own feelings of insecurity in this area.

A study carried out by Hurst in 1981 maintained that the main disincentives for using television, expressed by teachers themselves, tended to be technical (that is, they had insufficient knowledge of video usage), to do with time-tabling restrictions, and locality and availability of the television and video-recorder. Many teachers believed that children watched too much television at home and that therefore it was bad in principle for them to view in school. It was felt that a surfeit of television could encourage passivity or laziness in children and that perhaps teachers who used television too frequently could be shirking their responsibilities. The attitudes revealed in this survey also highlighted the general lack of awareness in teachers as to the real potential of educational television.[24]

As the first part of this chapter showed, there is no definite proof that television alone can hinder the educational achievement and school performance of individual children. In fact, it now seems likely that used sensibly, with the right encouragement from both parents and teachers alike, it can help to enhance the learning process. However, as the next chapter reveals, many parents rarely get involved with programmes that their children watch, so that many of today's youngsters are unlikely to be receiving the necessary in-put to make learning from television a real possibility.

Chapter eleven

How can parents influence children's viewing?

One recurring cosy picture of domesticity, frequently reinforced by the medium itself, is of the 'nuclear' family gathered together in front of a flickering screen, enjoying an entertaining evening's viewing. But how often do whole families sit together in this way, particularly in today's society where the traditional set-up of two parents, one of whom (usually the woman) chooses to stay at home and adopt a nurturing role, is becoming more of a rarity?

Modern child-rearing practices have resulted in young people being far more independent and less malleable than previous generations, which is reflected in the manner in which they strive to make their own decisions about when and what they watch on television. But at what point do parents step in and interfere with this decision-making process? Is it only when bedtime approaches or do parents make value judgements about the programmes themselves and act accordingly? Researchers have attempted to investigate both these questions.

Viewing decisions within the family

There is a wide range of factors that can influence the ways in which different families establish their viewing habits. As research has shown, the matter of what to watch on television can be the scene of some conflict in the home. When more than one member of the family wants to take over a television set for different reasons, there may be long arguments as to who gets to watch their preferred programme. In these days of multi-set homes, one might imagine that conflicts would be reduced or more quickly resolved, but this may not always be the case if it is the best set in the house which is being strongly competed for.

The evidence on who controls the television set and how viewing decisions are made does not offer a consistent picture of what goes on. Idiosyncratic family viewing patterns and rule-based controls over the use of the television set do exist and can be important mediators of the impact of television on children.[1] However, decisions over how the set is used, by whom and under what circumstances can vary a lot. For example, one family may not exert as much control over what the children watch as another; although parents may often claim to take care over what they allow younger members of the family to watch, this may well be far removed from what actually happens in practice. Added to this, in these days of two- and three-set households, and unnecessary numbers of sets in children's bedrooms, parents may not always know when or what their children are watching. Should the parents be out, youngsters are then free to watch whatever they like.

We can begin by taking a look at some early research on family television watching. Some of the evidence suggests that families behave democratically and take joint decisions on which programmes they will watch but this pattern may well be restricted to certain hours of the day. For example, a joint decision may be taken as to what to watch at night, when presumably the family are most likely to be gathered together as a group in front of the set, but during the day it is more likely for individual family members to assume control of the set. This early evidence also shows that children were more likely than their parents to be happy with programmes selected by the family.[2]

Another study found that, in family households, wives were the most likely to select shows at night, with general agreement or husbands tying for second place in the decision-making. Children were invariably in the minority, with only one out of seven decisions being left to them. This study also showed that in families, where the education level of either one or both parents was high, there was more likelihood of programmes being selected by general agreement instead of more authoritarian measures.[3]

Steven Chaffee and Albert Tims observed in 1976 that programme selection is partly dependent on other members of the family who are watching. In a study of about 200 junior and senior high school students, a relationship was found between the presence of others and the type of programme viewed. Brothers and sisters were often present for humorous shows, parents were more likely to be present for aggressive and 'real' shows, for example, news programmes. It is not known whether children adapt their viewing to who is present or whether they seek certain kinds of company for certain shows. George Comstock noted that viewers often watch programmes that are selected by someone else in the family, although much viewing is non-selective anyway and viewing is often determined by channel loyalty and inheritance of audiences from one programme to another. But the picture can get highly complex when families decide to watch television. A focus groups study undertaken by the Corporation for Public Broadcasting in 1974 revealed that programme selection decisions are often complicated inter-personal communication activities involving intra-family status relations, temporal context, the number of sets available and rule-based communication conventions within the household.[4]

One Canadian researcher found that choosing which programmes to watch did not always lead to family togetherness. Mothers were found to dominate fathers when they disagreed over which TV shows to watch, even though fathers were generally perceived by members of the family to be in charge of the set. This finding was corroborated by James Lull, who observed that fathers were regarded by other family members as the most influential person in family discussions about which shows to watch. In general, fathers, mothers and older children (13–18 years) were more likely than younger children to get their own way in choosing what the family should view.[5]

Another observation which underlined the father's dominance was that they were less likely to ask others before changing channels. Trained monitors spent two days observing the families watching television and then returned on the third day to conduct interviews with each family member. Observers actually joined in other family activities so that the main purpose of the study was less obvious.[6]

Ninety-three families were observed, of which seventy-four were two-parent families which formed the focus of the study. Fathers were named most often as the person or one of the persons who controlled the selection of television programmes. Children and mothers were more likely to regard fathers in this way than were the fathers themselves. Fathers believed that their spouses or partners were more responsible than any other single person or specific combination of individuals for determining the choice of programmes. Overall, however, family members were just as likely to say that one of the children rather than the mother decided what was viewed on the main television set. Children often perceived themselves, or one of their siblings, as the primary controller of the set. Family consensus was another procedure that was mentioned.

These perceptions were supported only in part by the observed instances of control of the main television set that were documented by the researchers who lived with families. Observers noted who turned the set on, who changed the channel and who turned the set off. They also noted whether or not these actions were undertaken with any discussion of what would be viewed. The observations indicated that fathers controlled more programme decisions than any other single family member or combination of family viewers. They were more than twice as likely as their female partners to do so. Further, they acted alone in more than 90 per cent of these decisions. One of the children was next most likely to turn the set on, turn it off or change the channel. Children were responsible for 30 per cent of these actions (compared to 36 per cent for their fathers) and they were also extremely likely to do so without discussion (93 per cent of the time acting alone).

Mothers were observed to be far less involved in the actual manipulation of the set than were either their husbands (or live-in male friends) or children. They were the initiators of only 15 per cent of these actions. They were far less likely than either fathers or children to negotiate action alone. Three-quarters of all set alterations were made by one family member – mostly without observable negotiations.

This observation study conflicts with the earlier research, which cites the mother as the person who makes most of the viewing decisions, implying that people's self-reported behaviour is often in direct opposition to what they actually do in practice.

Influence of family communication patterns

Another source of influence to which mass communication researchers have given increasing significance is the manner in which parents communicate with each other and how this interacts with the way in which the television set is used in the family home. One assumption here is that children are socialised into particular styles of television viewing as one consequence of the prevailing climate of parental control and disciplinary practices in the home.

Early studies of the media use of children had suggested that youngsters learn patterns of television viewing through imitating their parents.[7] More recently, however, other researchers have pointed out that this modelling explanation may be an over-simplification of how children's viewing behaviours develop. It fails to take into account the role of other factors such as the common social class of parents and children which might account for the similarities in their respective viewing patterns, quite apart from direct copying by one of the other's television-related habits. And another possibility is that the child's viewing behaviours may sometimes influence those of parents, thus giving rise to a reversal of the initial hypothesis.[8]

We have already seen that the evidence for the implementation of direct control over children's viewing by parents is equivocal. The notion of a sphere of influence which operates in a less direct fashion through the climate of parent–child interactions has produced evidence that the family can affect the amount and type of television viewing indulged in by children.

This social interaction view puts forward the idea that children's viewing behaviours are shaped and controlled by norms and values concerned with the conduct that generally occurs in the family context. Attempts to investigate the significance of interpersonal relationships between family members for the development of certain patterns of media use have derived from research by Steven Chaffee and his colleagues, beginning in the early 1970s.[9]

According to this perspective, parent–child communication patterns are among the most persuasive influences in child socialisation and development. Parental values and norms need not be transmitted directly, however, in order to have an impact. It is not simply the existence of certain rules within the home that matters; the way in which they are applied is equally important. Chaffee and two colleagues, Jack McLeod and Daniel Wackman, developed a two-dimensional model of family communication patterns, labelled *socio-orientation* and *concept-orientation*. In a socio-oriented family setting, parents encourage their children to maintain a harmonious climate of personal relationships, to avoid arguments, anger and any form of controversial expression or behaviour. In a concept-oriented family, children are invited to express their ideas and feelings, even if they are controversial, and to challenge the beliefs of others.[10]

These patterns of family communications are known to be associated in part with social class. Thus, the socio-oriented climate is more characteristic of working-class families, while concept-orientation is more typical of middle-class families.[11] But the effects of family communication patterns are not believed to be wholly explicable by social class alone.[12] Although the above class differences in orientations do exist, they are not strong, and the orientations themselves have relationships with cognitive processes which are more than simply an outcome of social class.[13]

Another interesting question was whether families were either socio-oriented types *or* concept-oriented types, or whether they could be a little bit of both. Further research showed that these two orientations were positively correlated, but only to a slight extent.[14] Nevertheless, it emerged that it was possible to develop a fourfold typology by dichotomising families at a half-way point along each dimension. This gave rise to the following four family types:

1 *Laissez-faire* families in which neither socio- nor concept-orientation were strongly emphasised. This meant that there was little parent–child communication of any sort, and the child instead was influenced more by friends and peer groups outside the home.
2 *Protective* families in which socio-oriented relations only were emphasised, with little impetus provided to the child from parents to develop a broad-minded thoughtful outlook on the world.
3 *Consensual* families in which both socio- and concept-orientation were encouraged. In this context the child was encouraged to take an interest in what was going on in the world but to avoid taking up controversial positions and disturbing the internal harmony of the family.
4 *Pluralistic* families in which concept-orientation only was stressed, and where the child was encouraged to be exploratory, to challenge existing norms and values, though again without disrupting family harmony.

A Swedish study of adolescents' use of television in the family context reported that at a basic level of analysis low concept and high socio-orientation in the family were associated with heavy television viewing by adolescents in the household. Family communication patterns, however, did not stand up as significant predictors of young people's television viewing in the presence of multiple statistical controls for social class and other socialisation variables such as parental attitudes towards television.[15]

James Lull observed that both the socio-oriented (harmony and agreement) and concept-oriented (emphasis on dissent and expression of opinion) dimensions were related to uses of television as a resource for the accomplishment of interpersonal objectives in the home. That is, television can be used to create occasions when family members come together as a unit; it can act as a source of mutual interest and conversation. The socio-oriented families watched more television and were more likely to use it to reach these interpersonal objectives. Concept-oriented families saw television as not being useful to them as a social resource, although they did use it for transmission of values and exercising authority.[16]

Lull examined patterns of how families talked to and got on with each other in relation to specific television-linked attitudes and activities. Family members answered questionnaire items designed to determine the degree to which they were 'concept' or 'socio'-oriented. Concept-oriented families were those who value the presentation of personal points of view on issues under discussion and did not discourage disagreement or argument about these issues. Socio-oriented homes, on the other hand, were characterised by an environment where social harmony was prized and children were told to repress expression of ideas if it would cause friction in the home. Some interesting differences were found in how these families watched television.

First, the overall amount of television viewing carried out in these households was negatively associated with concept orientation and uncorrelated with socio-orientation. That is to say that, on the whole, concept-oriented families watched less television than the socio-oriented families. However, satisfaction with the family's selection of television programmes was not related to either concept or socio-orientation scores. However, sensitivity to others' preferences when choosing programmes was stronger among concept-oriented families and weaker among socio-oriented ones. Second, selective viewing was more typical of concept-oriented families than it was of socio-oriented families. Concept-orientation was negatively associated with watching programmes that were not selected by the individual or watching 'television' instead of particular shows. Socio-orientation was unrelated to both of these indices. Third, concept-oriented families were less likely to be satisfied with television as a form of family entertainment. Socio-orientation was linked with more arguments over the selection of television programmes, while concept-orientation scores were not thus correlated. Concept-orientation related to fewer such developments.

It seems, then, that concept-oriented families are more likely to be selective in their viewing, switching on only for specific programmes rather than out of habit; they are also more considerate of other people's viewing habits. This more responsible attitude towards television, in which the content of programmes is given due consideration, presumably influences children's responses to the medium and possibly results in a higher degree of critical awareness.

Other people's influences on children's use of TV

Parents and other people can both influence children's television viewing behaviour. They may influence how much children watch television generally, or, more specifically, affect what types of programmes children watch. This in turn can control the impact television has on children by limiting the extent to which they watch certain types of programmes. In addition, the strength of impact of particular TV shows can be affected by parental intervention.

The influence of others on viewing behaviour can operate through two mechanisms. First, direct intervention with a child's viewing may occur when parents lay down rules about television watching or encourage or discourage in explicit terms the watching of particular kinds of programmes or amounts of television.

For example, parents may limit children's viewing to a set number of hours per day or impose an early bedtime, thus restricting the viewing of 'unsuitable' material. Perhaps they insist that youngsters watch only programmes that are produced specifically for children or ones that are perceived to have educational content.

Second, influence from parents may be less direct and without specific intent, whereby parents provide models of viewing which are matched by their offspring. As already pointed out, if parents themselves are both selective and critical when viewing television, this kind of behaviour might well rub off on their children. However, young people, particularly when reaching adolescence, also respond to peer pressure and are far more likely to insist on watching material their parents might well regard as unsuitable if the majority of their school friends are allowed to watch it.

Parental concern and awareness

A good deal of survey evidence shows that parents are concerned with the violent and sexual content of television, although that concern is extended by only some of them to worry about the amount of time their own children spend watching television. One reason for this lack of worry is that parents may underestimate their child's viewing time and may not be aware of the extent of the violent content in what they watch.

Bradley Greenberg has found that children gave estimates of their own viewing time that were twice as great as those given by their mothers when estimating how much time their children devoted to viewing. This finding has since been repeated and extended. For instance, there is some suggestion that mothers report more rules, higher levels of watching with their children, and lower estimates of the child's susceptibility to TV advertising compared with the child's own responses on these questions.[17]

There is also some evidence that mothers may not recognise the extent of their child's response to television content. Children tend to perceive more violence in the same set of television programmes than their mothers do.[18] Furthermore, mothers apparently under-report their children's fright reaction to scary television programmes and movies and also the extent to which they intervene to control what their children watch or to explain programmes to their youngsters.[19]

There is even more evidence which casts doubt on how much influence parents exert over their children's viewing. One major survey asked a question of parents with children under the age of 15 at home: 'Are there any rules or regulations in your home about when and what the children watch, or do you let them make their own decisions?' While 41 per cent said they had definite rules, 30 per cent said they had no rules at all. Another 6 per cent said they made an effort to control children's viewing, but did not go so far as to say they had definite rules. Even though an attempt was made here to balance the wording of the question, there was probably still some bias towards giving rules as a socially desirable response. Among the rules mentioned were those relating to hours when viewing is permitted; duties, such as homework or chores, which must be done first; programme-specific rules relating to prohibition of watching particular programmes; and supervision while watching other programmes. Mothers (31 per cent) and fathers (29 per cent) were fairly equally likely to mention rules governing circumstances of viewing; while mothers (38 per cent) were more likely than fathers (30 per cent) to mention programme guidance.[20]

One form of programme control was conspicuously small. In the same sample that designated 'violence' the number one irritant, only about 5 per cent specifically mentioned some attempt at regulation in this regard. More significant still, this figure was not substantially higher among those parents who actually cited violence as a disadvantage (about 7 per cent to 5 per cent of those who did not).

On the whole, few relationships were observed between the disadvantages the parents cited and the controls they mentioned. For instance, those who worried about television's interference with chores or other activities were only slightly more likely to mention appropriate limitations on the circumstances under which children can watch (14 per cent vs. 12 per cent).

A few years later, this 1960s survey was followed up by a new survey at the beginning of the 1970s among children aged 5–6, 11– 12 and 15–16 years and their parents. When questioned, 27 per cent of 11- to 12-year-olds and 38 per cent of 15- to 16-year-olds said their parents never complained about their television watching. When complaints were received, they fell usually into one of three categories, in which concern was expressed about watching too much television, watching too late, and about the types of programmes watched. When asked directly if their parents exhibited any control over their television viewing, over one in three 11- to 12-year-olds and 15- to 16-year-olds felt that they either currently were or in the past had been under a limit. Mothers of the youngest children interviewed in this survey said that the form of control they used most often with their youngsters was supervision of programme selection. Mothers of girls reported more control than did mothers of boys. Very little use of the television to keep the child occupied or indoors was reported.[21]

Later research found that parents were unlikely to control the quantity or the character of viewing, although there are certain restrictions in some families. These restrictions tend to decline sharply as children reach their teens. Some 39 per cent of 11- to 12-year-olds and only 18 per cent of 15- to 16-year-olds reported rules about the time spent watching television. Mothers were more likely to report rules, with 69 per cent of the mothers of 11- to 12-year-olds and 31 per cent of mothers of older children reporting rules about viewing. In both cases, however, rules about television viewing were much less prevalent than rules about other things.[22]

What about parental guidance in connection with specific programmes? One study reported that 6- to 12-year-olds were likely to say that parents control but do not guide their television watching in the sense of telling them what and what not to watch.[23] Another found that both mothers and their children (9- to 14-year-olds) reported very little parental guidance with 85 per cent of both groups saying 'none' for guidance about specific programmes.[24]

An Australian study measured parental control of children's television viewing by asking parents to list the programmes they considered unsuitable viewing fare for their youngsters. Parents who were unable to specify either a particular programme or programme type were assumed to be non-discriminating in relation to their child's viewing. It emerged that parental knowledge regarding the potential harm of commercial television did not necessarily lead to a reduced amount of such viewing by children.[25]

Parents were also asked to specify the extent to which the television viewed by their pre-schoolers in the past week was selected by a parent, siblings or the pre-schoolers themselves. The finding here was that pre-schoolers who selected their own television had higher viewing rates. Parental attitudes to television were important too. Children who were heavy users, or who watched proportionately more of commercial stations, had parents who were less likely to express concern over the negative side-effects of watching television. Such children also tended to have parents who perceived less need to control their child's use of the medium.

Parental influences on the impact of television

Parents can have an impact on what their children take from television, although few parents actually become involved in or actively exercise control over their children's consumption, interpretation and use of television information. When parental intervention is used, through for instance discussion about programmes, it can be influential on the child. However, while some parents may forbid their children from viewing certain 'adult' or 'offensive' programmes, set bedtime limits on viewing, or make comments on the nature of the content being viewed, the majority tend not to participate in their child's television viewing. The most common form of control seems to take the form of rules about how late to watch, but even that kind of intervention may be neither widespread nor consistent. Watching with children can be effective in influencing what they view but a great deal of the time children watch unsupervised.

There is evidence too that parents can be induced to exert guidance on their children's television viewing. A leading market researcher, Gordon Heald, posted TV guides to a sample of parents over a six-week period.[26] A significantly greater proportion of the experimental groups reported receiving their parents' positive and negative recommendations about programmes than of a control group who were not mailed guides. Unfortunately, there is no indication of the extent to which parental recommendations influenced the children's viewing of programmes. Other researchers, however, have found that even when supplied with an external source of information about the negative impact of television on children, the majority of parents may be unlikely to participate in their children's television viewing behaviour to any significant degree.[27]

Although these investigations indicate that few parents establish explicit rules and practices regarding television, they fail to take into consideration other forms of social interaction that might have an impact on children's learning from the medium.[28] It is possible that more implied or global forms of mediation exist in the household. Parental disciplinary practices, for example, may also serve to mediate what and how children learn from television. Research elsewhere has demonstrated that disciplinary practices are related to children's social behaviour in general.

This issue has been explored by attempting to specify some of the conditions under which children's modelling of anti-social television portrayals was minimised and maximised. Enduring parental styles of discipline and behaviour towards each other and their children should mediate the degree to which children acquire and express anti-social predispositions modelled after television offerings. In practice, children with mothers who primarily discipline with reasoning and explanation seem to be least affected by anti-social television content.[29]

Another consideration is the role of parental disciplinary practices on children's learning of pro-social behaviour from television. Television contains as much pro-social behaviour as anti-social behaviour. There is evidence that mothers who discipline by acts or threats of physical punishment or the deprivation of material objects or privileges tend to be less likely to be aware of or to learn from television's portrayals than children whose mothers engage in other forms of discipline.[30]

What are the mediating effects of parental disciplinary practices on television's impact on their children? Do styles of parental discipline make a difference to children's television viewing patterns? One researcher looked at two modes of parental discipline which were labelled induction and sensitisation. Induction techniques include the use of reasoning, explanation and appeals to the child's pride and achievements, and exert little external power over the child. Parents who engage in this form of discipline typically point out to the child why one course of action may be better than another for the child's own well-being or because of effects on others.

Sensitisation techniques are basically punitive, threatening children with negative consequences – material or emotional – unless the children behave as their parents wish. External rewards or threat of removal of such rewards are characteristic of this mode of discipline.[31] Abelman obtained information about disciplinary patterns from parents and about television viewing habits, programme preferences and how well or badly their children generally behave. The results indicated that inductive discipline – a style which encourages the development of some internalised standard of morality and behaviour – tends to have a positive impact on children's pro-social behaviour and viewing of programmes whose characters are generally well-behaved, as well as a negative impact on children's viewing of programmes containing violence. Sensitising discipline would seem to contribute to the overall amount of television viewing as well as their preference for disruptive, uncivilised ways of resolving disagreements with others and violence-containing TV programmes.

It was also found that the disciplinary style used by their mothers has a greater impact on the way children resolve arguments and disagreements than does the disciplinary style employed by fathers. Mothers may also have more influence over children's television viewing. Regardless of whether fathers are sensitising or inductive, children from households whose mothers are inductive are more likely to react to conflict in a pro-social manner and expose themselves to a greater amount of pro-social television content.

Practical advice for parents

Various publications have now been introduced that can act as a guide to those parents who would really like their children to become more critical viewers. Unfortunately, there is no indication as to whether the activities suggested in some of these books have any degree of success when transferred to the home environment. For example, M.R. Kelley's *A Parent's Guide to Television* provides a detailed list of aggregated activities that parents can encourage their children to do in response to a wide range of television genres from soap operas to documentaries.[32] Some of these activities, however, appear to replicate those of the classroom; for example, writing programme reviews or imaginary news forecasts, interpreting new vocabulary or making up bar charts to display information collected from the screen. It seems doubtful if many children could be persuaded to carry out these tasks at the end of a busy school day; furthermore, how many parents would be willing to supervise these kinds of activities on a regular basis?

Perhaps Laurene Krasny Brown's advice in *Taking Advantage of Media* would be more useful, particularly in the light of the research findings outlined earlier in this chapter.[33] As she points out, if parents adopt responsible attitudes towards their own viewing, that is, they are seen to be making informed decisions as to when and what to watch, they can act as role models for their children. Furthermore, parents should try to discourage children from indulging in long hours of solitary viewing by sitting with them when possible and demonstrating that they value opinions they might have about individual programmes. By encouraging discussion about televised material, parents can then help their offspring to clarify and interpret not only character behaviour and narrative structure, but also examples of biased information and stereotyping. Children might then approach the medium in a more serious fashion. These kinds of positive attitudes within the home as well as the exertion of some kind of reasonable control over amount and content of viewing might then not only assist in making children more critical viewers but also more resistant to any potential harmful effects. More structured activities such as those outlined by Kelley are probably better left to educationalists, who, as we shall see in the next chapter, are now beginning to adopt a more active role as far as children and television are concerned.

Chapter twelve

How can schools influence children's viewing?

Throughout this book, we have tried to describe not only the manner in which children watch television but also the ways in which they attempt to make sense of it. It seems from the research so far that there might well be a need to educate young viewers to become more intelligent consumers of television. One way of achieving this could be through specially designed courses which can be taught to children in the classroom. As they grow older, children become more sophisticated about television and learn its conventions. Through natural viewing experiences, children develop a better understanding of television content, becoming able to make finer distinctions between programmes and more sophisticated and critical judgements about them. With further guidance from adults – parents and teachers alike – who discuss programmes with them, children's understanding of television can be further enhanced and the way they use television can be substantially modified.

The past twenty years, therefore, have seen the beginning of a new effort to teach children to understand the television medium. In the United States, which is probably ahead of any other country in this field, a number of school curricula have been developed that incorporate teacher-taught lessons, specially provided documentary and instructional programmes, practical assignments in the actual use by students themselves and audio-visual and other technical equipment to produce their own television programmes.[1]

Evidence is accumulating to suggest that such curricula are welcomed by teachers and pupils and that these educational projects produce changes in awareness of specific aspects of television such as how programmes and advertisements are made, and of more global aspects of the medium such as the economics and politics of the TV industry, and the influence television can have on intellectual development, and social attitudes and behaviour.[2] It is usually intended that through enhanced understanding of television children will become more critical and discerning viewers and less vulnerable to harmful television effects. Teaching about television is considered by many television researchers to be one of the most important practical developments in the last decade, and one that needs to be continued, expanded and improved in the coming years. Our initial intention then is to look at the broad theoretical perspectives from which television literacy projects were derived.[3]

Perspectives on teaching television

The notion of critical skills directing the processing of information is an old one. The application of these skills to information presented via a particular medium – as in critical reading skills, listening skills or television viewing skills – is an acknowledgement that the medium of presentation is an integral part of the message. It also implies that there are elements of grammar, syntax, symbols and meaning which are medium-specific and which presumably can be taught. Television literacy curricula have derived from four principal theoretical perspectives. Some critical viewing projects have been influenced largely by one of these perspectives only, whilst others have attempted to achieve instructional objectives specified by two, three or all four perspectives. James Anderson of the University of Utah,[4] a leading authority on the development of television literacy curricula, has labelled the four theoretical stances:

1 Impact mediation or intervention
2 Goal attainment
3 Cultural understanding
4 Visual literacy.

Impact mediation or intervention

This perspective derives from the experimental research that has been concerned with the effects of the mass media. This research has typically assumed that different types of media content can have different effects on the way individuals behave subsequent to their exposure to it. Perhaps the best example of this is the belief that violent television leads to subsequent viewer aggression, even though the results of behavioural effects research have not indicated consistent one-to-one relationships between certain types of television content and later behaviour changes among viewers. Nevertheless, one line of thought is that an appropriate television literacy curriculum can help students to recognise portrayals of undesirable social behaviour and to distinguish these from the portrayals of desirable conduct.

The aim is to teach young viewers to realise that certain forms of TV conduct are acceptable in real life, and that others are not. It is explained to children, for instance, that unacceptable behaviours, such as violence, are often added to programmes as ingredients designed to enhance the entertainment value of fictional storylines. However, they are not to be taken as examples to be copied or used as justification for similar conduct by the children themselves.

The main goal of curricula derived from the impact mediation perspective, therefore, is to control the influence of television and ensure that through teaching children to make full and proper interpretations of portrayals, only socially appropriate lessons are learned from the events it portrays.

Goal attainment

This perspective derives from an area of research and theory known as use-and-gratifications. Instead of looking at the effects of television on viewers, this research model examines the reasons why people use television, some of which have been outlined in Chapter 2.

Instructional curricula within this perspective focus children's attention on their motives for viewing television. Next, they help children develop standards by which television viewing can be evaluated as the most appropriate method of satisfying their needs – social, emotional, intellectual and so forth. Finally, tuition is designed to encourage students to make careful and selective decisions about television usage, and to manage the amount of viewing they do. The idea is to teach children to become more critical consumers of television, and to realise that there may be other, more profitable ways of spending one's time than sitting in front of the TV screen.

Cultural understanding

Television is an aspect of the culture in which it is produced, and it conveys the dominant values, beliefs and attitudes of that culture. Instructional frameworks deriving from this perspective attempt to convey the fact that television is simply an element of the culture. At the same time, however, television often exaggerates or distorts aspects of the socio-cultural milieu out of which it is born, and the images it conveys may not always be entirely faithful reflections of social reality.

One area of concern, relating to TV's impact on children, is that the medium tends to depict various social groups – women, old people and ethnic minorities in particular – in relatively traditional and demeaning roles, and that such portrayals cultivate stereotypes and negative attitudes about these groups among young, impressionable viewers. These effects can be counteracted by making children more aware of how television can, through its statistical representation or by the characteristics it attributes to certain social groups, distort the way things are in the real world.

Visual literacy

This perspective focuses on the production techniques of television programmes, and in this respect contrasts with the cultural understanding model which emphasises the nature of the content of television. According to this approach, understanding television is founded in knowledge of the way programmes are made. This includes an awareness of the various ingredients of programmes, development of a concept or theme, writing of scripts, shooting film or video-tape recording and matching of narratives to visuals. An underlying assumption is that the impact of a programme may be determined as much by its technical quality as by its content. Special camera and editing effects are given particular attention and learning is evaluated in terms of students' abilities to describe and appraise specific techniques. This perspective usually includes a strong practical teaching element in which students are taught how to handle technical equipment and produce different kinds of programmes for themselves.

These perspectives are not so distinct in their procedures and divergent in their aims as to be mutually incompatible and much of the television literacy curricula that have now emerged incorporate elements from all four. But how successful have some of these televised literacy projects been and what indications do they provide as to the value of educating children to become more TV literate?

Television literacy in the United States

Much of the work on television literacy has been conducted in the United States, although this has still been on a limited scale. Many of the studies were stimulated by Parent–Teacher Association interaction with parents, educators and network officials about the negative consequences of television on children's lives. Different television literacy curricula have had different emphases. Some have emphasised management of viewing, whilst others have focused on teaching children about the techniques of television as a means of inoculation against possible harmful effects of watching certain types of television content (e.g. violence).[5]

One of the most comprehensive studies has been carried out by the Yale Family Television Research and Consultation Centre, which received funding from the ABC network. The researchers developed a series of eight lessons for use in elementary schools to teach children to understand television and to capitalise on their interest in this medium in conjunction with reading, writing and discussion skills. The study was carried out in a school system near a large city and replicated twice in the same state.[6]

After many improvements in the video-tapes and teachers' guides had been made, it was tested on a larger sample in ten school districts in cities scattered throughout the United States. An additional curriculum was also developed for kindergarten, first- and second-grade children (ages 4, 5 and 6 respectively), and subsequently tested in one community. This was a refinement of the elementary school curriculum but geared to younger children and emphasised more non-verbal activities.

The curriculum was designed to teach children the following things:

1 To understand the different types of television programmes – news, documentaries, variety, game shows, situation comedies, dramas, etc.

145

2 To understand that programmes are created by writers, producers, directors, etc, and that they use actors and props.
3 To understand how television works in terms of simple electronics.
4 To distinguish fantasy from reality on the screen, and to be aware of and able to recognise camera techniques and special effects.
5 To learn about the purpose and types of advertisements, including public service announcements and political broadcasts.
6 To understand how television influences feelings, ideas, self-perceptions and identification.
7 To become aware of television as a source of information about the world – and to become aware of the ways in which stereotypes are presented.
8 To help children to be more critical of violence on television; to become aware that television rarely shows someone recovering from an act of violence or the aggressor being punished; and to understand the distinction between verbal and physical aggression.
9 To use these lessons within a language arts framework so that children can gain experience in using correct grammar and spelling; writing letters; abstracting ideas, critical thinking, expressive language, and oral discussion and reading.

The first study ran an experimental and a control group; in order to evaluate the impact of the curriculum, pre- and post-tests and follow-up tests were used which included questions relating to the eight topics being taught. These topics were: Introduction to Television; Reality and Fantasy on Television; Camera Effects and Special Effects; Commercials and the Television Business; Identification with Television Characters; Stereotypes on Television; Violence and Aggression; and How Viewers Can Influence Television.

Results indicated that children in the experimental school showed a greater increase in knowledge about television than those in the control school. Differences were greatest between the two groups in the measures of knowledge and understanding of special effects, commercials, and advertising. The children in the experimental school also learned more lesson-related vocabulary words and showed more improvement in their ability to identify video-taped examples of camera effects and special effects than did children in the control school.

Tests were also run to find out if the knowledge gained from the curriculum could be generalised to another situation – tests were on new material involving the area of special effects. Results demonstrated that the children could transfer their learning to the new situation, and indeed understood camera techniques and special effects when used in different shows from the ones used in the lessons. After this initial development, a follow-up study was conducted with a refined curriculum. Children aged 4 to 9 years took part, with lessons taught once a week. Modified materials were used for the youngest children, whose lessons included more play activities, puppets and so on.

Results for kindergarten (4-year-olds) through second grade (6-year-olds) indicated that at each level there was clear evidence of improvement in understanding the material covered in the curriculum. Particularly strong effects were found for the children's learning about camera techniques, the nature of editing, and the distinction between reality and fantasy characters.

In another important study it was found that young children were able to learn the contents of television literacy curricula and to apply them in discussions about television reality, but such learning did not seem to mediate television's impact on social attitudes. In a project begun originally in 1974, Dorr and her colleagues were concerned with modifying the effects of entertainment television via the cultivation of critical viewing skills in children.[7] This research was broken down initially in terms of a number of objectives. The first was to decrease the extent to which children perceived fictional television programmes as real. The second was to increase children's tendencies and abilities to compare television content with information from other sources. The third aim was to diminish the credibility children ascribed to television through teaching about the industry's economic goals, about production and about other legitimate sources of information. The final aim was to teach children to apply the knowledge they gained from the first three areas to the evaluation of television content.

To incorporate these four areas, two curricula about television and one control curriculum about social reasoning were used. All three curricula had separate versions for kindergarteners (aged 4) and for second- (aged 6) and third-graders (aged 7–8). They were designed to be taught to small groups of boys and girls in six one-hour lessons; they involved viewing audio-visual material, group discussion, drawing, role-playing, games, and commentary by the teacher.

Most emphasis was placed on games and role-playing, since these were effective ways to engage the children and to make the lessons concrete, and all curricula attempted to use analogies from the children's own experiences. The two television curricula used segments of programmes taped off-air to teach, illustrate, and test informally the achievement of each lesson's goals.

The first television curriculum (the 'industry' curriculum) was designed to teach children about the production of entertainment programmes and the industry's economic system. Children were to learn eight facts, four about television production and four about broadcast economics, and apply them to reasoning about the reality/fantasy of entertainment programming. The eight facts were

1 plots are made up
2 characters are actors
3 incidents are fabricated
4 settings are often constructed
5 programmes are broadcast to make money
6 money for programmes comes from advertisers' purchasing airtime
7 ads are to sell products to the viewer
8 audience size determines broadcaster income.

The second television curriculum (the 'process' curriculum) was designed to teach children processes and sources for evaluating television content. Children were to learn four facts, three about television programmes and one about sources for judging television realism, and apply them in reasoning about the reality/fantasy of entertainment programming.

The four facts were

1 entertainment programmes are made up
2 entertainment programmes vary in how reliable they are
3 viewers can decide how realistic they find entertainment programmes
4 television content may be evaluated by comparing it to one's own experience, asking other people, and consulting other media sources.

In this curriculum most of the effort was devoted to teaching children about the sources available to them to evaluate television content. Teaching about realism of entertainment programmes was less extensive here than in the industry curriculum. Moreover, while the process curriculum emphasised the extent to which programmes vary in their realism, the industry curriculum emphasised only their lack of realism.

The control curriculum on 'social reasoning' was designed to teach children role-taking skills. Children were to learn that other people have their own perspectives and feelings which matter in interactions with others, and that one can learn about them by asking, observing, talking with others, and trying out different interaction strategies. Children were expected to use this information in reasoning about social dilemmas common to them.

The children were pre-tested and the curricula were taught for two weeks. About three days after the last class, the children were tested on reality/fantasy judgements of entertainment content and knowledge of television production, industry economics and number of known sources for evaluating the reality of television. The children also viewed a half-hour episode of *The Jeffersons*, judged to present mildly uncomplimentary views of Blacks. About seven days later, the children were further tested, interviewed about reality/fantasy of television in general, of one of their favourite programmes and about the episode of *The Jeffersons* they saw.

The results showed that young children can, in as short a time as six hours, learn much about television and alternative sources of information, and can apply that information when asked to reason about the reality of television content. The two curricula each in their own way helped young children to understand better and evaluate television content. Each was effective for both kindergarteners and second- or third-graders. Improvement was more likely to be in areas where children do not have to engage in much reasoning. The study found that children can learn more about the television medium and how to evaluate it and can apply that knowledge in discussing its content.

Another study explored the effectiveness of an instructional film about television advertising which was designed to reduce children's susceptibility to commercial appeals.[8]

Here the researchers were interested in the possibility that children might be taught how to process and evaluate all commercials in a more 'adult' rational way. They conducted two studies: the first used an instructional film called *The Six Billion Dollar Sell*, a five-minute film designed for classroom use. Children (aged 9, 11 and 13) were split into two groups – one saw the instructional film and the other saw a film unrelated to commercials or persuasion. Immediately after viewing the children filled out a questionnaire that asked how much they liked the film and how much they felt they had learned from it. It also repeated questions about general attitudes to commercials which had originally been given to them ten days before.

Five days later they watched a video-tape with five commercials and answered questions dealing with general issues covered in *The Six Billion Dollar Sell*. The results showed that the children who viewed *The Six Billion Dollar Sell* were more sceptical than children who viewed the control film; this was particularly noticeable with the 9-year-olds.

The second study therefore focused on younger children (aged 7, 8 and 10) and was of similar design. Children saw either one of two educational films (either *The Six Billion Dollar Sell* or one called *Seeing Through Commercials*), or a control film, not concerned with advertising. Results showed greater increases in scepticism in the youngest age group, assumed to be more susceptible to commercial appeals due to their immaturity. This was borne out by pre- and post-test data. They, of course, had greater room to move or change.

Broadcasters themselves have also attempted to educate children to become more television literate. It was in 1978 that NBC took the first steps towards direct industry participation in developing and airing television literacy information. A small number of short segments designed to inform children about some aspects of television were created by NBC and broadcast on Saturday mornings; they were known collectively as *How To Watch TV* (HTWTV).[9]

Television literacy curricula have various ultimate goals. These may include that children will watch less television, that they will watch better television, that they will believe or be influenced by less of what they see on television, and/or that they will be less influenced by the 'bad' things they see on television. Attaining these goals is usually thought to come about by making children aware of their viewing practices, teaching them how and why programmes are produced and broadcast, and helping them to be more analytical and evaluative about programme and advertising content.

The NBC experiments sought only to inform children about some of the illusions that can be created by television, to explain why commercials are broadcast, and to advocate certain desirable practices *vis-à-vis* television viewing patterns and response to commercials.

The HTWTV segments were designed to be inserted into the Saturday morning schedule in the same way that commercials are. Each was therefore self-contained and addressed one idea. Each message was about thirty seconds and featured a male actor who was the lead in a half-hour 'pro-social' children's programme which NBC had also broadcast. As far as possible, the message was acted out and ended with a visual and audio presentation saying 'There's a smart way to watch TV'.

Aimee Dorr and her colleagues investigated the impact of this educative material on a group of ninety-five ethnically mixed children in the Los Angeles area. The youngsters were invited to view a selection of children's programmes over a five-day period which included a variety of HTWTV drop-ins.[10]

The children were then asked if they recalled having seen something on television about 'how to watch TV' or a 'smart way to watch TV'. The majority of children believed they had recently seen something about how to watch television. Older children were more likely than younger children to say they had seen it, and boys were more likely than girls to say so. There was greater recall the closer in time to viewing recall was tested. When asked to describe the content of programmes on how to watch television, many could not. Only 62 per cent of those who claimed to have seen such programming could actually describe any of the HTWTV content.

Each child was asked about a drop-in just seen, and if he or she could recognise the main point of it; 61 per cent of the children correctly selected the appropriate main idea from among three alternatives. Many more older than younger children and more girls than boys were able to select the correct alternative. Younger boys performed no better than chance on this item, and older boys performed only about as well as younger girls. This suggests that the ideas behind HTWTV messages were not communicated very effectively to boys, especially younger boys.

Did the children see these messages as presenting new ideas? Did they think the idea was worth presenting? Sixty-four per cent of children believed they already knew the information in the drop-in they had just viewed. Older more than younger children and girls more than boys were likely to feel they already knew it. Many believed they learned something new from HTWTV drop-ins. Overall, 54 per cent of the children who said they did not already know a drop-in's information indicated that they had wondered about it. Also, 81 per cent of all children felt that the drop-ins' information was worth knowing.

Did children see these short messages within programmes as programmes themselves or as commercials or what? Fifty-one per cent categorised drop-ins as adverts. The remainder were split between seeing them as part of the programme or as something else. The HTWTV drop-ins were a positive contribution to children's television viewing experiences. They presented information which children judged to be worthwhile, whether or not they believed they already knew it, and adults certainly judged the information to be beneficial for children.

Examples of TV literacy projects in Britain

So far there has been little in the way of continuous and systematic assessment of the efficiency of teaching television in the classroom, even though in recent years a series of publications has emerged under the IBA's Educational Fellowship Scheme, and several television series for schools have been produced on the subject of television. In his book *Teaching About Television*, Len Masterman proposed a television studies curriculum for schools and colleges which aimed to achieve specific television literacy goals. Whilst this book is a mine of very good ideas for TV literacy curriculum development, it did not go on to report examples of their practical implementation and educational usefulness in the classroom.[11]

Nevertheless, more recently, particularly with the advent of new examinations for 16-year-olds (the GCSE), media studies is gradually becoming an acceptable component of the secondary school curriculum. These courses invariably include a section on television and attempt to combine critical analysis and theory with practical work.

One early practical attempt to teach television was made by Edward Buscombe, who piloted a number of experimental courses on television during the 1973–74 academic year in several schools and colleges of further education in and around London.[12] One course, for example, consisted of three class periods per week for six weeks, in which 14-year-old boys at a London comprehensive school examined the content of a television series in detail. The chosen series was *Kung Fu* and because no video-recording equipment was available, the teacher had to rely on the boys watching the programme in their own time at home.

A second course was developed in a different school similar to the above in that it focused on the genre of TV series, but with the additional advantage that available video-recording equipment meant that programmes could be watched in class. This course was for two periods a week over ten weeks and examined events in programmes and attributes of leading characters, their life-styles, personal histories, attitudes towards sex, violence, crime, money, etc. Essay exercises were set at regular intervals based on specific topics of classroom discussion about the series under examination. Other courses in schools and colleges where facilities were even better included practical exercises in making programmes. Buscombe believed that pupils and students gained something from each of these courses, although he stressed that they were experimental and did not all look at or attempt to teach the same things. An amalgam of these courses would probably bring most benefits, and even then, there were many television topics he did not cover. However, Buscombe's effort at the time represented a very important initiative.

More recently a further attempt has been made to explore the best ways to teach with or about television. The Television Literacy Project reported a pilot study for a course taught to 14- to 15-year-old children, aimed at explaining television production techniques and approaches, and at evaluating critically television news broadcasts and drama. The course involved analysis of specific broadcasts and the planning, preparation and production of video programmes by the pupils themselves. Detailed course evaluation, by careful pre- and post-testing of experimental and control groups, demonstrated clear improvements of the children's understanding of those aspects of television on which tuition was given.[13]

This initial study was designed to develop, test and eventually further refine a course that would teach children to understand better how television is made and to become more critical in the way they watch programmes. The course gave equal emphasis to teaching about the practical problems of television production and to cultivating more active and critical thinking about programmes. In addition to the efficacy of the course as it stood, the researchers hoped to gain experience from this exercise which would serve as a pilot for the development of a more detailed and extensive course in the future.

Broadly, the aims of the course were to improve children's awareness on a number of specific topics:

1 To understand techniques of production and the meanings conveyed by certain types of camera work such as cuts, fades and zooms; awareness of special effects and what they signified.
2 To become more aware of different settings and contexts and to distinguish between realism and fantasy in programmes on television.
3 To improve understanding of the news on television and to think more carefully about the value and credibility of the news; news was considered as a form of entertainment as well as information and thought was given to why television news tends to stress certain kinds of events and depict them in a certain way.
4 To evaluate the portrayals of characters and events in television dramas more critically and to consider how they compare with people and events in the real world.

In all, forty-two 14- to 15-year-old pupils from a single school on Humberside took part in this pilot exercise. Twenty-six children were selected for the experimental group (who were taught the course) and sixteen were allocated to the control group (who were not taught about television in class). While the former were taught about television, the latter were given normal English lessons which involved reading and essay writing exercises on non-television topics. Half of each group were boys and half were girls.

The course lasted eight weeks and was taught in English lessons. During six weeks there were six forty-minute classroom periods per week. Another week was devoted to a field trip on which pupils made their own video-recordings. During the eighth week of the course, school examinations meant that only two forty-minute classroom periods were available. Pupils on the course spent about half their time on practical exercises, making their own news and drama programmes with video-recording equipment, and the other half discussing television in general or particular programmes from which extracts were viewed in class. The children also completed three pieces of written work on discussion topics about different aspects of television.

Both experimental and control groups were given tests on their understanding of drama on television and of news on television before the course began, and re-tests on both topics after completion of the course. Experimentals and controls were tested at the same time. The tests were constructed, marked and checked by a team of teachers from the school. In the drama tests and re-tests both groups were shown a fifteen-minute excerpt from two television dramas, not seen by any of them before. Tests probed children's memory and understanding of the plot of each programme, perceptions of how realistic the setting appeared to be, and impressions about the characters and their lives. In the news tests, both groups saw an edited network television newscast recorded several days earlier from a lunch-time bulletin which none of the children would have seen because they were all at school at the time of transmission. Questions probed recall and comprehension of the news stories in the bulletin.

Results showed that the scores of children in the experimental group improved substantially from initial to final tests of television drama and television news, whilst the scores of the controls improved slightly for news and fell for drama. On the initial drama test there were no significant differences between experimental and control group children, while on the final test, the former performed significantly better than the latter. On the initial news test, control group children actually performed better than the experimentals, while on the final test, their positions were reversed, as the children who had undergone the television literacy course were able to remember and understand more than were those children who had not taken the course.

Thus, in a relatively short spell of lessons lasting only two months, it was possible to enhance teenage children's understanding of and abilities to learn from television.

However, very little appears to have been done for the younger age group. Most activities carried out with primary school children (aged 5 to 11) seem to depend on the interests of individual teachers. The British Film Institute is attempting to redress this imbalance, with support from the DES, and has set up a working party to examine the possibility of introducing a standardised media studies curriculum for younger children. A small group of enthusiastic and committed teachers has designed and tested various methods of introducing media studies to younger children, but this seems to be in a fairly haphazard and unstructured way, making no provision for any kind of formal assessment to be applied.

As in the United States, beginning in the late 1970s, there have been several notable television series, produced by the industry itself, that have attempted to improve young people's understanding of television. Accompanying each series was a booklet, published by the television company concerned, in which synopses were provided of each programme and questions raised by it, and around which classroom lessons or written exercises could be built. One series examined the influence of television, and two looked at the inner structure and production process of television. *Viewpoint 2* was a series of four programmes produced by Thames Television in 1979 about the mass media and the way different groups of people, notably young people, Blacks, workers and those out of work are represented in them. The aim of the series was to get young viewers to think more carefully about the media images of different social groups and to consider whether these images are often accurate or unreliable, and whether media portrayals might influence public attitudes and beliefs. In 1978, Yorkshire Television produced a series of eight programmes called *Looking At Television*, which examined a number of different aspects of television – measuring the audience, the historical development of the TV industry, the production of drama, regional programming, light entertainment and the news, the role of advertising in TV, and future developments in the industry.

More recently (September–October 1983) Thames Television transmitted five programmes on *Understanding Television* as the first unit of the 1983–84 series of *The English Programme*. The aim of this unit was to introduce school children to aspects of television with which they may not hitherto have been familiar. Topics covered included how programmes are constructed and the production process, the history of broadcasting in Britain, audience research and how its findings may influence programme-making and scheduling, and future technological developments in the television industry.

Each of these television productions and publications illustrates the efforts of the industry to enhance young people's understanding of television, and to encourage and sponsor research in curriculum development. Unfortunately, there is very little evidence emanating from the United Kingdom that these various television literacy curricula have been 'field' tested and found feasible and successful in real school situations.

Conclusion

Concern about the impact of television on the lives of children has existed since broadcasts began. For a long time the predominant assumption was that television acted upon young viewers whose behaviours and outlook on life were changed through constant passive exposure. However, there is a growing awareness now that television can be turned to educational advantage as a tool for instruction, a source of information about the world and as a subject matter in its own right. Furthermore, children's natural interest in television may function as a powerful motivating force which can facilitate rapid learning about the medium itself and encourage youngsters to practise other skills in reading, writing and critical thinking which they normally face up to only with reluctance.

It is easy enough to join those who criticise television for its destructive social and intellectual influences; but rather more imagination and effort is required to use the medium for its socially and educationally constructive value. Let us hope that schools do not shy away from this challenge.

Chapter thirteen

Making the best of television

Television is an inescapable part of family life – and this means of children's lives too. We have presented a broad overview of what is known about children's use of television, their understanding of what it broadcasts, and of the impact that it has, or is often assumed to have, on their lives.

Public discussion about children's relationship with the small screen has been dominated over the years by the supposed harm it does to them. The daily press regularly abounds with stories which report on adverse influences of television portrayals of violence, sex, drinking, drug-taking and affluence in programmes, and of uncontrolled consumerism in advertisements. Television has been accused of encouraging children and teenagers to become more aggressive, to begin drinking under-age, to use bad language, and to adopt sexist and racist points of view. Television is also seen as undermining the educational development of young people through cultivating mental passivity and laziness and by keeping children up too late.

While it may be true that over-indulgence with television, as with most other things, can bring problems, it is equally true that when it is used properly and constructively television can have many positive influences on young viewers. All too often, these influences are ignored or under-played simply because they don't make such good news copy as stories about its supposed negative effects.

Television can provide children with a breadth of experiences, not all of which can in any way be construed as bad. Indeed, television can bring to children knowledge and other personal benefits which may be unavailable to them through any other source. People who dwell on the negative side of television fail to do the medium justice in terms of identifying and elaborating the role it actually plays in children's lives.

Television is not invariably bad for children. Thankfully, the balance of opinion has been redressed at least in part by recent writings such as those of Maire Messenger Davies, who chooses to emphasise some of the good things that can happen to children contingent upon their sensible use of television.[1]

Television can and does influence children. Its effects can be either good or bad, depending on how the medium is used. Either way, television's effects on youngsters are rarely simple or direct. For a start, television's influences can occur at a number of levels. It can affect children's knowledge, beliefs and values; it can produce shifts in attitudes or feelings about things; and it can cause certain courses of action and changes in patterns of behaviour.

What children get out of television, however, can depend crucially on what they bring to it. Children do not simply sit passively and watch the images displayed before them on the screen, absorbing anything that is presented without question or interpretation.[2] Instead, they often actively select what to watch to satisfy particular needs or moods, and they place their own meanings on programming and advertising content. Some programmes may indeed wash over children, leaving behind no clear trace of having been viewed. Others may have a profound impact on them, perhaps shifting a belief about or in something, or radically altering a particular view of the world. In the case of most programmes, however, their influence falls somewhere in between these two extremes with the precise nature and strength of television's impact being determined and limited by the reasons children have for watching at all, and by their understanding and interpretation of what was shown.

The effects of television on children can also depend on what kinds of programmes they are watching and how the programmes are made. Some programmes are designed to inform and educate, while others are made principally to entertain. Programmes do not always sit comfortably in these convenient categories, though. Nor do they always or necessarily attract viewers by their major functions. Entertainment programmes may excite, enthral, amuse and in other ways move their audiences, but they may also cultivate awareness of certain aspects of life, influence beliefs and values, or provide insights into how to deal with personal and social problems. In addition to their entertainment function, therefore, these programmes also have an educational impact. This educational impact may be perceived by viewers who turn to such programmes not simply to be entertained but also because they believe they can learn something of personal value from them. Television's fictional narratives often contain elements of truth or insights into everyday reality which viewers – young and old – can pick up on and recall at some later date for their own use where relevant or appropriate.

Programmes that are made to inform may also need to be entertaining in order to win and maintain their audience. In peak-time television in the United Kingdom, the schedules regularly feature magazine shows whose principal aim is to inform or advise the public about social and consumer issues (e.g. holidays, gardening, health and medical matters) together with the latest news about scientific and technological development. These programmes, which often contain film reports as well as studio anchors, employ entertainment formats, visual effects and background music. The popularity of such television series may often be put down to their production qualities as much as to the value of the information they provide.

Young viewers soon learn to make up their own minds about programmes. They learn to distinguish between different categories of programming by genre and in terms of the kinds of functions different programmes have. Children come to recognise that some programmes are good for entertainment reasons and others are good as sources of learning – but learning which touches on issues of importance to them.

There is an accumulating body of academic research evidence, some of which we have pulled together, which demonstrates the very positive learning potential of television. This learning function can be implemented throughout all stages of childhood with appropriate programming for different age-bands. Studies carried out among pre-school children in the United States using programmes such as *Sesame Street*, and in Britain with *Play School* and *Rainbow*, show that children can and do learn many valuable lessons from such television – particularly when they watch with other people like their mothers or older children. Young children can benefit most from television if parents, or other adults watching with them, discuss what they have seen.

Schools too can play their part. Educationally oriented programmes, when carefully integrated into a structured course framework involving input from other source materials, can have an influential teaching impact. It is essential, however, that television is used in a controlled and systematic fashion, rather than in a haphazard, hit-and-miss sort of way, in order to be effective in a formal educational context.

At the same time as drawing attention to the good effects of television, a more considered and cautious appraisal is needed of the so-called bad effects of the medium. Without diminishing the very genuine concern that exists among some critics about the possible harms of television, we believe there is a tendency to make television a scapegoat for some of society's ills. Television is often unjustifiably accused of misleading children on very flimsy evidence and a very poor understanding of how young viewers respond to programmes.

The research on the effects of television violence, for example, is voluminous, but far from conclusive. It might be argued that where there is doubt, caution should prevail. We would not dispute this. We would point out, though, that the broadcasters in the United Kingdom already implement comprehensive codes of practice on the portrayal of violence on television, and these codes are made known to programme-makers. Furthermore, we cannot see that it is of benefit to anyone to distract attention from the significant causes of social violence by unreasonably laying the blame at the door of television.

The fact that there is a great deal of research on the effects of television violence does not necessarily make the case stronger. Research techniques commonly employed by researchers in this field can be questioned for the robustness and veracity of the findings they produce. Research which takes place under artificial conditions may have doubtful relevance to what happens between children and television in reality. Even when children's use of television and the impact it has upon them has been studied under real-world conditions, shortcomings on the part of respondents to supply accurate or complete information about their viewing and other social habits may often undermine the validity of the research findings.

Looked at in a broader context, studies of children's aggression, and its relationship with television viewing and upbringing, suggest that family lifestyle, local neighbourhood, school and peers are more influential than television programmes. Television can show children how other people, including 'bad' people, behave, but it cannot bring them up to be good or bad. Indeed, television may show that bad behaviour is something not to be copied or to be proud of. There is evidence that far from wanting to imitate 'bad examples', children can become quite moralistic and disapproving of televised bad behaviour.

Intellectually, television-watching can stimulate conversational skills, co-operation with other children, imaginative play, the development of logical inferences, the understanding of stories and insight into, and sympathy with, other people's human dilemmas. Adults can encourage this learning. The study of television in school can introduce children to complex literary concepts of plot and style, persuasive techniques, and critical appraisal through a medium that is both accessible and interesting to them. These benefits do not all happen by accident or good luck; however, they can be cultivated and controlled. We must learn how to use television to enjoy its full benefits, and we must teach our children to do likewise.

The next few years will witness a rapid and unprecedented expansion in the number of television channels available to the public. Increased public anxiety about this development stems not only from worries about what it will mean for the quality and diversity of broadcasting, but also from the ways in which it will affect children. Will they spend more time watching the box? Will they be exposed more often to material that is unsuitable for them? In regard to the last two questions, we can probably be reassured by the fact that children do not use television haphazardly, but selectively. And they do not accept impassively everything that is shown to them in programmes; instead they learn to question and discriminate. These faculties can be strengthened through teaching management of viewing and critical television literacy. Children's understanding of television can also be aided by the attention of parents to what their offspring watch. With this help, children can become careful and sensible users of television who recognise its positive qualities and eschew its negative ones.

References

Chapter one: What is the nature of children's viewing?

1. Svennevig, M. and Wynberg, R. Viewing is viewing is viewing ... or is it? A broader approach to television research. *Admap*, 1986, May, 267–274.
2. Bechtel, R.B, Achelpohl, C. and Akers, R. Correlates between observed behaviours and questionnaire responses on television viewing. In E.A. Rubinstein, G.A. Comstock and J.P. Murray (Eds) *Television and Social Behaviour, Vol 4, Television in Day-to-Day Life: Patterns of Use*. Washington, DC: US Government Printing Office, 1972.
3. Anderson, D.R., Alwitt, L.F., Lorch, E.P. and Levin, S.R. Watching children watch television. In G. Hale and M. Lewis (Eds) *Attention and Cognitive Development*. New York: Plenum, 1979.
4. Schramm, W., Lyle, J. and Parker, E.B. *Television in the Lives of Our Children*. Stanford, Calif: Stanford University Press, 1961.
5. Levin, S.R. and Anderson, D.R. The development of attention. *Journal of Communication*, 1976, *26*(2), 126–135.
6. Anderson, D.R. and Levin, S.R. Young children's attention to *Sesame Street*. *Child Development*, 1976, 47, 806–811.
7. Wober, J.M. The extent to which viewers watch violence containing programmes. *Current Psychology: Research and Reviews: Special Issue: Violence on Television*, (B. Gunter, Ed.) 1988, *7*(1), 43–57.
8. Wober, J.M. 1988, *op. cit.*
9. Himmelweit, H.T., Oppenheim, A.N. and Vince, P. *Television and the Child: An Empirical Study of the Effects of Television on the Young*. London: Oxford University Press, 1958.
10. Gunter, B. and Greenberg, B.S. Media-wise. *Times Educational Supplement*, 1986, October 10.
11. Brown, J.R., Cramond, J.K. and Wilde, R.J. Displacement effects of television and the child's functional orientation to media. In J. Blumler and E. Katz (Eds) *The Use of Mass Communication: Current Perspectives on Gratifications Research*. Beverly Hills, Calif: Sage, 1974.
    Williams, T.M. (Ed.) *The Impact of Television: A National Experiment in Three Communities*. New York and London: Academic Press, 1986.
12. Robinson, J.P. Television and leisure time: Yesterday, today and (maybe) tomorrow. *Public Opinion Quarterly*, 1969, *33*, 210–222.
13. Himmelweit *et al.* 1958, *op. cit.*

Brown *et al.* 1974, *op. cit.*

14. Murray, J.P. and Kippax, S. Children's social behaviour in three towns with differing television experience. *Journal of Communication*, 1978, *28*, 19–29.
15. Williams, T.M. 1986, *op. cit.*
16. Selnow, G.A. and Reynolds, H. Some opportunity costs of television viewing. *Journal of Broadcasting*, 1984, *28*(3), 315–322.
17. Gunter, B. and Greenberg, B.S. 1986, *op. cit.*

Chapter two: Why do children watch TV?

1. Gunter, B. and Svennevig, M. *Behind and In Front of the Screen: Television's Involvement with Family Life*. London: IBA and John Libbey, 1987.
2. Katz, E., Blumler, J. and Gurevitch, M. Utilization of mass communication by the individual. In E. Katz and J. Blumler (Eds) *The Uses of Mass Communications: Current Perspectives in Gratifications Research*. Beverly Hills, Calif: Sage, 1974.
3. Herzog, H. What do we really know about daytime serial listeners? In P.F. Lazarsfeld and F. Stanton (Eds) *Radio Research 1942–3*. New York: Duell, Sloan & Pearce, 1944.
4. Schramm, W., Lyle, J. and Parker, E.B. *Television in the Lives of Our Children*. Stanford, Calif: Stanford University Press, 1961.
5. Greenberg, B.S. Viewing and listening parameters among British youngsters. In R. Brown (Ed.) *Children and Television*. London: Collier Macmillan, 1976.
6. Rubin, A. Television usage, attitudes and viewing behaviours of children and adolescents. *Journal of Broadcasting*, 1977, *21*, 355–369.
   Rubin, A. Television use by children and adolescents. *Human Communication Research*, 1979, *5*, 109–120.
7. Greenberg, B.S. 1976, *op. cit.*
8. Dembo, R. and McCron, R. Social factors in media use. In R. Brown (Ed.) *Children and Television*. London: Collier Macmillan, 1976.
9. Greenberg, B.S. 1976, *op. cit.*
10. Gunter, B. and Svennevig, M. 1987, *op. cit.*
11. Maccoby, E.E. Television: Its impact on schoolchildren. *Public Opinion Quarterly*, 1951, *15*, 421–441.
12. Gantz, W. and Masland, J. Television as babysitter. *Journalism Quarterly*, 1986, *63*(3), 530–536.
13. Howitt, D. and Cumberbatch, G. The parameters of attraction to mass media figures. In R. Brown (Ed.) *Children and Television*. London: Collier Macmillan, 1976.
14. Johnsson-Smaragdi, V. *TV Use and Social Interaction in Adolescence: A Longitudinal Study*. Stockholm: Almqvist and Wiksell International, 1983.
15. Himmelweit, H.T., Oppenheim, A.N. and Vince, P. *Television and the Child: An Empirical Study of the Effects of Television on the Young*. London: Oxford University Press, 1958.
16. Himmelweit *et al.* 1958, *op. cit.*
17. Freedman, J. and Newtson, R. *The Effect of Anger on Preference for Filmed Violence*. Paper presented at the annual conference of American Psychological Association, Chicago, September, 1975.
18. Goldstein, J.H. *Preference for Aggressive Movie Content: The Effects of Cognitive Salience*. Unpublished manuscript, Temple University, Philadelphia.

19. Gunter, B. Do aggressive people prefer violent television? *Bulletin of the British Psychological Society*, 1983, *36*, 166–168.
20. Dominick, J.F. and Greenberg, B.S. Attitudes toward violence: The interaction of television response, family attitudes and social class. In G.A. Comstock and E.A. Rubinstein (Eds) *Television and Social Behaviour, Vol 3, Television and Adolescent Aggressiveness*. Washington, DC: US Government Printing Office, 1972.

   McIntyre, J.J., Teevan, J.J. and Hartnagel, T. Television violence and deviant behaviour. In G.A. Comstock and E. A. Rubinstein (Eds) *Television and Social Behaviour, Vol 3, Television and Adolescent Aggressiveness*. Washington, DC: US Government Printing Office, 1972.

   McLeod, J.M., Atkin, C.K. and Chaffee, S.H. Adolescents, parents and television use: Adolescent self-report measures from Maryland and Wisconsin samples. In G.A. Comstock and E.A. Rubinstein (Eds) *Television and Social Behaviour, Vol 3, Television and Adolescent Aggressiveness*. Washington, DC: US Government Printing Office, 1972.
21. Atkins, C., Greenberg, B.S., Korzenny, F. and McDermott. S. Selective exposure to televised violence. *Journal of Broadcasting*, 1979, *21*, 5–13.
22. Zillmann, D., Hezel, R.T. and Medoff, N.J. The effect of affective states on selective exposure to televised entertainment fare. *Journal of Applied Social Psychology*, 1980, *10*(4), 323–339.
23. Schramm *et al.* 1961, *op. cit.*
24. Boyanowsky, E.O. Film preferences under condition of threat: Whetting the appetite for violence, information or excitement? *Communication Research*, 1977, *4*, 133–144.
25. Medoff, N.J. Selective exposure to televised comedy programmes. *Journal of Applied Communication Research*. 1982, *10*(2), 117–132.
26. Masters, J.C., Ford, M.E. and Arend, R.A. Children's strategies for controlling affective responses to aversive social experience. *Motivation and Emotion*, 1983, *7*, 103–116.

Chapter three: How do children watch TV?

1. Svennevig, M. *The Viewer Viewed*. Paper presented to ESOMAR. Seminar on Research for Broadcasting Decision-Making, Amsterdam: ESOMAR, 1987.
2. Svennevig, M. 1987, *op. cit.*
3. Anderson, D.R. and Lorch, E.P. Looking at television: Action or reaction? In J. Bryant and D.R. Anderson (Eds) *Children's Understanding of Television: Research on Attention and Comprehension*. New York: Academic Press, 1983.
4. Singer, J.L. The power and limitations of television: A cognitive-affective analysis. In P.H. Tannenbaum (Ed.) *The Entertainment Functions of Television*, Hillsdale, NJ: Lawrence Erlbaum Associates, 1980.
5. Anderson, D.R. and Levin, S.R. Young children's attention to *Sesame Street*. *Child Development*, 1976, *47*, 806–811.
6. Anderson, D.R. and Lorch, E.P. 1983, *op. cit.*
7. Calvert, S.L., Huston, A.C., Watkins, B.A. and Wright, J.C. The relation between selective attention to television forms and children's comprehension of content. *Child Development*, 1982, *53*, 601–610.

   Alwitt, L.F., Anderson, D.R., Lorch, E.P. and Levin, S.R. Pre-school children's visual attention to attributes of television. *Human Communication Research*, 1980, 7, 52–67.

Welch, A. and Watt, J.H. Visual complexity and young children's learning from television. *Human Communication Research*, 1982, 8, 133–145.

8. Singer, J.L. 1980, *op. cit.*

9. Hollenbeck, A.R. and Slaby, R.G. Infant visual responses to television. *Child Development*, 1979, 50, 41–45.

10. Anderson, D.R. and Levin, S.R. 1976, *op. cit.*
Carew, J.V. Experience and the development of intelligence in young children at home and in daycare. *Monographs of the Society for Research in Child Development*, 1980, 45(187), 1–89.

11. Alwitt, L.F. *et al.* 1980, *op. cit.*
Anderson, D.R. and Levin, S.R. 1976, *op. cit.*
Calvert, S.L. *et al.* 1982, *op. cit.*

12. Collins, W.A. Children's comprehension of television content. In E. Wartella (Ed.) *Children Communicating: Media and Development of Thought, Speech, Understanding*. Beverly Hills, Calif: Sage, 1979.

13. Singer, J.L. 1980, *op. cit.*
Singer, J.L. and Singer, D.G. *Television, Imagination and Aggression: A Study of Pre-schoolers*. Hillsdale, NJ: Lawrence Erlbaum Associates, 1981.
Tower, R.B., Singer, D.G., Singer J.L. and Biggs, A. Differential effects of television programming on pre-schoolers' cognition, imagination and social play. *American Journal of Orthopsychiatry*, 1979, 49, 265–281.

14. Anderson, D.R., Lorch, E.P., Field, D.E. and Saunders, J. The effects of TV programme comprehensibility on pre-school children's visual attention to television. *Child Development*, 1981, 52, 151–157.

15. Lorch, E.P., Anderson, D.R. and Levin, S.R. The relationship of visual attention to children's comprehension of television. *Child Development*, 1979, 50, 722–727.

16. Anderson, D.R. *et al.* 1981, *op. cit.*

17. Anderson, D.R. and Lorch, E.P. 1983, *op. cit.*

18. Huston, A.C. and Wright, J.C. Children's processing of television: The informative functions of formal features. In J. Bryant and D.R. Anderson (Eds) *Children's Understanding of Television: Research on Attention and Comprehension*. New York: Academic Press, 1983.

19. Anderson, D.R. and Lorch, E.P. 1983, *op. cit.*
Huston, A.C. and Wright, J.C. 1983, *op. cit.*

20. Anderson, D.R., Alwitt, L.F., Lorch, E.P. and Levin, S.R. Watching children watch television. In G. Hale and M. Lewis (Eds) *Attention and Cognitive Development*. New York: Plenum, 1979.

21. Anderson, D.R. and Lorch, E.P. 1983, *op. cit.*

22. Steiner, G.A. *The People Look at Television*. New York: A. Knopf, 1963.
Lyle, J. and Hoffman, H.R. Children's use of television and other media. In E.A. Rubinstein, G.A. Comstock and J.P. Murray (Eds) *Televison and Social Behaviour, Vol 4, Television in Day-to-Day Life: Patterns of Use*. Washington, DC: US Government Printing Office, 1972.

23. Anderson, D.R. and Lorch, E.P. 1983, *op. cit.*

24. Bechtel, R.B., Achelpohl, C. and Akers, R. Correlates between observed behaviour and questionnaire responses on television viewing. In E.A. Rubinstein, G.A. Comstock and J.P. Murray (Eds) *Television and Social Behaviour, Vol 4, Television*

in Day-to-Day Life: Patterns of Use. Washington, DC: US Government Printing Office, 1972.

25. Anderson, D.R., Levin, S.R. and Lorch, E.P. The effects of TV programme pacing on the behaviour of pre-school children. *AV Communication Review*, 1977, *25*, 159–166.

26. Wright, J.C. and Huston, A.C. *The Information Processing Demands of Television and 'Media Library' in Young Viewers.* Paper presented at the Annual Meeting of the American Educational Research Association, New York, March 1982.

27. Huston, A.C. and Wright, J.C. 1983, *op. cit.*

28. Anderson, D.R. and Lorch, E.P. 1983, *op. cit.*

29. Wright, J.C., Calvert, S.L., Huston-Stein, A. and Watkins, B.A. *Children's Selective Attention to Television Forms: Effects of Salient and Information Production Features as Functions of Age and Viewing Experience.* Paper presented at the Meeting of the International Communication Association, Acapulco, Mexico, 1980.

Chapter four: How well do children follow and understand TV?

1. Anderson, D.R. and Lorch, E.P. Looking at television: Action or reaction? In J. Bryant and D.R. Anderson (Eds) *Children's Understanding of Television: Research on Attention and Comprehension.* New York: Academic Press, 1983.
   Huston, A.C. and Wright, J.C. Children's processing of television: The informative functions of formal features. In J. Bryant and D.R. Anderson (Eds) *Children's Understanding of Television: Research on Attention and Comprehension.* New York: Academic Press, 1983.

2. Alwitt, L.F., Anderson, D.R., Lorch, E.P. and Levin, S.R. Pre-school children's visual attention to attributes of television. *Human Communication Research*, 1980, *7*, 52–67.

3. Collins, W.A. Interpretation and inference in children's television viewing. In J. Bryant and D.R. Anderson (Eds) *Children's Understanding of Television: Research on Attention and Comprehension.* New York: Academic Press, 1983.

4. Rydin, I. *Information Processes in Pre-School Children II. The Tale of the Seed.* Stockholm, Swedish Broadcasting Corporation, Project No 72-7-114, 1976.

5. Collins, W.A. Learning of media content: A developmental study. *Child Development*, 1970, *41*(4), 1133–1142.
   Collins, W.A. The developing child as viewer. *Journal of Communication*, 1975, *25*(4), 35–44.
   Collins, W.A., Wellman, H., Keniston, A. and Westby, S. Age-related aspects of comprehension and inference from a televised dramatic narrative. *Child Development*, 1978, *49*, 389–399.

6. Collins, W.A. *et al.* 1978, op. cit.

7. Collins, W.A. 1970, *op. cit.*
   Collins, W.A. 1983, *op. cit.*
   Collins, W.A. *et al.* 1978, op. cit.
   Newcomb, A.F. and Collins, W.A. Children's comprehension of family role portrayals in televised dramas: Effects of socioeconomic status, ethnicity and age. *Developmental Psychology*, 1979, *15*(4), 417–423.

8. Collins, W.A. 1983, *op. cit.*
   Collins, W.A. and Wellman, H. Social scripts and developmental changes in

representations of televised narratives. *Communication Research*, 1982, *9*(3), 380–398.

9. Newcomb, A.F. and Collins, W.A. 1979, *op. cit.*

10. Gross, L. and Jeffries-Fox, S. What do you want to be when you grow up, little girl? In G. Tuchman, A. Daniels and J. Benet (Eds) *Hearth and Home: Images of Women in the Mass Media*. New York: Oxford University Press, 1978.

11. Fernle, D.E. *Ordinary and Extraordinary People: Children's Understanding of Television and Real-Life Models*. Paper presented at the Society for Research in Child Development Biennial Meeting, Boston, Mass., April, 1981.

12. Dorr, A. No shortcuts to judging reality. In J. Bryant and D.R. Anderson (Eds) *Children's Understanding of Television: Research on Attention and Comprehension*. New York: Academic Press, 1983.

13. Dorr, A. 1983, *op. cit.*

14. Fernie, D.E. 1981, *op. cit.*

15. Hawkins, R.P. The dimensional structure of children's perceptions of television reality. *Communications Research*, 1977, *4*(3), 299–320.

16. Dorr, A. 1983, *op. cit.*

17. Dorr, A. 1983, *op. cit.*

18. Dorr, A. 1983, *op. cit.*

19. Rarick, D.L., Townsend, J.E. and Boyd, D.A. Adolescent perceptions of police: Actual and as depicted in TV drama. *Journalism Quarterly*, 1973, *50*, 438–446.

20. Reeves, B. and Lometti, G. The dimensional structure of children's perceptions of television characters: A replication. *Human Communication Research*, 1979, *5*, 247–256.

21. Dorr, A., Graves, S.B. and Phelps, E. Television literacy for young children. *Journal of Communication*, 1980, *30*(3), 71–83.

22. Collins, W.A. 1983, *op. cit.*

23. Dorr, A. 1983, *op. cit.*
Collins, W.A. 1983, *op. cit.*

24. Collins, W.A. and Westby, S. *Moral Judgements of TV Characters as a Function of Programme Comprehension*. Paper presented at the Society for Research in Child Development Biennial Meeting, Boston, Mass., April, 1981.

Chapter five: Does TV improve children's knowledge?

1. Gunter, B. *Poor Reception: Misunderstanding and Forgetting Broadcast News*. Hillsdale, NJ: Lawrence Erlbaum Associates, 1987.

2. Gunter, B. 1987, *op. cit.*

3. Robinson, J.P. and Levy, M.R. *The Main Source*. Beverly Hills, Calif: Sage, 1985.

4. Chaffee, S.H., McLeod, J.M. and Wackman, D.B. Family communication patterns and adolescent political participation. In J. Dennis (Ed) *Socialisation to Politics*. New York: Wiley, 1973.
Greenstein, F.I. Political socialisation. In *International Encyclopaedia of the Social Sciences*, Vol 1b. New York: Macmillan, 1968.

5. Gunter, B. 1987, *op. cit.*

6. Dominick, J.R. Television and political socialisation. *Educational Broadcasting Review*, 1972, *6*, 48–56.

7. Conway, M.M., Stevens, A.J. and Smith, R.G. The relation between media use and

children's civic awareness. *Journalism Quarterly*, 1975, *8*, 240–247.

8. Furnham, A. and Gunter, B. Political knowledge and awareness in adolescents. *Journal of Adolescence*, 1983, *6*, 373–385.
9. Atkin, C. and Gantz, W. Television news and political socialisation. *Public Opinion Quarterly*, 1978, *42*, 183–197.
10. Cairns, E., Hunter, D. and Herring, L. Young children's awareness of violence in Northern Ireland: The influence of Northern Irish television in Scotland and Northern Ireland. *British Journal of Social and Clinical Psychology*, 1980, *19*, 3–6.
11. Cairns, E. Television news as a source of knowledge about the violence for children in Ireland: A text of the knowledge-gap hypothesis. *Current Psychological Research and Reviews*, 1984, *3*, 32–38.
12. Cairns, E. 1982, *op. cit.*
13. Drew, D. and Reeves, B. Learning from a television news story. *Communication Research*, 1980, *7*, 121–135.
14. Drew, D. and Reese, S.D. Children's learning from a television newscast. *Journalism Quarterly*, 1984, *61*, 83–88.
15. Furnham, A. and Gunter, B. Sex, presentation mode and memory for violent and non-violent news. *Journal of Educational Television*, 1985, *11*, 99–105.
16. Salomon, G. *Interaction of Media, Cognition and Learning*, San Francisco: Jossey-Bass, 1979.
17. Meringoff, L.K. Influence of the medium on children's story apprehension. *Journal of Educational Psychology*, 1980, *72*, 240–249.
18. Beagle-Rous, J. and Gat, I. Specific impact of radio and television on children's story comprehension. *Journal of Educational Psychology*, 1983, *75*, 128–137.
19. Singer, J.L. The power and limitations of television: A cognitive-affective analysis. In P.H. Tannenbaum (Ed.) *The Entertainment Functions of Television*, Hillsdale, NJ: Lawrence Erlbaum Associates, 1980, p. 51.
20. Salomon, G. Beyond the formats of television: The effects of student preconceptions on the experience of televiewing. In M. Meyer (Ed.) *Children and the Formal Features of Television*. Munich: K.G. Saur, 1983.
21. Salomon, G. 1983, *op. cit.*
22. Salomon, G. 1983, *op. cit.*

Chapter six: Does TV teach children about social roles?

1. Fauls, L.B. and Smith, W.D. Sex-role learning in 5-year-olds. *Journal of Genetic Psychology*, 1956, *89*, 195–217.
2. Gunter, B. *Television and Sex-Role Stereotyping*. London: IBA and John Libbey, 1986.
3. Beuf, F.A. Doctor, lawyer, household drudge. *Journal of Communication*, 1974, *24*, 110–118.
4. Frueh, T. and McGhee, P.E. Traditional sex-role development and amount of time spent watching television. *Developmental Psychology*, 1975, *11*, 109.
5. McGhee, P.E. Television as a source of learning sex-role stereotypes. In S. Cohen and T.J. Comiskey (Eds) *Child Development: Contemporary Perspectives*. Ithace, Ill: Pecork Publishers, 1975.
   McGhee, P.E. and Frueh, T. Television viewing and the learning of sex-role stereotypes. *Sex Roles*, 1980, *2*, 179–188.

6. Morgan, M. Television and adolescents' sex role stereotypes: A longitudinal study. *Journal of Personality and Social Psychology*, 1982, *43*, 947–955.
7. Williams, T.M. *The Impact of Television*. London: Academic Press, 1986.
8. Wober, J.M., Reardon, G. and Fazal, S. *Personality, Character Aspirations and Patterns of Viewing Among Children*. London: IBA Research Paper, 1987.
9. Johnston, J. and Ettema, J.S. *Positive Images*. Beverly Hills, Calif: Sage, 1982.
10. Durkin, K. *Sex Roles and Children's Television*. A report to the Independent Broadcasting Authority, University of Kent, Canterbury, Social Psychology Research Unit, 1983.
11. Charters, W.W. *Motion Pictures and Youth: A Summary*. New York: Macmillan, 1933.
12. Lambert, W.E. and Klineberg, O. *Children's Views of Foreign Peoples: A Cross-National Study*. New York: Appleton-Century-Crofts, 1967.
13. Bogatz, G.A. and Ball, S. *The Second Year of Sesame Street: A Continuing Evaluation*. Princeton, NJ: Educational Testing Service, 1977.
14. Gorn, G.I., Goldberg, M.E. and Kanningo, R.N. The role of educational television in changing intergroup attitudes of children. *Child Development*, 1976, *47*, 277–280.
15. Nelson, B. *The Statement of Goals and Objectives for Vegetable Soup*. Unpublished manuscript, University of Massachusetts, Amherst, 1974.
16. Mays, L., Henderson, E.H., Seidman, S.K. and Steiner, V.S. *An Evaluation Report on Vegetable Soup: The Efforts of a Multi-Ethnic Children's Television Series on Intergroup Attitudes of Children*. Unpublished manuscript, New York State Department of Education, 1975.
17. Roberts, D.F., Herold, C., Hornby, M., King, S., Sterne, D., Whiteley, S. and Silverman, T. *Earth's a Big Blue Marble: A Report of the Impact of a Children's Television Series on Children's Opinions*. Unpublished manuscript, Stanford University, Calif., 1974.
18. Greenberg, B.S. Children's reactions to TV blacks. *Journalism Quarterly*, 1972, *49*, 5–14.
   Greenberg, B.S. and Hanneman, G.J. Racial attitudes and the impact of television blacks. *Educational Broadcasting Review*, 1970, *4*, 27–34.
19. Graves, S.B. *Racial Diversity in Children's Television: TV's Impact on Racial Attitudes and Stated Programme Preferences*. Unpublished doctoral dissertation, Harvard University, Cambridge, Mass., 1975.
20. Leckenby, J.D. and Surlin, S.H. *Race and Social Class Differences in Perceived Reality of Socially Relevant Television Programmes for Adults in Atlanta and Chicago*. Paper presented at the International Communication Association annual convention, Chicago, April, 1975.
21. Vidmar, N. and Rokeach, M. *Archie Bunker's Bigotry: A Study in Selection Perception and Exposure*. Paper presented at the review meeting of the Eastern Psychological Association, Washington, DC, May, 1973.
22. Hartmann, P. and Husband, C. The mass media and recall conflict. *Race*, 1971, *12*, 3.
   Hartmann P. and Husband, C. The mass media and racial conflict. In S. Cohen and J. Young (Eds) *The Manufacture of News: A Reader*. Beverly Hills, Calif: Sage, 1973.
23. Atkin, C.K., Greenberg, B.S. and McDermott, S. *Television and Racial Socialisation*. Paper presented at meeting of the Association for Education in Journalism, Seattle, Wash., 1978.
24. Bayton, J.A., Austin, L.J. and Burke, K.R. Negro perception of negro and white personality traits. *Journal of Personality and Social Psychology*, 1965, *3*, 250–253.

Bronfenbrenner, U. The psychological waste of quality and equality in education. *Child Development*, 1967, *38*, 909–925.

Jones, J.M. *Prejudice and Racism*. Reading, Mass: Addison-Wesley, 1972.

Powell, G.J. Self-concept in white and black children. In C.V. Willie, B.M. Krumer and B.S. Brown (Eds) *Racism and Mental Health*. Pittsburgh, Pa: University of Pittsburgh Press, 1973.

Spurlock, J. Some consequences of racism for children. In C.V. Willie, B.M. Kramer and B.S. Brown (Eds) *Racism and Mental Health*. Pittsburgh, Pa: University of Pittsburgh Press, 1973.

25. Clark, K.B. and Clark, M.P. Racial identification and preference in Negro children. In H. Proshansky and B. Seidenberg (Eds) *Basic Studies in Social Psychology*. New York: Holt, Rinehart & Winston, 1955.

Greenwald, H.J. and Oppenheim, D.B. Reported magnitude of self-misidentification among Negro children – artifact? *Journal of Personality and Social Psychology*, 1968, *8*, 49–52.

26. Neely, J.J., Heckel, R.V. and Leichtman, H.M. The effect of race of model on imitation in children. *Journal of Social Psychology*, 1973, *89*, 225–231.

27. Heckel, R.V. Cited in S.B. Graves. Psychological effect of black portrayals on television. In S.B. Withey and R.P. Abeles (Eds) *Television and Social Behaviour: Beyond Violence and Children*. Hillsdale, NJ: Lawrence Erlbaum Associates, 1980.

28. Greenberg, B.S. 1972, *op. cit.*

Chapter seven: Does TV influence aggressive behaviour?

1. Schramm, W., Lyle, J. and Parker, E.B. *Television in the Lives of Our Children*. Stanford, Calif: Stanford University Press, 1961.

Smyths, D.W. *Three Years of New York Television: 1951–1955*. Urbana, Ill: National Association of Education Broadcasters, 1954.

2. Gerbner, G. Violence in television drama: Trends and symbolic functions. In G.A. Comstock and E.A. Rubinstein (Eds) *Television and Social Behaviour, Vol 1, Media Content and Control*. Washington, DC: US Government Printing Office, 1972.

Gerbner, G. and Gross, L. Living with television: The violence profile. *Journal of Communication*, 1976, *26*, 173–199.

3. British Broadcasting Corporation. *Violence on Television: Programme Content and Viewer Perceptions*. London: BBC, 1972.

Halloran, J.D. and Croll, P. Television programmes in Great Britain. In G.A. Comstock and E.A. Rubinstein (Eds) *Television and Social Behaviour, Vol 1, Media Content and Control*. Washington, DC: US Government Printing Office, 1972.

4. British Broadcasting Corporation 1972, *op. cit.*

5. Van der Voort, T.H.A. *Television Violence: A Child's Eye View*. Amsterdam, Holland: Elsevier Science Publishers, 1988.

6. Zillmann, D. Attribution and misattribution of excitatory reactions. In J.H. Harvey, W. Ickes and R.F. Kidd (Eds) *New Directions in Attribution Research*. New York: Lawrence Erlbaum Associates, 1978, Vol 2.

7. Berkowitz, L. Some aspects of observed aggression. *Journal of Personality and Social Psychology*, 1965, *2*, 359–369.

8. Bandura, A. Vicarious processes: A case of no-trial learning. In L. Berkowitz (Ed.)

Advances in Experimental Social Psychology, Vol 2. New York: Academic Press, 1965.

9. Bandura, A. and Walters, R.H. *Social Learning and Personality Development*. New York: Holt, Rinehart & Winston, 1963.
   Baron, R.A. *Human Aggression*. New York: Plenum, 1977.

10. Drabman, R.S. and Thomas, M.H. Does media violence increase children's toleration of real-life aggression? *Developmental Psychology*, 1974, *10*, 418–421.

11. Osborn, D.K. and Endsley, R.C. Emotional reactions of young children to TV violence. *Child Development*, 1971, *42*, 321–331.

12. Bandura, A. 1965, *op. cit.*
    Bandura, A., Ross, D. and Ross, S.A. Imitation of film-mediated aggressive models. *Journal of Personality and Social Psychology*, 1963, *66*, 3–11.

13. Baron, R.A. 1977, *op. cit.*
    Kniveton, B.H. Social learning and imitation in relation to TV. In R. Brown (Ed.) *Children and Television*. London: Collier Macmillan, 1976.

14. Berkowitz, L. 1965, *op. cit.*

15. Drabman, R.S. and Thomas, M.H. 1974, *op. cit.*
    Osborn, D.K. and Endsley, R.C. 1971, *op. cit.*

16. Gunter, B. Video violence. *Stills Magazine*, 1984, (Feb–Mar), *10*, 36–37.

17. Steuer, F.B., Applefeld, J.M. and Smith, R. Televised aggression and the interpersonal aggression of pre-school children. *Journal of Experimental Child Psychology*, 1971, *81*, 442–447.

18. Parke, R.D., Berkowitz, L., Leyens, J.P., West, S.G. and Sebastian, R.J. Some effects of violent and non-violent movies on the behaviour of juvenile delinquents. In L. Berkowitz (Ed.) *Advances in Experimental Social Psychology*, Vol 10, New York: Academic Press, 1977.

19. Dominick, J.F. and Greenberg, B.S. Attitudes towards violence: The interaction of television exposure, family attitudes and social class. In G.A. Comstock and E.A. Rubinstein (Eds) *Television and Social Behaviour, Vol 3, Television and Adolescent Aggressiveness*. Washington, DC: US Government Printing Office, 1972.
    McIntyre, J.J., Teevan, Jr, J.J. and Hartnagel, T. Television violence and deviant behaviour. In G.A. Comstock and E.A. Rubinstein (Eds) *Television and Social Behaviour, Vol 3, Television and Adolescent Aggressiveness*. Washington, DC: US Government Printing Office, 1972.

20. National Institute of Mental Health. *Television and Behaviour: Ten Years of Scientific Progress and Implications for the Eighties*. D. Pearl, L. Bouthilet and J. Lazar (Eds) Rockville, Md: NIMH, 1982.

21. Stipp, H. and Milavsky, J.R. US television programming's effects on aggressive behaviour of children and adolescents. *Current Psychology: Research and Reviews*, 1988, *7* (1), 76–92.

22. Belson, W.A. *Television Violence and the Adolescent Boy*, Farnborough, England: Saxon House, 1978.

23. Milavsky, J.R., Kessler, R.C., Stipp, H. and Rubens, W.S. *Television and Aggression: A Panel Study*. New York: Academic Press, 1982.

24. Williams, T.M. (Ed.) *The Impact of Television: A National Experiment in Three Communities*. New York and London: Academic Press, 1986.

Chapter eight: Does TV encourage good behaviour?

1. Gunter, B. The cathartic potential of television drama. *Bulletins of the British Psychological Society*, 1980, *33*, 448–450.
2. Copeland, G.A. and Slater, D. Television, fantasy and various catharsis. *Critical Studies in Mass Communication*, 1985, *2*, 352–362.
   Gunter, B. 1980, *op. cit.*
3. Biblow, E. Imaginative play and the control of aggressive behaviour. In J.L. Singer (Ed.) *The Child's World of Make-Believe*. New York: Academic Press, 1973.
4. Feshbach, S. The stimulating versus cathartic effects of a vicarious aggressive activity. *Journal of Abnormal and Social Psychology*, 1963, *63*, 381–385.
5. Feshbach, S. and Singer, J. *Television and Aggression*, San Francisco, Calif: Jossey-Bass, 1971.
6. Copeland, G.A. and Slater, D. 1985, *op. cit.*
   Gunter, B. 1980, *op. cit.*
7. Noble, G. *Children in Front of the Small Screen*, London: Constable/Sage, 1975.
8. Biblow, E. 1973, *op. cit.*
9. Gunter, B. Can television teach kindness? *Bulletin of the British Psychological Society*, 1981, *34* 121–124.
10. Bandura, A. and Menlove, F. Factors determining vicarious extinctions of avoidance behaviour through symbolic modelling. *Journal of Personality and Social Psychology*, 1968, *8*, 99–108.
11. Poulos, R.W. and Davidson, E.S. *Effects of a Short Modelling Film on Fearful Children's Attitudes Towards the Dental Situation*. Unpublished manuscript, State University of New York, Stony Brook, 1971.
12. O'Connor, R.D. Modification of social withdrawal through symbolic modelling. *Journal of Applied Behaviour Analysis*, 1969, *2*, 15–22.
    O'Connor, R.D. Relative efficacy of modelling, shaping and the combined procedures for modification of social withdrawal. *Journal of Abnormal Psychology*, 1972, *79*, 327–334.
13. Stein, G.M. and Bryan, J.H. The effect of a television model upon role adoption behaviour of children. *Child Development*, 1972, *43*, 268–273.
14. Stein, G.M. and Bryan, J.H. 1972, *op. cit.*
15. Wolf, T.M. and Cheyne, J.A. Persistence of effects of live behavioural, televised behavioural and live verbal models on resistence to deviation. *Child Development*, 1972, *43*, 1429–1436.
16. Bryan, J.H. Model effect and children's imitative behaviour. *Child Development*, 1971, *42*, 2061–2065.
17. Bryan, J.H. and Walbeck, N.H. Preaching and practising self-sacrifice: Children's actions and reactions. *Children's Development*, 1970a, *41*, 329–353.
    Bryan, J.H. and Walbeck, N.H. The impact of words and deeds concerning altruism upon children. *Child Development*, 1970b, *41*, 747–757.
18. Rushton, J.P. and Owen, D. Immediate and delayed effects of TV modelling and preaching on children's generosity. *British Journal of Social and Clinical Psychology*, 1975, *14*, 309–310.
19. Fryrear, J.L. and Thelen, M.H. Effect of sex of model and sex of observer on the imitation of affectionate behaviour. *Developmental Psychology*, 1969, *1*, 299.
20. Silverman, L.T. *Effects of Sesame Street Programming on the Cooperative Behaviour*

of Pre-Schoolers. Unpublished doctoral dissertation, Stanford University, Calif., 1977.

21. Friedrich, L.K. and Stein, A.H. Prosocial television and young children: The effects of verbal labelling and role-playing on learning and behaviour. *Child Development,* 1975, *46,* 27–38.

22. Coates, B. and Pusser, H.E. Positive reinforcement and punishment in *Sesame Street* and *Mister Rogers' Neighbourhood. Journal of Broadcasting,* 1975, *19,* 143–151.
    Coates, B., Pusser, H.E. and Goodman, I. The influence of *Sesame Street* and *Mister Rogers' Neighbourhood* on children's social behaviour in the pre-school. *Child Development,* 1976, *41,* 138–144.

23. Rubinstein, E.A., Liebert, R.M., Neale, J.M. and Poulos, R.W. *Assessing Television's Influence on Children's Prosocial Behaviour* (Occasional Paper 74-11). Stony Brook, New York: Brookdale International Institute, 1976.
    Sprafkin, J.N., Liebert, R.M. and Poulos, R.W. Effects of a prosocial televised example on children's helping. *Journal of Experimental Child Psychology,* 1975, *20,* 119–126.

24. Murray, J.P. and Ahammer, I.M. *Kindness in the Kindergarten: A Multidivisional Programme for Facilitating Altruism.* Paper presented to the biennial meeting of the Society for Research in Child Development, New Orleans, March, 1977.

25. Baron, S.J., Chase, L.J. and Courtright, J.A. Tele-drama as a facilitator of prosocial behaviour: *The Waltons. Journal of Broadcasting,* 1979, *23,* 277–284.

26. Sprafkin, J.N. and Rubinstein, E.A. Children's television viewing habits and prosocial behaviour: A field correlational study. *Journal of Broadcasting,* 1979, *23,* 265–276.

27. Lee, B. Prosocial content on prime-time television. In S. Oskamp (Ed.) *Television as a Social Issue.* Beverly Hills, Calif: Sage, 1988.

Chapter nine: Does TV advertising affect children?

1. Choate, R.B. *Petition of the Council on Children, Media and Merchandising to Issue a Trade Regulation Rule Governing the Private Regulation of Children's Television.* Advertising Filed before the Federal Trade Commission, Washington, DC, March, 1975.

2. Choate, R.B. 1975, *op. cit.*
   Rossiter, J.R. and Robertson, T.S. Children's TV commercials: Testing the defenses. *Journal of Communication,* 1974, *24,* 137–45.

3. Brumbaugh, F. Cited in L. Bogart, *The Age of Television.* New York: Frederick Ungar Publishing Co. 1958, p. 258.

4. Packard, V. *The Hidden Persuaders.* London: Longman.

5. Brooks, R. In the dark over TV ads. *Observer,* 1987, November 8.

6. Ward, S., Levinson, D. and Wackman, D. Children's attention to advertising. In E.A. Rubinstein, G.A. Comstock and J.P. Murray (Eds) *Television and Social Behaviour, Vol 4, Television in Day-to-Day Life: Patterns of Use.* Washington, DC: US Government Printing Office, 1972.

7. Bechtel, R., Adelpohl, C. and Akers, R. Correlations between observed behaviour and questionnaire responses on television viewing. In E.A. Rubinstein, G.A. Comstock and J.P. Murray (Eds) *Television and Social Behaviour, Vol 4, Television in*

Day-to-Day Life: Patterns of Use. Washington, DC: US Government Printing Office, 1972.

8. Wartella, E., Wackman, D., Ward, S., Shamir, J. and Alexander, A. The young child as consumer. In E. Wartella (Ed.) *Children Communicating, Media and Development of Thought, Speech, Understanding.* Sage Annual Reviews of Communication Research. Beverly Hills, Calif: Sage, 1979.

9. Zuckerman, P., Ziegler, M. and Stevenson, A. Children's viewing of television and recognition memory of commercials. *Child Development*, 1978, *49*, 96–106.

10. Blatt, J., Spencer, L. and Ward, S.A. Cognitive-developmental study of children's reactions to television advertising. In E.A. Rubinstein, G.A. Comstock and J.P. Murray (Eds) *Television and Social Behaviour, Vol 4, Television in Day-to-Day Life: Patterns of Use.* Washington, DC: US Government Printing Office, 1972.
Ward, S., Beale, G. and Levinson, D. Children's perceptions, explanations and judgements of television advertising: A further explanation. In E.A. Rubinstein, G.A. Comstock and J.P. Murray (Eds) *Television and Social Behaviour, Vol 4, Television in Day-to-Day Life: Patterns of Use.* Washington, DC: US Government Printing Office, 1972.
Wartella, E. and Ettema, J.S. A cognitive-developmental study of children's attention to television commercials. *Communication Research*, 1974, *1*(1), 69–88.

11. Ward, S. *et al.* 1972, *op. cit.*

12. Ward, S. and Wackman, D. Children's information processing of television advertising. In F.G. Kline and P. Clark (Eds) *New Models for Mass Communication Research*, Vol III. Sage Annual Reviews of Communication Research. Beverly Hills, Calif: Sage, 1973.

13. Zuckerman, P. *et. al.* 1978, *op. cit.*

14. Ward, S. *et al.* 1972, *op. cit.*

15. Levin, S.R. and Anderson, D.R. The development of attention. *Journal of Communication*, 1976, *26*(2), 126–135.

16. Ward, S., Wackman, D. and Wartella, E. *How Children Learn to Buy.* Beverly Hills, Calif: Sage, 1977.
Caron, A. and Ward, S. Gift decisions by child and parents. *Journal of Advertising*, 1975, *15*, 12–30.

17. Wright, P. and Barbour, F. The relevance of decision process models in structuring persuasion messages. *Communications Research*, 1975, *2*, 246–259.

18. Rubin, R.S. *An Exploratory Investigation of Children's Responses to Commercial Content of Television Advertising in Relation to their Stages of Cognitive Development.* Unpublished doctoral dissertation, University of Massachusetts, 1972.

19. Sharp, T., Dyer, R. and Divita, S. An experimental test of the harmful effects of premium-orientated commercials on children. *Journal of Advertising Research*, 1976, *3*, 1–11.

20. Donohue, T.R., Meyer, T.P. and Hencke, L.L. Black and white children's perceptions of television commercials. *Journal of Marketing*, 1978, *42*, 34–40.
Meyer, T.P., Donohue, T.R. and Hencke, L.L. How black children see TV commercials. *Journal of Advertising Research*, 1978, *18*(5), 51–62.
Robertson, T.S. and Rossiter, J.R. *Stimulus Dispositional Variables in Children's Responses to Advertising.* Paper presented at the annual meeting of the American Psychological Association, September, 1975.
Sheikh, A., Prasad, K. and Rao, T. Children's TV commercials: A review of research. *Journal of Communications*, 1974, *24*, 126–136.

21. Greenberg, B.S., Fazal, S. and Wober, M. *Children's Views on Advertising*, London: Independent Broadcasting Authority. Research Report, February, 1986.
22. Donohue, T.R., Hencke, L.L. and Donohue, W.A. Non-verbal assessment of children's understanding of television commercial content and programme market segmentation. *Journal of Advertising Research*, 1980, *20*(5), 51–57.
23. Gaines, L. and Esserman, J.F. A quantitative study of young children's comprehension of televison programmes and commercials. In J.F. Esserman (Ed.) *Television Advertising and Children*, New York: Child Research Service, 1981.
    Rossiter, J.R. and Robertson, T.S. 1974, *op. cit.*
24. Greenberg, B.S. *et al.* 1986, op. cit.
25. Robertson T.S. and Rossiter, J.R. 1975, *op. cit.*
26. Greenberg, B.S. *et al.* 1986, op. cit.
27. Atkin, C. and Block, M. *Content and Effects of Alcohol Advertising*. Prepared for the Bureau of Alcohol, Tobacco and Firearms. No. PB82 -123142. Springfield, Va: National Technical Information Service, 1981.
28. Atkin, C. and Block, M. 1981, *op. cit.*
29. Aitken, P., Leathar, D.S. and Scott, A.L. *Ten- and Sixteen-Year Olds' Perceptions of Advertisements for Alcoholic Drinks*. Unpublished paper, University of Strathclyde, Glasgow, 1987.

Chapter ten: Does TV affect school performance?

1. Himmelweit, H.T., Oppenheim, A.N. and Vince, P. *Television and the Child: An Empirical Study of the Effects of Television on the Young*. London: Oxford University Press, 1958.
   Schramm, W., Lyle, J. and Parker, E.B. *Television in the Lives of Our Children*. Stanford, Calif: Stanford University Press, 1961.
   Brown, J. R., Cramond, J.K. and Wilde, R.J. Displacement effects of television and the child's functional orientation to media. In J. Blumler and E. Katz (Eds) *The Uses of Mass Communications: Current Perspectives on Gratification Research*. Beverly Hills, Calif: Sage, 1974.
2. Furu, T. *Television and Children's Life: A Before–After Study*. Tokyo: Japan Broadcasting Corporation, 1962.
   Furu, T. *The Function of Television for Children and Adolescents*. Tokyo: Sophia University Press, 1971.
   Werner, A. Children and television in Norway. *Gazette*, 1971, *16*, 133–151.
3. Himmelweit, H.T. *et al.* 1958, *op. cit.*
4. Schramm, W. *et al.* 1961, *op. cit.*
5. Murray, J.P. and Kippax, S. Children's social behaviour in three towns with defining television experience. *Journal of Communication*, 1978, *28*, 18–29.
6. Furu, T. *Cognitive Style and Television Viewing Patterns of Children*. Tokyo: Research reports, Department of Audio-Visual Education, International Christian University, 1977.
7. Zuckerman, D.M., Singer, D.L. and Singer, J.L. Children's television viewing, racial and sex-role attitudes. *Journal of Applied Psychology*, 1980, *10*, 281–294.
8. Singer, J.L. The power and limitation of television: A cognitive-affective analysis. In P.H. Tannenbaum (Ed.) *The Entertainment Functions of Television*. Hillsdale, NJ: Lawrence Erlbaum Associates, 1980.

9. Scott, L.F. Relationships between elementary school children and television. *Journal of Educational Research*, 1958, *52*, 134–137.
   Sharman, K. *Television and School Achievement*. Report to Australian Council for Educational Research. In *Research Information for Teachers*, 2.
10. Schramm, W. *et al.* 1961, *op. cit.*
11. Morgan, M. and Gross, L. Television and educational achievement aspirations. In D. Pearl, L. Bouthilet and J. Lazar (Eds) *Television and Behaviour: Ten Years of Scientific Progress and Implications for the Eighties*. Washington, DC: US Government Printing Office, 1980.
12. Singer, S.L. and Singer, D.G. Implications of childhood television viewing for cognitions, imagination and emotion. In J. Bryant and D.R. Anderson (Eds) *Children's Understanding of Television: Research on Attention and Comprehension*. New York: Academic Press, 1983.
13. Pierce, C. (Ed.) *Television and Education*, Beverly Hills, Calif: Sage, 1978.
14. Lesser, G.S. Assumptions behind the production and writing methods in *Sesame Street*. In W. Schramm (Ed.) *Quality in Institutional Television*. Honolulu: University Press of Hawaii, 1972.
   Lesser, G.S. *Children and Television: Lessons from Sesame Street*. New York: Random House, 1974.
15. Lesser, G.S. 1974, *op. cit.*
16. Bogatz, G.A. and Ball, S. *The First Year of Sesame Street: An Evaluation*. Princeton, NJ: Educational Testing Service, 1970.
17. Bogatz, G.A. and Ball, S. *The Second Year of Sesame Street: A Continuing Evaluation*. Princeton, NJ: Educational Testing Service, 1971.
18. Bogart, J., Alexander, A.F. and Brown, D. Learning from educational television programmes. In M.J.A Howe (Ed.) *Learning from Television: Psychological and Educational Research*. London: Academic Press, 1983.
19. Bryant, J. *et al.* 1980, *op. cit.*
20. O'Bryan, K.G. and Silverman, H. *Research Report: Experimental Programme Eye Movement Study*. Children's Television Workshop, New York, 1976.
21. Chen, M. *Verbal Response to The Electric Company: Qualities of Programme Material and the Viewing Conditions Which Aspect Verbalisation*. Children's Television Workshop, New York, 1972.
22. Ball, S. and Bogatz, G.A. *Reading with Television: An Evaluation of The Electric Company*. Princeton, NJ: Educational Testing Service, 1973.
23. McAleer, J. and Gunter, B. An investigation into the use and perceived value of an educational TV programme made for schools. *Journal of Educational Television*, 1988, *14*(2), 123–135.
24. Hurst, P. The utilization of educational broadcasts. *Educational Broadcasting International*, 1981, *14*(3), 104–107.

Chapter eleven: How can parents influence children's viewing?

1. Gunter, B. and Svennevig, M. *Behind and In Front of the Screen: Television's Involvement with Family Life*. London: IBA and John Libbey, 1987.
2. Niven, H. Who in the family selects the TV programmes? *Journalism Quarterly*, 1960, *37*, 110–111.

3. Smith, D.C. The selection of television programmes. *Journal of Broadcasting*, 1961, *6*, 35–44.

4. Chaffee, S.H. and Tims, A.R. Interpersonal factors in adolescent TV use. *Journal of Social Issues*, 1976, *32*, 98–115.

5. Wand, B. Television viewing and family differences. *Public Opinions Quarterly*, 1968, *32*, 84–94.

6. Lull, J. How families select television programmes: A mass-observational study. *Journal of Broadcasting*, 1982, *26*, 801–811.

7. Schramm, W., Lyle, J. and Parker, E.B. *Television in the Lives of Our Children*. Stanford, Calif: Stanford University Press, 1960.

8. McLeod, J. and Brown, J.D. The family environment and adolescent television use. In R. Brown (Ed.) *Children and Television*. London: Collier Macmillan, 1976.

9. Chaffee, S.H., McLeod, J.M. and Atkin, C.K. Parental influences on adolescent media use. *American Behavioural Scientist*, 1971, *14*, 323–340.

10. Chaffee, S.H., McLeod, J.M. and Wackman, D. Family communication patterns and adolescent political participation. In J. Dennis (Ed.) *Socialisation to Politics*. New York: John Libbey, 1973.

11. Wade, S.E. Interpersonal discussions: A critical predictor of leisure activity. *Journal of Communications*, 1973, *23*, 426–445.

12. Chaffee, S.H. *et al*. 1973, *op. cit.*

13. McLeod, J.M. and Brown, J.D. 1976, *op. cit.*

14. Chaffee, S.H. *et al*. 1971, *op. cit.*
    Chaffee, S.H. *et al*. 1973, *op. cit.*

15. Hedinsson, E. *TV, Family and Society: The Social Origins and Effects of Adolescents' TV Use*. Stockholm: Almquist and Wiksell International, 1981.

16. Lull, J. The social uses of television. *Human Communication Research*, 1980, *6*, 97–109.

17. Greenberg, B.S., Ericson, P.M. and Vlahos, M. Children's television behaviour as perceived by mother and child. In E.A. Rubinstein, G.A. Comstock and J.P. Murray (Eds) *Television and Social Behaviour, Vol 4, Television in Day-to-Day Life: Patterns of Use*. Washington, DC: US Government Printing Office, 1972.

18. Abel, J.D. and Bennison, M.E. Perceptions of TV programme violence by children and mothers. *Journal of Broadcasting*, 1976, *20*, 355–363.

19. Cantor, J. and Reill, S. Adolescents' fright reactions to television and films. *Journal of Communications*, 1982, *32*, 87–99.

20. Steiner, G.A. *The People Look at Television*. New York: A. Knopf, 1963.

21. Lyle, J. and Hoffmann, H.R. Children's use of television and other media. In E.A. Rubinstein, G.A. Comstock and J.P. Murray (Eds) *Television and Social Behaviour, Vol 4, Television in Day-to-Day Life: Patterns of Use*. Washington, DC: US Government Printing Office, 1972.

22. McLeod, J.M., Bybee, C.R. and Durrell, J.A. *Decision-Making by Adolescent Children and their Mothers*. Unpublished manuscript, Mass Communication Research Centre, University of Wisconsin, Madison, 1978.

23. Streicher, L. and Bonney, N. Children talk about television. *Journal of Communication*, 1974, *24*, 54–61.

24. Mohr, P.J. Parental guidance of children's viewing of evening television programmes. *Journal of Broadcasting*, 1979, *23*, 213–228.

25. Holman, J. and Braithwaite, V. Parental lifestyles and children's television viewing. *Australian Journal of Psychology*, 1982, *34*, 375–382.

26. Heald, G.R. Television viewing guides and parental recommendations. *Journalism Quarterly*, 1980, *57*, 141–144.
27. Cohen, A., Abelman, R. and Greenberg, B.S. The impact of child and adult-orientated TV literacy information on high and moderate conscience. *Journal of Broadcasting*, 1988, in press.
28. Abelman, R. *Sex Differences in Parental Disciplining Practices: An Antecedent of Television's Impact on Children*. Paper presented at the annual International Conference, Honolulu, Hawaii, May, 1985.
29. Korzenny, F., Greenberg, B.S. and Atkin, C.K. *Styles of Parental Disciplining Practices as a Medium of Children's Learning from Antisocial Television Portrayals*. Unpublished manuscript, Department of Telecommunication, University of Michigan, East Lansing, 1978.
30. Abelman, R. 1985, *op. cit.*
31. Abelman, R. 1985, *op. cit.*
32. Kelley, M.R. *A Parent's Guide to Television: Making the Most of It*. New York: Wiley, 1983.
33. Brown, L.K. *Taking Advantage of Media: A Manual for Parents and Teachers*. London: Routledge & Kegan Paul, 1986.

Chapter twelve: How can schools influence children's viewing?

1. Anderson, J.A. Television literacy and the critical viewer. In J. Bryant and D.R. Anderson (Eds) *Children's Understanding of Television: Research on Attention and Comprehension*. New York: Academic Press, 1983.
2. Anderson, J.A. 1983, *op. cit.*
3. Anderson, J.A. 1983, *op. cit.*
   Dorr, A., Graves, S.B. and Phelps, E. Television literacy for young children. *Journal of Communication*, 1980, *30* (3), 71–83.
4. Anderson, J.A. 1983, *op. cit.*
5. Fransecky, R.B. and Ferguson, R. New ways of seeing: The Milford visual communication project. *Audiovisual Instruction*, April, 1973, *18*, 44–49.
6. Singer, D.G. and Singer, J.L. Television and the developing imagination of the child. *Journal of Broadcasting*, 1981, *25*(4), 373–387.
   Singer, D.G., Zuckerman, D.M. and Singer, J.L. Helping elementary school children learn about TV. *Journal of Communication*, 1980, *30*(3), 84–93.
7. Dorr, A. *et al.* 1980, *op. cit.*
8. Christenson, P.G. Children's perceptions of TV commercials and products: The effects of PSAs. *Communication Research*, 1982, *9*(4), 491–524.
9. cf. Singer, D.G. and Singer, J.L. Learning how to be intelligent consumers of television. In M.J.A. Howe (Ed.) *Learning from Television: Psychological and Educational Research*. London: Academic Press, 1983.
10. Dorr, A. When social scientists cooperate with broadcasting. In S. Oskamp (Ed). *Television as a Social Issue*. Beverly Hills, Calif: Sage, 1988.
11. Masterman, L. *Teaching About Television*. London: Macmillan, 1980.
12. Buscombe, E. *Television in Schools and Colleges*. London: Independent Broadcasting Authority. Educational Fellowship Report, 1977.
13. Kelley, P., Buckle, L. and Gunter, B. The television literacy project. *Secondary Education Journal*, 1988, *15*, 21–22.

Kelley, P. and Gunter, B. Television literacy. *Times Educational Supplement*, 1984, October 12.

Kelley, P., Gunter, B. and Kelley, C. Teaching television in the classroom: Results of a preliminary study. *Journal of Educational Television*, 1985, *11*, 57–63.

Chapter thirteen: Making the best of television

1. Davies, M.M. *Television is Good For Your Kids*. London: Hilary Shipman, 1989.
2. See Bryant, J. and Anderson, D.R. (Eds) *Children's Understanding of Television: Research on Attention and Comprehension*. New York: Academic Press, 1983.

Index

ABC network 145
Abelman, R. 139
ability *see* intelligence
acquisitiveness and advertising 105,
 113–14, 118
action-adventure programmes 9, 40, 46,
 77, 78, 80, 99, 121
active nature of viewing 29–31, 61, 157,
 159
addiction to TV 22
adolescents: and advertising 116–17, 149;
 attention levels 32; and family
 communication patterns 134; parental
 guidance for viewing 138; political and
 news awareness 50, 51, 54–5; race-role
 perceptions 71–3; sex-role perceptions
 63, 66–7; and violence 87, 89; *see also*
 teenagers
adult viewing 6
adults: attention levels 33; comprehension
 of plot 39–40; and fragmentation of
 programme sequence 38; perception of
 violence 79–81, 90–1; reinforcement of
 educational programmes 128, 142, 159
advertising 32, 33, 38, 57, 104–18; and
 acquisitiveness 105, 113–14, 118;
 awareness of 42, 104, 107–8, 109, 110,
 111, 117; behavioural effect 114–17,
 118; belief in 112–13; immorality and
 105–6; reactions to 105–6; selling
 purpose of 83, 111–12, 117–18; and
 TV literacy curricula 146, 149;
 understanding of 108–10, 117
advertising agencies 104
age: for commencing viewing 4; and
 knowledge of news 53; related to
 advertising 107–8, 109, 112, 113–14;
 related to viewing 5, 28–9; and

understanding of programmes 37–40,
 41, 42–4
aggressive behaviour: and catharsis 92–5,
 102; influence of TV on 75–91, 97,
 101, 143, 159
aggressive humour 24
alcohol consumption and advertising
 115–17, 118
All in the Family 71, 72
Anderson, D.R. 3, 31, 32
Anderson, J.A. 143
Annenberg School of Communications,
 University of Pennsylvania 76
anti-social behaviour 139–40, 159; *see
 also* aggressive behaviour
Aristotle 92
arousal: viewing as 23, 24, 81, 83
Aston University Communications
 Research Group 78
Atkin, C.K. 72
attention levels 32–4
attention to TV 2–3, 26–7; to advertising
 107–8, 109–10, 112–13; and catharsis
 93; commencement of 4; and
 distraction 29–30, 36; ways of
 controlling 27–9, 31, 33–4, 36–7
attentional inertia 31–2
Audits of Great Britain 4

baby-sitting function of TV 20–1, 137
bad behaviour 159; *see also* aggressive
 behaviour
Bandura, A. 84
BARB 4
BBC Audience Research Department
 77–8
BBC: violence on 77–9
behaviour: bad 159; *see also* aggressive

178